THE BRITIS

For
Mary Quicke and Tom Langdon-Davies

The British Empire

A History and a Debate

JEREMY BLACK
University of Exeter, UK

Routledge
Taylor & Francis Group
LONDON AND NEW YORK

First published 2015 by Ashgate Publishing

Published 2016 by Routledge
2 Park Square, Milton Park, Abingdon, Oxon OX14 4RN
711 Third Avenue, New York, NY 10017, USA

First issued in paperback 2017

Routledge is an imprint of the Taylor & Francis Group, an informa business

British Library Cataloguing in Publication Data
A catalogue record for this book is available from the British Library.

The Library of Congress has cataloged the printed edition as follows:
Black, Jeremy, 1955-
The British Empire : a history and a debate / by Jeremy Black.
pages cm
Includes bibliographical references and index.
ISBN 978-1-4724-5966-4 (hardcover)
1. Great Britain--Colonies--History. 2. Commonwealth countries--History.
3. Imperialism--History. I. Title.
DA16.B576 2015
909.09'71241--dc23

2015009327

ISBN 13: 978-1-138-09958-6 (pbk)
ISBN 13: 978-1-4724-5966-4 (hbk)

Contents

Preface

What was the course and consequence of the British Empire? The rights and wrongs, strengths and weaknesses of empire are a major topic in global history, and deservedly so. The topic links the historical accounts of, and from, former colonies with those of the former imperial metropoles (homelands). This book focuses on the most prominent and wide-ranging empire in world history, the British empire. It does so not only in order to provide a history of that empire, but also so as to provide a perspective from which to consider the issues of strengths and weaknesses, and rights and wrongs, and how they are debated today. In short, this is history both as the past and as the present-day discussion of the past, and with the political dimension of the latter engaged with explicitly. This approach also offers a way to consider the empires of other states and, in particular, to assess the parallels and contrasts between the British and American empires, which provide the subject of Chapter 7. Moreover, debate over empire has become more common because of questions about the situation in many states today. Discussion over historical empires is in part a reflection of the consideration of contemporary states, notably their weaknesses.

This book therefore seeks to weave together an overview of the British empire, across the centuries, with a considered commentary on both the public historiography of empire and the politically charged character of much discussion of it. There is a coverage here of social as well as political and economic dimensions of empire, and both the British perspective and that of the colonies is considered. The role of both practicalities (such as strategic and commercial issues) and values as important forces of imperialism is emphasised. The chronological dimension is set by the need to consider not only imperial expansion by the British state, but also the history of Britain within an imperial context. As such, this is a story of empires within the British Isles, Europe, and, later, world-wide. It shows Britain as a colony, part of an empire, or as an empire, from its earliest history. It covers Roman Britain, Anglo-Saxon England, medieval imperial expansion, colonisation in the British Isles and later across the oceans, through to the heyday of empire in the eighteenth and nineteenth centuries. The book follows with global decline, decolonisation, and the complex nature of post-colonialism and different imperial activity in modern and contemporary history. The approach is revisionist. There is no automatic assumption that imperialism, empire, and colonialism were 'bad' things. Instead, there is a dispassionate and evidence-based evaluation of the British empire as a form of government, an economic system, and a method of engagement with the world, one with both faults and benefits for the metropole and the colony.

This book draws both on my own research, notably as seen with *The British Seaborne Empire* (2004), and on the work of others. The strength of scholarship, both British and non-British, on the history of the British empire is notable, and I would like to pay tribute to the work of many other academics. Throughout, it has proved helpful and stimulating. The range, scale, and quality of the scholarship is truly impressive. If I have only had space to engage with a portion of this scholarship, that is a reflection of the range of what I have had to cover and of the historiographical focus being on popular and public history, and not its academic counterpart. I would like to thank Jerry Bannister, Bill Gibson, John Griffiths, Will Hay, Kwasi Kwarteng, Luigi Loreto, Marc-William Palen, Murray Pittock, Kaushik Roy, Tony Stockwell, Richard Toye, and an anonymous reader for commenting on all or part of an earlier version. They are not responsible for any remaining errors and do not necessarily agree with particular assessments. I would also like to thank Michael Mosbacher of the Social Affairs Unit for allowing me to use material from a publication for that Unit. An exemplary publisher, Tom Gray has proved most helpful with this book. This book benefits greatly from the opportunity to teach for the Medieval and Early Modern first-year Introductory World History course at the University of Exeter and its Modern first-year counterpart in 2013–15. I have also benefited, while working on this book, from invitations to speak at Mary Washington University, William Paterson University, the Sorbonne, the University of Rheims, the Seconda Università di Napoli, and the Catholic University of Portugal.

I would like to thank all those who have provided opportunities to visit parts of the one-time empire, formal or otherwise, from Belize and Raritan to the Andaman Islands and Tasmania; from Chennai and Singapore to Palmerston Island and Beveridge Reef. I am delighted to dedicate this book to two good Devon friends who are tremendous fun and also shrewdly sensitive about people. I have benefited greatly from both aspects of their friendship.

List of Abbreviations

Add.	Additional manuscripts
BL.	London, British Library, Department of Manuscripts
CAB.	Cabinet Papers
NA.	London, National Archives, formerly Public Record Office
UN	United Nations

Chapter 1
Debating Empire

This is a call to reject a slavish adherence to fashion, to recognise the complexity of Britain's imperial past, and to avoid being ahistorical in passing judgement on it. History is both the past and the accounts in the present we provide about it. Empire and notably Britain's imperial past, have been very much affected by this interaction. Much of the modern popular discussion of empire, and part of its academic construction, especially by some scholars of colonial literature, rest on a criticism of empire and imperialism, these generally equated with rule by foreign powers, as inherently undesirable and therefore unnatural. Indeed, the very word empire has been demonised, and both across the political spectrum and with reference to popular culture. It is no coincidence that the *Star Wars* films chose 'the Empire' as the enemy, or that Ronald Reagan stigmatised the Soviet Union in 1983 as an empire. Empire is at once a term of abuse, or, at least, criticism, as well as a means of analysis, and the same is true for related words such as imperial. In contrast, supporters of empire, past and present, have often shied away from the term imperialism.

This situation makes discussion of empire difficult, and that is compounded by the apparent need to adopt a position on the British empire, in other words a single position. To do so, however, is not only to risk adopting anachronistic and ahistorical criteria, but also to look at a situation that lasted for many hundreds of years and is therefore difficult to treat as a single and unchanging unit or as a simple process. That, obviously, is not the case. Instead, it is the shifting character of what is discussed that is most apparent, that character, moreover, reflecting changes in the imperial metropole, in the colonies, and in the context provided by developments elsewhere.

Aside from disagreements in assessing these changes and their interaction, they engage the sympathy of commentators in very different fashions. In part, there is the problem that this response comes to the fore. In the nineteenth century, it tended to be favourable to empire, although not invariably so; today, the situation is the opposite. In each case, the opinions of those who were/are outside the mainstream are of particular interest, but the normal view is more apparent and instructive. It is unclear, however, why present-day criticism of empire should automatically command more approval than nineteenth-century support for empire.

Imperialism, today, is frequently presented, explicitly or implicitly, in Britain and across the world, as a pathology of power and as an anachronistic and redundant state in human development, each apparently helping to define the other. Because the British empire was the largest in world history, its purpose and reputation have proved topics of particular attention, indeed criticism, if not condemnation. This criticism is crucial to the foundation accounts and, therefore, public histories of many of the countries of the world. Indeed, linked to this, much of the debate about empire involves a contemporary struggle for dominance. One side, which sees itself as progressive, uses the history of empire in order to deny the moral legitimacy of its real or apparent opponents. That approach imposes a highly presentist view of history that is not historical at all. It is not only politics that is at stake. A strand of the current discussion of the British empire is essentially neo-Whiggish, with present commentators showing every bit as clear a sense of their own judgement as the Whig commentators of the past; only with human rights, transnationalism, and diversity all replacing the older values of constitutional liberal democracy and nationalist self-determination as both goal and means. More generally, there is a widespread tendency to see the present as considerably more moral than the past, and to write as if it is necessary to condemn the actions and beliefs of those who have gone before them.

The scholarly discussion of the imperial past is deeply grounded in the archives and in an understanding of the cultural mores and ideological precepts of the past. That does not preclude value judgements, but they tend to be measured.[1] This scholarly approach, however, does not dominate public attention. Instead, the latter has been, and is, affected by views and images that are more clear cut. At times, the theme has been one of imperial nostalgia. *Lagaan* (2001), an ahistorical Indian film with the most important Bollywood actors, set at the end of the nineteenth century, deals with taxation and a cricket match for which the stake is the taxes due. In the match, the Indian peasant team beats a team of British officers. The British are bad chaps, but not too bad; rather, they are somewhat comical. Nevertheless, in recent decades, the general note, both in popular works and on film, has frequently been more critical. The tone has often been strident. To give an example, one that can be readily duplicated in the 'history wars' to which empire has given rise, Richard Gott, the author of

1 For a very good introduction, B. Porter, *The Lion's Share: A Short History of British Imperialism 1850–2011* (5th edn, London, 2012). For a more strident approach, P. Chatterjee, *The Black Hole of Empire: History of a Global Practice of Power* (Princeton, New Jersey, 2012).

Britain's Empire: Resistance, Repression and Revolt (2011), in essence an account of 1755–1858, declared:

> Throughout the period of the British Empire, the British were for the most part loathed and despised by those they colonised ... Resistance, revolt and rebellion was a permanent fact of empire, and the imperial power, endlessly challenged, was tireless in its repression.[2]

In practice, resistance in any given colony was not a permanent feature. Comparison in Gott's book with Attila the Hun (*c.*406–53), who, while wide-ranging in his campaigning and devastation, scarcely created a lasting empire nor one with any positive features, did not apparently suffice, and the text,[3] back cover and catalogue copy of the book, was happy to rank the leaders of the British empire alongside Adolf Hitler, a highly inappropriate comparison:

> This revelatory new history punctures the widely held belief that the British Empire was an imaginative and civilizing enterprise. Instead, *Britain's Empire* reveals a history of systemic repression and almost perpetual violence, showing how British rule was imposed as a military operation and maintained as a military dictatorship. For colonized peoples, the experience was a horrific one, of slavery, famine, battle and extermination ... the British Empire provided a blueprint for the annihilation of peoples in twentieth-century Europe, and argues that its leaders must rank alongside the dictators of the twentieth century as authors of crimes against humanity on an infamous scale.[4]

Gott, himself a former Latin America correspondent and features editor for *The Guardian*, is the somewhat partisan author of works on Cuban history and Hugo Chávez, the left-wing authoritarian President of Venezuela from 1999 to 2013, and therefore has a committed position on American imperialism. It is interesting to note that the London publisher Verso, which claims to 'challenge the apologists of Empire and Capital', brought out, at the same time, an attack on capitalism and the 'imperialist-dominated Kyoto regime' in the *Planet or Death: Climate Justice Versus Climate Change* by Evo Morales, President of Bolivia. This comment is made not to suggest a conspiracy theory, but, rather, to imply an agenda.

---

2 R. Gott, *Britain's Empire* (London, 2011), p. 5.
3 Gott, *Britain's Empire*, p. 5.
4 Gott, *Britain's Empire*, p. 5.

Gott's book, ironically, had on the book cover (and in the catalogue) illustrations relating to the British conflict with Tipu Sultan of Mysore (r. 1782–99), which led, finally, to the overthrow of the latter in 1799 with the storming of his capital, Seringapatam. Tipu is a longstanding symbol of resistance to imperialism, but both he and his father, Haidar Ali, a soldier of fortune who took over the territory of Mysore in 1761, were also Muslim imperialists whose brutal expansion was a cause of great instability in southern India. Gott, however, was not really interested in contextualising British or Western imperialism in terms of a wider pattern of such rule across history and the world.[5] Nor was he concerned with the widespread discussion of the 'middle ground' of empire, the practice of relations that were not simply those of conquest.

Ghosts of Empire: Britain's Legacies in the Modern World (2011) by the Conservative MP Kwasi Kwarteng was far less strident. Nevertheless, he argued that the empire was poorly run (which, in practice, is the case with most government), and that the malign consequences are still apparent today. Kwarteng's focus on Iraq, Nigeria, Burma, Sudan, and Kashmir, however, again produced a somewhat slanted view, as British rule in all of them was short lived, and notably so in Iraq. None of Kwarteng's choices, moreover, comprised settler colonies. To a varying degree, these colonies were characterised by the harsh, sometimes murderous, treatment of the indigenous populations. Nevertheless, the former settler colonies can be regarded as a vindication of the hopes of imperialists. If imperialism is to be judged by legacies, some of which are very bleak, it is appropriate to note that, alongside the grim fate of the indigenous populations, Australia, New Zealand, and Canada have become highly successful countries. That, however, was not the case for many other colonies. Kwarteng again lacked much wider contextualisation in terms of other empires.

There were also popular histories on the Right that offered problematic accounts. In particular, Niall Ferguson's celebration of the empire as 'Anglobalisation'[6] was, at times, as presentist and simplistic as some approaches on the Left. The right-wing approach to Britain's recent imperial history is amplified by the range of books on Churchill, most of which are favourable.

---

5 Gott, *Britain's Empire*, pp. 138–9. For measured and valuable accounts of the period on which Gott focuses, C.A. Bayly, *Imperial Meridian: The British Empire and the World 1780–1830* (Harlow, 1989) and B. Collins, *War and Empire: The Expansion of Britain, 1790–1830* (London, 2010).

6 N. Ferguson, *Empire: How Britain Made the Modern World* (London, 2003).

The thesis of this book is that there is a need, as part of the public debate, to contest what may be seen as the 'politically correct' version of British empire history and to offer a narrative of the empire that will have greater complexity and that will avoid a simplistic moral condemnation of the past. In doing so, there is no intention to overlook the extent to which violence was involved both in imperial expansion and as a systematic and integral instrument of British imperial government. However, that imperial rule does not match current understandings of how human beings ought to organise themselves has been, and is, read back, in popular accounts of the past that very much offer the present as both superior and a frame of judgemental reference. This owes much to the extent to which the modern treatment of human and state development towards the present is largely focused, not on the role of empires, but, instead, on self-determination, democracy, and human rights. The last is understood in a collective as well as an individual fashion, and with this collective character being particularly clearly expressed in, and through, self-determination and democracy. During the 1950s and 1960s, anti-colonialists made use of the language of human rights to advance their central demands of self-determination and racial equality, and even to redefine human rights according to anti-colonial principles; although more in international forums (most obviously the United Nations) than domestically.

In contrast, as a reflection of the justifications of power, by the 1970s newly independent African and Asian states were increasingly apt to discredit what was called Westminster-style parliamentary democracy as an expression of Western imperialist and neo-colonial designs. As a result, they were able to rebut foreign criticism of an authoritarianism that was sometimes more marked than that of colonial powers. This pattern continues to this day, with the criticism more commonly focused on the application of human rights legislation. Thus, in 2013–14, there was African criticism about the International Criminal Court at The Hague, notably as it sought to prosecute senior Kenyan politicians, such as Uhuru Kenyatta, for murderous electoral violence at the time of the presidential election of 2007. There was a cruel irony that this rejection of international jurisdiction by Kenya took place at the same time that the British courts and press were used, and more successfully, to pursue claims for redress arising from the brutal treatment of Kenyans during the Mau Mau insurrection against British imperial rule in the 1950s.

As a consequence of the emphasis on self-determination, indeed of the present politics of knowledge, imperialism appears as an undesirable 'other', an intrusion and interference on the history of peoples, and a stage that had to be overcome to reach the present and/or a desired future. The Hegelian–Marxist tradition of analysis in terms of thesis and antithesis ensures that this theme of overcoming is presented as necessarily involving strife and struggle, and thus as entailing the overthrow of empires. More specifically, imperialism is not only seen as ending self-determination by ensuring foreign rule. It is also presented as compromising internal liberties, either explicitly or implicitly, not only in colonies but also in imperial metropoles or homelands, and as creating a false superiority/inferiority between 'equal' peoples, and thus as blocking democracy and appropriate development. In addition, imperialism serves for many critics as an equivalent to, or surrogate for, capitalism, and, indeed, is commonly treated as a particularly brutal and coercive aspect of capitalism. Appropriation is a key term for critics of imperial rule.

The undesirable character of imperialism is taken further as a result of the foundation or origin-accounts of many states, governments, political movements, and social and cultural tendencies. These bodies frequently present themselves, and assert their legitimacy, in terms of the overthrow of alien imperial control; alien and imperial being seen as conditions of each other. The necessity of overthrow becomes an explanation of past, present, and future, at once teleological and self-serving. It is very attractive for countries to have a heroic foundation born from self-liberation, the pattern seen with the USA. A gender dimension is added, and has been so increasingly in recent decades, by arguing that imperialism is quintessentially a form of aggressive and dangerous masculinity, and notably one that ravishes the colonised.[7] Such attitudes are then looked for in imperial conduct and attitudes.

Blaming imperial rule served, and serves, a variety of intellectual and political strategies. Within former imperial metropoles, such as Britain, for example, it can be employed to try to integrate immigrant communities as part of a rejection of a past. This rejection plays a related role in stigmatising aspects of the present that are undesirable: thus opposition to imperialism is used to characterise and condemn racialism, while racialism is held to characterise, and thus to condemn, imperialism. In practice, imperialism was about far more than racialism, and many racists, moreover, operated, and operate, in non-imperial contexts. A similar point can be made about imperialism and slavery.

At the global level, criticism of empires serves a similar purpose to that within specific states. It is employed in order to try to transform, or at least ease, political relations between one-time imperial powers and colonies, notably as an aspect of an explicit or implicit truth and reconciliation process. Specific political strategies build on a longer-lasting hostility to imperialism as a process

7 R. Hyam, *Empire and Sexuality* (Manchester, 1990).

that supposedly distorted both the imperialists and the colonists, and, in doing so, represented the full toxicity of imperial rule. Each of these views also represents a rejection of the one-time culture of imperialism. Thus, the debate over imperialism constitutes a prime instance of what is otherwise termed culture wars or history wars.[8]

Anti-imperial origin-accounts are the case not only for the states in the Third World that replaced European colonies after 1945, particularly India, which became independent from Britain in 1947, but also for other groups of countries. These include those countries in the Americas, from the USA to Chile, that, between 1775 and 1825, defeated attempts to maintain European imperial rule; and the nations that, in 1989–91, won independence as a result of the overthrow of Communist power in Eastern Europe (1989) and the collapse in 1991 of the Soviet Union and of Yugoslavia. This list, which can be extended, captures part of the range of empire[9] and the manner in which narrow and unchanging definitions of empire are of limited value. Indeed, the meaning of the words empire and imperialism changed across time.[10] In 1815, *Encyclopaedia Britannia* offered the definition, 'Empire, in political geography, a large extent of land, under the jurisdiction or government of an emperor'.[11]

However, aside from the issue of which rulers were legally entitled to call themselves emperors, and which deserved the designation for functional reasons, this definition failed to engage with republican governments. Moreover, the relationship between emperors and empires is no longer pertinent. One of the central elements in this book, indeed, is that empire was a dynamic, continually evolving, phenomenon. As a consequence, no one definition works, while the British empire we perceive today is overly shaped by our sense of the nineteenth century.

Recent decades provide instances of the continuing nature of the creation of new opportunities for anti-imperial discussion. Examples include the opposition to Pakistani rule of East Pakistan (now Bangladesh), which was overthrown in 1971, and the rejection of Serbian policy and power in the 1990s, notably in Bosnia and Kosovo. This situation is not tangential to the history of the British empire, because the more general global experience of imperialism and of decolonisation greatly helps condition responses to the British empire elsewhere

---

8 J. Black, *Contesting History: Narratives of Public History* (London, 2014).

9 A.L. Stoler, C. McGranahan, and P.C. Perdue (eds), *Imperial Formations* (Santa Fe, New Mexico, 2007).

10 R. Koebner, *Empire* (Cambridge, 1961) and, with H.D.R. Schmidt, *Imperialism: The Story and Significance of a Political Word, 1840–1960* (Cambridge, 1964).

11 *Encyclopaedia Britannia*, VIII (Edinburgh, 1815), p. 34.

in the world, as well as in Britain. For example, the view of an American on that empire may well be affected if he or she is of Ukrainian descent and has opinions about Russian imperial rule and ambitions.

The range of anti-imperial experience extends, more controversially, to current or very recent attempts to overthrow unwelcome rule, for example persistent separatist tensions within India, Indonesia, and China. Although these views are controversial, the Kashmir imbroglio thus becomes, in one light, an opposition to Indian imperialism, while Indian policy in Sri Lanka and the Himalayan chain towards Sikkim, Bhutan, and Nepal, can also be regarded as imperialist in tone and tendency. Independent in 1947, India and Pakistan can be treated not only as successor states to British India, but also as heirs to its expansionist attitudes. Indian competition with China and other powers, in these areas and further afield, especially in Afghanistan, appears as a new imperialist 'Great Game', redolent of the competition between Britain and Russia in the nineteenth century that has been described in these terms.

Indonesia succeeded in 1949 to the imperialist position and policies of the Dutch East Indies. Indeed, the Dutch created the state that became Indonesia. The legacy of Dutch imperialism contributed to regional opposition to Indonesian rule, notably in Achin (Atceh) and Papua New Guinea, but that rule was imperialist in itself, notably with the Indonesian occupation of the Portuguese colony of East Timor in 1975, as the Portuguese empire collapsed, against the wishes of the local population. After a bitter struggle, East Timor finally won independence in 2002.

The language of imperialism might change with the end of Western control, and that was certainly true of India and Indonesia. However, in each case, the reality of power remains that of rule over a large territory incorporating areas that have distinctive histories and cultures. Thus, in Sulawesi/the Celebes, Indonesia means rule from Java, which is the centre of power and the island with the most people, whatever the identity of those exercising rule. An emphasis on such a wide-ranging scope for imperialism offers a major qualification to any presentation of imperialism as essentially Western. This point also emerges from a consideration of the Chinese position in Tibet and Xinjiang, positions established by successive conquests, notably in the eighteenth century, and by the subsequent suppression of rebellions. Chinese rule in both definitely matches criteria usually employed to discuss empires.

The wider range of empire can also be seen in the case of the USA. Repeated mention, in the USA and elsewhere, of the American Declaration of Independence in 1776, and of the related liberation from an allegedly overbearing British empire, underlines the extent to which anti-imperialism is a central feature in the ideology of the modern world and of modernisation of politics and government.[12] The American Patriots presented opposition to George III of Britain (r. 1760–1820), and to the Westminster parliament, as anti-imperial as well as advancing freedom. Thereafter, the USA adopted that history and took that approach as a key theme in its attitudes towards the outside world. This approach could serve not only as a continuing critique of the British empire, but also for other empires. This anti-imperial stance was seen in President Woodrow Wilson's support for national self-determination at the close of World War One, particularly in Eastern Europe and China; in President Franklin Delano Roosevelt's anti-imperial attitudes during World War Two, notably at the expense of the British empire;[13] and in American policy at the time of the Suez Crisis of 1956.

This process of continuing hostility to empire was encouraged by the extent to which many immigrants to the USA fled imperial rule elsewhere, as with Jews leaving Russia, both under the Romanov dynasty and under the Communists, or could see themselves or be presented as doing so. The Irish, another important immigrant group in the USA, had, and still have, a generally very hostile view of the British empire. As a result of the Anglo-Irish Act of Union of 1800, the Irish were represented in the Westminster parliament. However, although they eventually gained the vote as a result of Catholic Emancipation in 1829, many Irish Catholics did not feel that this situation secured their interests. There was major Irish participation in the British empire, notably in the army, but this can be presented as a consequence of a lack of other opportunities, although, in turn, it is a less than full account of this participation. Participation in the empire tends to be ignored in Irish popular memory, with the exception of the increasing interest in the Irish role in World War One. Instead of shared Anglo-Irish roles, it is the devastating Irish Famine of 1845–49, and the resulting large-scale emigration, that attract lasting attention, and then are used to characterise the British empire in a hostile light, not least in the USA.

Anti-imperialism proved a key theme in American policy. American hostility to imperial rule was seen in the opposition to European intervention in the Americas, as with the Monroe Doctrine of 1823, and the hostility of Emperor Maximilian, the unsuccessful French-backed Austrian ruler of Mexico in the 1860s; and also in opposition to the maintenance of the European empires after World War Two. For example, the Americans proved unwilling to back

12 D. Armitage, *The Declaration of Independence: A Global History* (Cambridge, Massachusetts, 2007).

13 F.J. Harbutt, *Yalta 1945: Europe and America at the Crossroads* (Cambridge, 2010).

the French presence in Algeria, which, in contrast, was seen in France as part of metropolitan France and not as a colony, or to support the Portuguese position in Goa, which was seized by India in 1961.

It was an irony, unappreciated by most Americans and resented by many of them, that the USA, which definitely took an imperialist course in North America in the nineteenth century, at the expense of Native Americans, in addition to Spain, Mexico, and British rule in Canada,[14] was itself to be regarded as the leading imperial power, initially in the Americas, and subsequently in the Pacific and then across the world. Indeed, seeking to find parallels and precursors for the current American position,[15] some of the modern literature about empire looks at nineteenth-century expansion, American, British, and elsewhere, in that light. This theme is considered in Chapter 7.

Any comparison of American and British power and settlement raises the vexed question of the definition of empire.[16] America, indeed, refused to treat what others regarded as in effect its colonies, for example Cuba and the Philippines, in that light. In these cases, issues of informal, as opposed to formal, empire come to the fore. Each type of empire can be seen in the case of both America and Britain, and it is accordingly mistaken to adopt too rigid a definition of empire. Practices of informal empire permitted each power to reconcile its influence with respect for the sovereignty of other states and/or with anti-imperial ideology.[17]

The comparison of American and British power and settlement also raises the distinction between what can be seen as 'internal' and 'external' empires. The former, with its emphasis on contiguous landward expansion, is closer to the American trajectory at least prior to the 1890s, and to that of China, and the latter, with the stress on trans-oceanic expansion, to the British. At the same time, landward or nearby expansion was also seen with the British empire. Considering this point helps to relate what happens to the 'Four Nations', English, Scottish, Welsh, and Irish, the British peoples at home,[18] to what

14 J. Black, *The Shaping of Mastery in North America, 1519–1871* (Bloomington, Indiana, 2012).

15 M.B. Cosmopoulos (ed.), *Experiencing War: Trauma and Society in Ancient Greece and Today* (Chicago, Illinois, 2007); E.N. Luttwak, *The Virtual American Empire: War, Faith, and Power* (New Brunswick, New Jersey, 2009).

16 J. Darwin, *After Tamerlane: The Global History of Empire since 1405* (London, 2007).

17 J. Van Vleck, *Empire of the Air: Aviation and the American Ascendancy* (Cambridge, Massachusetts, 2013).

18 H. Kearney, *The British Isles: A History of Four Nations* (Cambridge, 1989).

happened in the wider empire, the British people(s) overseas. This approach to the British empire became more pressing in 2013–14 as the debate over Scottish independence moved forward to a referendum.

The contrast in attitudes to American power, between attitudes within America and those without, is, and was, a familiar one, and one where an historical perspective is useful. Indeed, states that had an anti-imperial slant in their foundation accounts or public history were frequently to be regarded as empires themselves, and correctly so. This process can be taken back to the origins of anti-imperial discussion in Antiquity. That lineage is significant for Britain and the USA due to the long and central role of the Classics in the education of their élites, a role, however, that has largely ceased in recent decades. The Greeks presented Persian rule, as experienced by Greek cities in Asia Minor (Turkey) from the sixth century BCE, and as threatened for the rest of Greece with the unsuccessful Persian invasions of 490 and 480 BCE, as both despotic and barbarian; and saw each of despotism and barbarianism as demonstrating the other. The cultural legacy of Greece ensured that this set of beliefs was to be important subsequently to critical discussion about imperialism. As foreign, imperialism could be presented as barbarian and despotic, and, as barbarian and despotic, foreign. Other aspects of the Classical legacy were significant for the discussion of empires. The distinction between bad and good monarchs provided a way to explain why rule by an individual could be both undesirable, and thus imperialising, and yet also desirable, and therefore appropriate. As such, discussion of imperial rule overlapped with that about tyrants in the Greek city-states. A reminder of the very different echoes of the Antique world as far as imperialism is concerned was provided by the 'out of Africa' debate of the twentieth century. In this, it was argued that Classical and modern Western imperialising tendencies led to a failure to appreciate the strengths of African culture and, notably, and less accurately, the alleged African character of Ancient Egypt.[19]

Ascribing barbarian and foreign characteristics to imperial rule complicated the discussion of such practices within the Classical Greek world. Having created an anti-imperial language directed against the Persians, the Greeks then faced difficulties in using it effectively against other Greeks. Yet, Athens, and other leading city-states, were, with reason, to be regarded as imperial powers. In the fifth century BCE, Athens employed a form of 'informal empire' to direct the Delian League, a loose maritime confederation of Aegean states based on

19 R.H. Fritze, *Invented Knowledge: False History, Fake Science and Pseudo-Religions* (London, 2009), pp. 201–55.

the island of Delos, but one that Athens increasingly governed in a high-handed fashion. The resulting rebellions can be seen as anti-imperial. Athens' policies helped cause the Peloponnesian War with Sparta in 431–404, and affected its course.

Some of the Classical Greeks, notably Demosthenes (*c*.383–22 BCE) in his *Philippics*, subsequently developed anti-imperial language against the expansionist Philip II of Macedon (r. 359–36 BCE), who ruled a territory to the north of Classical Greece that many Greeks appear to have regarded as barbarian. Once absorbed (a word meaning conquest for some, notably after the battle of Chaeronea in 338 BCE, and co-operation for others) within the Macedonian world, the Greeks found themselves part, and only a minor part, of a widespread Macedonian empire. For Philip's son, Alexander the Great (r. 336–23 BCE), conquered the Persian empire and advanced as far as India, which he reached in 326 BCE. If Alexander's empire lacked cohesion, and fell apart after his early death, the Hellenistic successor empires in South-West Asia, Egypt, and the Balkans in turn were far flung, especially that of the Seleucids from the fourth to the first century BCE: in 305 BCE Seleucus ruled from the Indus to the border of modern Syria.

These empires faced anti-imperial opposition, notably with the Maccabees in Israel after 166 BCE. The significance of Jewish history for Christendom, ensured that this opposition was absorbed into the general anti-imperial tradition of the West. In turn, the Maccabees provided a prime instance of the subsequent use of opposition to the empires of Antiquity in order to vindicate assertions of national independence. Thus, modern Israel looked back to the Maccabees and, even more, to the later, self-sacrificing resistance of the garrison at Masada to the conquering imperial forces of Rome in 74 CE, not least because these instances provided a more assertive and forceful account of an origin for Israel than in terms of the Holocaust at the hands of the Germans in World War Two. The latter lacked the fighting resistance, as well as the location in Israel, that many Israeli commentators thought necessary.

Opposition to Rome repeatedly proved a rallying symbol for later nationalists, who, ironically, were dependent for their information about this opposition on the writers of Classical Rome, such as Tacitus (*c*.55–118). His *Agricola*, a biography of the great Roman general and his father-in-law, recorded resistance for example in Caledonia, later Scotland. German hostility to Papal power at the time of the Protestant Reformation in the early sixteenth century was given historical depth by reference to resistance to the Roman empire, and notably to the destruction by German tribesmen under Arminius of three legions commanded by Varus in the Teutoburger Wald in 9 CE. The location of the Papacy in Rome provided a clear reference point at the time of the Reformation. The battle was the subject of literary work by Ulrich von Hutten (1488–1523), who influenced Martin Luther, the founder of German Protestantism. Moreover, this episode was to be powerfully revived by German nationalists in the nineteenth century, notably after the formation of the Second German Empire in 1871. A commanding statue of Arminius brandishing the Sword of Vengeance, completed in 1875 under the Second Empire, can still be seen near Detmold. This Prussian-centred empire was soon to become an imperial power in Africa and the Pacific, as it chased its 'place in the sun', often brutally so. The German conquest of what is now Namibia in South-West Africa in 1904–05 was far more deadly than the British or French conquest of any of their colonies; not that that excuses brutalities in the case of the latter. Moreover, in 1914, Germany helped launch a war in which it revealed extensive plans for imperial conquest in Europe, both in Eastern and Western Europe. The Germans had already annexed most of Alsace and part of Lorraine from France after victory in the Franco-Prussian War of 1870–71. Thus, as in Britain and France, a pedigree traced back to resistance to Roman imperialism did not prevent its modern counterpart.

Other uses of opposition to Classical Rome included the Dutch at the time of the successful Dutch Revolt against Philip II of Spain in the late sixteenth century making reference to Cluvius, who had led Frisian resistance to the Roman empire in this area. Seeking an exemplary past, Portugal emphasised resistance to Roman conquest.

There was also interest in Britain in the resistance to Roman imperialism. Caratacus, an unsuccessful leader of opposition in the 40s CE, was presented by Tacitus as an impressive figure of integrity. Tacitus's discussion of the Caledonians of Highland Scotland, an example of the theme of the bravery of primitive virtue in resistance to imperial conquest, was subsequently to be adopted and adapted by the British historian Edward Gibbon in his *Decline and Fall of the Roman Empire* (1776–88). Moreover, at the height of their own imperial power, the British, in 1898, erected Thomas Thornycroft's dramatic sculpture of Boudicca at Westminster Bridge in London, where it can still be seen. As ruler of the Iceni, a tribe in what was to be named East Anglia (after the Angles, successful later invaders in the fifth century CE), she had rebelled in 59–60 CE against the brutality of Roman imperial rule, although the details are impossible to recover and she is a creation of Roman writers offering differing accounts. Boudicca could be presented as a heroic failure.[20] Thornycroft's sculpture underlines the repeated ability of empire to incorporate a range of historical episodes and in a frequently

20 R. Hingley and C. Unwin, *Boudica: Iron Age Warrior Queen* (London, 2005).

inconsistent fashion; in this case, the British empire incorporating the Roman. Leading British political intellectuals discussed the relationship between Britain and Rome, as with James, Viscount Bryce's *The Ancient Roman Empire and the British Empire in India* (1914). Bryce also emphasised the significance of 'white' colonial ethnicity and institutions.[21] A statue of Agricola was put up over the entrance to Manchester Town Hall, a monument to the wealth and confidence flowing from the Industrial Revolution. Rome has repeatedly served as a point of comparison for the USA.[22]

Reference to the Dutch and the British serves as a reminder that, as with the Athenians and Americans, peoples with an anti-imperial account of their own history, nevertheless, could become major imperial powers in their own right. The English use of successful opposition to Philip II at the time of the Spanish Armada in 1588, and, subsequently, against Louis XIV of France (r. 1643–1715), Napoleon (in control of France, 1799–1814, 1815), and Germany at the time of both world wars (1914–18, 1939–45), can be readily fitted into this context.

In part, this situation captured the marked contrast between good empire and bad empire that was central to political thought and rhetoric. Legitimate authority was seen as sanctioned by God, as part of the divine plan, and as having a clear moral purpose. The defeat of imperial powers could therefore be presented as divine judgement on bad empires, or at least emperors, that lacked such a purpose, as with the fall of the Babylonian empire, a topic from Antiquity luridly depicted in the nineteenth century by the French painter Delacroix. He also castigated contemporary non-Western imperialism, notably the Turks shown oppressing the Greeks in *The Massacre at Chios* (1823). The contrast between good and bad, which, understandably, can be assessed as self-serving, was highly significant in giving purpose to imperialism. The dichotomy of good and bad empire drew on the longstanding difference between the existential empires of God and the Devil, a core theme in St Augustine's *City of God* (412–27). A product of the late and collapsing Roman empire, this book by a bishop was to be the fundamental text for medieval Christian thought.

---

21 J. de Groot, *Empire and History Writing in Britain c.1750–2012* (Manchester, 2013), p. 197.

22 C. Murphy, *Are We Rome? The Fall of an Empire and the Fate of America* (New York, 2007); T.F. Madden, *Empires of Trust: How Rome Built – and America is Building – a New World* (New York, 2008); A. Goldsworthy, *How Rome Fell: Death of a Superpower* (New Haven, Connecticut, 2009); E. Adler, 'Post-9/11 Views of Rome and the Nature of "Defensive Imperialism"', *International Journal of the Classical Tradition*, 15 (2008), pp. 587–610.

In a different context and with a very different language, the contrast between good and bad empire was also seen in a diffuse fashion in discussion by colonial administrators and others about their own imperial rule and destiny. Thus, the British debate about India prior to World War One was really a debate about the accountability, competency, and standards of the administration, and not about Indian fitness for self-government. Very few politicians thought the latter a realistic prospect within any meaningful timetable. The contrast between good empire and bad empire has only been replaced by an equation of empire itself and bad over the last century, with that equation then read back into history.

It was not necessary to turn back to the might of the Classical Romans to find accounts of the defiance of empires at and as key moments of national formation. The Middle Ages provided many instances. Scots have frequently referred to their war of independence from England in the run-up to the 2014 vote on Scottish independence. As a reminder that the meaning of the past is frequently transformed, the victories over English forces at Stirling (1297) and Bannockburn (1314) and the declaration of Scottish independence at Arbroath in 1320 were all presented in the nineteenth century not as a call for independence but as providing the background for the parliamentary union of England and Scotland in 1707, with Scotland able then to negotiate from a position of independence. In contrast, the growth of Scottish nationalistic separatism from the 1960s and, even more, 2000s, led to a focus on the medieval war of independence as an apparent precursor and example for a struggle against what was presented as modern English imperialism, with the existence of Britain regarded as an expression of this imperialism. In August 2014, the Scottish Cabinet met at Arbroath in order to draw on these resonances.

In, and from, the Middle Ages, there was a similar use of conflict by Flemings and Swiss, who pointed to glorious victories over the rulers of France and Austria respectively. William Tell, a probably legendary figure, became the key figure in accounts of the latter and provided Swiss history with an anti-imperial character. In turn, the imperial position of the Habsburgs, the rulers of Austria, gave this account later resonance. Subsequently, Habsburg support for the Catholic or Counter-Reformation, especially in the Thirty Years' War (1618–48), ensured that German Protestants and their foreign allies presented religious liberty in terms of opposition not only to the imperial religious pretensions of the papacy, but also to the cesaro-papalism of the Habsburg Holy Roman Emperors.

For the early-modern period, the Spanish empire of Philip II (r. 1556–98), the first empire on which, thanks to the establishment of Spanish positions in the Philippines from the 1560s, the sun literally never set, became the basis for accounts of Dutch and English independence. The defeat of the apparently overwhelming Spanish Armada in 1588, a fleet designed to make invasion possible, provided the key instance of the role of Spain in the English narrative, as well as substantiating beliefs in a providential dispensation for England. Celebrations were annually held thereafter as part of a new calendar of Protestant providentialism. From 1605, what became Guy Fawkes Day followed, to mark the failure of a Catholic plot to blow up parliament. Confidence in divine support was to prove an important bridge between belief in national destiny and confidence in imperial purpose.[23] The religious dimension in imperial history is always important, and clearly so for Britain. For example, during World War Two (1939–45), Winston Churchill sometimes presented the struggle with Hitler in religious terms. More generally, British attitudes towards Christian trusteeship and moral leadership were significant in encouraging support, first for imperial rule by Britain (and by others judged by Britain to act appropriately) and then for decolonisation by Britain and others.

Annual celebrations helped memorialise episodes of providential support, for example with the later treatment of the Armada of 1588 in Stuart England, creating a history that demonstrated purpose, and these episodes could also be brought forward at times of national emergency. Using the device of a play within a play, Richard Brinsley Sheridan's *The Critic* (1779) mocks the production of a play focused on the Armada at a time of concern about possible Bourbon (France and Spain) invasion during the War of American Independence; an invasion plan that year was unsuccessful. By then, as a reminder that different imperial roles could be played simultaneously, Britain was both a great power and also one whose imperial rule was itself under challenge. This challenge came not only from the Americans but also, in and after 1778, from their allies, the French, who were joined, in 1779, by Spain and in 1780 by the Dutch. As such, the War of American Independence appears as more than an anti-imperial struggle; although it has been presented as such both in America, and in India where the British fought first the Marathas and then Mysore. The Americans themselves had an imperial strategy, both in British-ruled Canada, which they invaded in 1775, being driven out in 1776,[24] and, more successfully and

23 K. Wilson, 'The Island Race: Captain Cook, Protestant Evangelicalism and the Construction of English National Identity, 1760–1800', in T. Claydon and I. McBride (eds), *Protestantism and National Identity: Britain and Ireland, c.1650–c.1850* (Cambridge, 1998), p. 290; S. Brown, *Providence and Empire, 1815–1914* (London, 2008). For the USA, F. Ninkovich, *Global Dawn: The Cultural Foundation of American Internationalism 1865–1890* (Cambridge, Massachusetts, 2009).

24 M.R. Anderson, *The Battle of the Fourteenth Colony: America's War of Liberation in Canada, 1774–1776* (Lebanon, New Hampshire, 2013).

lastingly, at the expense of the Native Americans. American control of African Americans can also be referred to as imperial, as slavery was a particularly harsh and cruel instance of control over people. Leaving this aside, the contest between the Bourbons (the ruling dynasties of France and Spain) and the British was one for imperial dominance, notably in the Caribbean and the western Mediterranean, while conflict with the Dutch and France added an important Indian Ocean dimension.

This point captures a central reality of imperial history, to employ it in the sense of world history from an imperial viewpoint. Despite the assumption widely propagated, the choice generally was not between empire and non-empire, as suggested or implied in many public myths and by numerous writers, both past and present, critical of imperialism. Instead, the choice was usually between different empires or, at best, and more particularly after 1945, different types of empire. Unless this point is appreciated, much of the discussion of imperialism and imperial legacies is of limited value as an accurate account of the past; but, if the point is appreciated, then much of the tone of the current discussion is inappropriate. If, for example, during the War of American Independence (1775–83), control of East and West Florida or St Lucia or Minorca, or the West African bases of the slave trade, such as Gorée, changed hands, it was not a case of the expulsion of imperial powers (which only occurred, during the war, in the Thirteen Colonies of North America), but, rather, of one imperial power replacing another. The latter, moreover, would have also happened if the Americans had conquered Canada. The Floridas, transferred from Spain to Britain in 1763 at the end of the Seven Years' War, were returned in 1783. In the French Revolutionary and Napoleonic Wars (1792–1815), France lost Saint-Domingue/Haiti to a slave revolution, but all its other overseas losses were to Britain, with the exception of Louisiana, which was sold to the USA in 1803. From the perspective of Native Americans, the USA was very much an imperial power.

This theme of transfer between empires remained important in World War One (1914–18), with the disposal by the victorious powers of German colonies and territories of the Ottoman (Turkish) empire as League of Nations mandates, in other words protectorates. Thus, German East Africa became British Tanganyika, while Syria was put under French control. The expansion of empires at the expense of others also appeared an option with Italian colonies after World War Two. Britain occupied Italian Somaliland and much of Libya during and after that conflict, and there was some consideration of annexation.

This aspect of imperial history is scarcely ignored by scholars, but, in comparison with the discussion when Britain was a major empire, it is badly underplayed today because the standard assumption in much of the public commentary is that of empire or non-empire. In part, this situation pertains because the emotional, intellectual, and political commitment to anti-imperialism, specifically the allegedly inherent self-determination of those defined as peoples, is so great. There is a belief in the self-determination of all peoples and the independent sovereignty of all states, a misleading historicising of this belief, and a reluctance to appreciate the extent to which such an outcome did not seem an option to major powers.

Instead, with imperialism often competitive, in practice, if not in theory, there was a determination on the part of imperial powers to prevent the rise of rivals. Areas outside imperial control could thus appear a source of vulnerability, and one that had to be secured by the extension of imperial control. This was the case, for example, with the competition between Ottomans and Safavids for control of the Caucasus region from the sixteenth to eighteenth centuries, a competition in which, once the Safavid empire collapsed in the 1720s, the Russians came to play a greater role. The Ottomans and Safavids were the ruling dynasties in empires that can be misleadingly described as Turkish and Iranian, but these terms reflected an anachronistic ethnogenesis that is rooted in modern ideas of national development. In practice, the Ottomans and Safavids were conquering groups from outside the boundaries of those modern states.

The tendency to provide security by expansion was also seen with Britain's African empire: the 'frontier' or non-colonialised areas represented a vacuum that apparently had to be filled, as was the case of Sudan once the British were established in Egypt in 1882. The move into Egypt itself was motivated by the drive to control the newly constructed Suez Canal, opened in 1869, and thus the route to India. Part of the Egyptian empire, Sudan was affected by a large-scale rebellion by the Mahdi, a Muslim revivalist. If, for the imperial powers, these areas apparently represented chaos, threat, and a vacuum, it was sometimes the case that this was indeed true. However, the British were able to put up with Mahdist rule in Sudan for a number of years after the Mahdist killing at Khartoum in 1885 of Charles Gordon, the British Governor General for the Egyptian Khedive, and a heroic figure for the Victorians.

The functionalist approach to imperialism, whether, as in this case, as dealing with an apparent source of vulnerability, or in other terms, for example economic advantage, underplays the values involved in seeking to rule others; values that frequently attract attention and opprobrium in the public debate in the modern world. The functionalist approach also opens up a contrast between empires operating in a highly competitive context (as Spain and the

Ottomans did in the Mediterranean in the sixteenth century, and Russia and Britain in the region of Afghanistan in the late nineteenth, or the Europeans in Africa in the same period during the 'Scramble for Africa'[25]) and, on the other hand, those empires that did not face, or acknowledge, comparable imperial powers. The last was the Chinese position until repeated defeat at the hand of foreign powers in the nineteenth century. That contrast is a realist one, to employ the vocabulary of international relations theory, but there is also the comparison between Western and Chinese imperialism offered by the extent to which the condescending and controlling Chinese attitude to neighbouring peoples, most successfully in Korea, displayed the type of superiority and values generally deplored when seen in the case of Western imperial powers. Moreover, in contrast to the standard theme of the Chinese as motivated by Confucian values and being essentially defensive, there has been an emphasis in the recent literature on China as an expansionist empire. This emphasis has a weight in current discussion of Chinese power.[26] In short, differences over the character of imperialism are, at least in part, linked to issues of political presentation and scholarly assessment.

Comparative contexts for the discussion of empire range widely: alongside imperial growth, limits, and overstretch as themes,[27] comes decline, real, threatening, or possible. Some comparisons in this case command attention, for example, for nineteenth-century thinkers, Classical Rome with Britain, or, for their modern counterparts, America in the early twenty-first century with Britain in the 1930s. Other comparisons appear less pertinent. The Ottoman empire struck contemporaries in the nineteenth century as a weak and declining empire, the 'Sick Man of Europe', but there is little helpful comparison in this case with the more recent decline of the British empire. So also for the Ottoman empire and nineteenth-century Brazil and, even more, Mexico, which were new (and very different) dynastic empires that came to nought with republicanism, instead, succeeding.

Much of the tension in the contention over imperialism focuses on the debate over its values, but these values were not the sole drive behind the establishment, expansion, and sustaining of empires. Instead, there was a host of practicalities

---

25 M.E. Chamberlain, *The Scramble for Africa* (3rd edn, London, 2010).

26 H. van de Ven (ed.), *Warfare in Chinese History* (Leiden, 2000); P.C. Perdue, *China Marches West: The Qing Conquest of Central Eurasia* (Cambridge, Massachusetts, 2005); P.A. Lorge (ed.), *Debating War in Chinese History* (Leiden, 2013).

27 T. Andrade and W. Reger (eds), *The Limits of Empire: European Imperial Formations in Modern World History* (Farnham, 2012); F.C. Schneid (ed.), *The Projection and Limitations of Imperial Powers, 1618–1850* (Leiden, 2012).

that came into play, principally the strategic competition referred to above and the related strategic cultures, but also, prominently, commercial issues. The drive for resources and that for markets played key roles.

Strategic competition does not tend to attract praise, but it was a factor seen over the last century in what were life-and-death struggles for the Western liberal order, those against Nazi Germany and the Communist Soviet Union. In the former case, there were clear instances of prophylactic imperial interventions, those designed to thwart the possibility that independent or quasi-independent states would turn to hostile patrons. This factor was seen in the British conquest of Iraq in 1940, and in the Anglo-Soviet invasion of Iran in August–September 1941. In both Iraq and Iran, there was, alongside the overthrow of nationalist governments, justified British concern about rising German influence in what were neutral states, and at a time when the British empire was under great pressure. A British force from the Indian Army advanced to Tehran for the first time. In 1940 and 1942, moreover, the British forced changes of government in Egypt in order to ensure opposition to Germany. In a different context, the establishment of Allied power in the Danish colonies of Iceland and Greenland after the German conquest of Denmark in 1940 was a prophylactic action designed to thwart the possibility of a German takeover. French nationalists feared that British imperialism played a role in interventions against Vichy rule in 1940–42, notably in Syria, Lebanon, and Madagascar.

Imperial power, largely indirect, but, at times, more overt, was also employed during the Cold War, in order to impose control, ensure cohesion, and prevent the risk of hostile action, as with American intervention in Iran in 1953 and, very differently in type and far more overt, that of the Soviet Union in Hungary in 1956, in Czechoslovakia in 1968, and, far less successfully, in Afghanistan in 1979. From the nineteenth century, American policy in Central America was frequently seen as imperial in character, with new ideologies and issues imprinted on old patterns of concern and intervention. By the time of the Cold War, however, imperial rule faced serious criticism from within the West (the metropoles), as well as large-scale opposition in the colonies and other areas subject to imperialist intervention and pressure. Western criticism of the purpose and/or nature of imperial control had increased from the 1920s, with George Orwell, who served in the Burma Police Service from 1922 to 1927, arguing that, 'When the white man turns tyrant, it is his own freedom that he destroys'.[28] The view that colonies are dangerous to the health of democracy was long held by political critics, going back to the Classical world, and, more

28 G. Orwell, *Burmese Days* (London, 1934).

specifically, the argument that imperial strivings harm the chances for an egalitarian social order.[29]

There was also a view on the Right in the second half of the twentieth century, and notably from what saw itself as the modernising Right, notably in Britain and France, that imperialism was redundant. This view was based in part on a perception that the colonial project was exhausted and that there was inadequate force to sustain it in the face of opposition. This was seen, for example, in the Gaullist response to the crisis in French control in Algeria, a response that led to independence for Algeria in 1962 in opposition to the views of many of the French colonists and part of the army. In Britain, a Labour government was responsible for the fundamental burst of decolonisation in 1947–48, notably independence for India, but also for what became Pakistan, Sri Lanka, Myanmar, and Israel. However, Conservative governments presided in 1957–64 when most of empire was wound up and when the first attempt to join the European Economic Community (which became the European Union) was launched. Harold Macmillan, prime minister from 1957 to 1963, saw both policies in terms of the modernisation of Britain: one with a different pattern of national strength coming to the fore than that of traditional imperialism.

In contrast, depending on the part of the world being discussed, and especially prior to 1500, earlier opposition to empire had often been to the particular identity of the ruling power, as much as to the fact of imperial rule. Thus, in Khurusan (North-East Persia) and western Afghanistan, which were repeatedly contested by the Safavids, Uzbeks, and Mughals, rival imperial powers, in the sixteenth century, the question pertained to which empire, not whether empire, was in command. A similar point can be made about Spanish success in 1519–21 in winning large-scale local support in Mesoamerica (Mexico) against Aztec rule, a case of one empire replacing another. The harshness of Aztec rule helps explain why Hernán Cortés, the Spanish leader, won considerable local support from those who had been subjugated by the Aztecs, support that played a major role in the campaigning of 1521.[30] This is a point, indeed a perspective, that tends to be ignored or underrated by modern Western and non-Western critics of Spanish expansion. Similarly, the Germans initially benefited from a degree of local support when they invaded the Soviet Union in 1941, notably in Ukraine and the Baltic republics. This support, which remains controversial to the present, included limited involvement in the Holocaust.

---

29 H. Lebovics, *Imperialism and the Corruption of Democracies* (Durham, North Carolina, 2006).

30 R. Hassig, *Mexico and the Spanish Conquest* (London, 1994).

There was not necessarily, in opposition to imperialism, any clear understanding of statehood, national identity, or frontiers. Indeed, all three tend to be exaggerated and read back by modern commentators seeking a long-term identity for present-day entities, and thus, in part, trying to validate them. Ethnogenesis played a major role in this process, as did a belief in inherent competition between peoples and states. Thus, a form of Social Darwinism fulfilled a part in providing long-term credibility for the opposition to imperial rule. Hostility to imperialism also reflects the extent to which a national basis for states became the norm in the twentieth century, a norm advanced by the Versailles Peace Settlement of 1919, the League of Nations, and the United Nations. This approach made alternatives appear inappropriate and wrong, and thus set up imperialism as the undesirable 'other'. This process was enhanced by the hostile and self-validating analysis of the supposed values of empires. The nationalist stance, however, appears of limited validity from the longer historical perspective, notably given the extent to which, across much of the world, there was only a limited sense of national identity for most of history.

Moreover, in many areas, particularly in cities, there were not homogenous nations, but, instead, a variety of ethnic groups. In a major instance of transnationalism, this variety can be seen as contributing greatly to the identity, character, and success of multi-national empires, which were therefore far more than states incorporating areas each of which had coherent national populations, the last a view at least implicit in the arguments of some critics of empire. Indeed, the ability, sometimes with considerable difficulty, to maintain peace in complex multi-ethnic communities was an aspect of successful imperial rule, one that underlines its value. Like the British empire, in, for example, Bombay (Mumbai) and Singapore, the Ottoman empire was a good instance of the mixture of ethnic groups, not least in cosmopolitan cities such as Alexandria, Smyrna (Izmir), Salonica, and Constantinople (Istanbul). Such cities contained large numbers of minority groups, notably Armenians, Greeks, and Jews.[31] Similarly, there were considerable numbers of Muslims in rural areas in the Balkans, especially in Kosovo and Albania.

Subsequent problems in such areas are not so much a legacy of empire, as Jack Straw, then British Foreign Secretary suggested in 2003, with reference to former British colonies, but, rather, a legacy of the end of empire, which is a very different point. If empires ended in the way they did because of what

31 B. Kolluoğlu and M. Toksöz (eds), *Cities of the Mediterranean: From the Ottomans to the Present Day* (London, 2010); P. Clark (ed.), *The Oxford Handbook of Cities in World History* (Oxford, 2013).

they were, this was partly because of their character, notably their ethnic heterogeneity. 'Ethnic cleansing' may appear logical from the perspective of ethnically based national states, based at least in part on a reaction against empire, such as twentieth-century Turkey, Egypt, and Serbia, but is not from that of polyglot empires. Thus, under the Treaty of Lausanne of 1923 ending the Greek–Turkish conflict following World War One and marking the replacement of the Ottoman empire by Turkey, there was a large-scale expulsion by Greece and Turkey of those Muslims and Christians who, on religious grounds, were judged alien. Similarly, although without such a clearance, Protestants in the new Irish Free State did not benefit from Irish independence in 1922. However, in newly separate Northern Ireland, their dominant position was reflected in the character of the government, and Catholics were denied opportunities.

From the perspective of many groups, empires such as those ruled by the Ottomans, Habsburgs (Austria), and Britain, could be more benign than the ethnically based nation-states that succeeded them. Not all empires were benign to minority ethnic groups, but many were. The British concept of imperial civilisation included religious tolerance (up to a point) and ethnic diversity. In addition, Britain eventually sought to end formal enslavement in its empire (and elsewhere), although the labour situation continued to be grossly inegalitarian on an ethnic basis in the colonies, and even more so than in the metropole.

Any debate about imperialism should address the question about its relationship with ethnic variety. Such variety itself was functionally an advantage for imperial systems, and notably for their commercial viability. This argument from the past is of interest today. In an increasingly multi-cultural world, marked by mass migrations and new intermixing of peoples, the wiser choice may well be the larger and more capacious political unit, rather than the narrower and more exclusive one. Empires, indeed, arouse particular scholarly interest at present because, for all their faults, they are perceived to embody a wealth of experience in the management of difference and diversity. The sympathetic BBC documentary series on the Ottoman empire broadcast in 2013 was particularly instructive in this respect.

This approach has become particularly pertinent over the last two decades with a shift towards transnationalism as both a means of analysis and a value-system, if not ideology. Transnationalism presents the present and future in terms of international communities that are not contained within, nor expressed in terms of, national states. Transnational accounts can lead in a variety of directions, and these accounts have a number of consequences for the discussion of imperialism. Transnationalism can be deployed both to defend imperialism, as a way to organise and protect a multi-ethnic world, and also to provide a basis for condemning imperialism as a form of national imposition on such a world. Again, there is a level of ahistoricism in both approaches. The idea that governance should automatically seek to protect diversity is, in many respects, a modern view. Moreover, the treatment of imperialism as a form of national imposition on other nations is highly problematic for periods prior to the nineteenth century, not least as it assumes the clear existence of nations.

The shifting nature of values is certainly part of the story. Today, there is an emphasis on universal values and institutions, expressed in, and through, human rights and international courts, as well as on the extent to which communications, culture, trade, and, in particular, migration, are making national criteria invalid. This account is then read back into the past. Universal criteria, such as self-determination, democracy, and human rights, undermined the mental world of traditional imperialism. This mental world was based on differences between people within, as well as between, empires. However, paradoxically, the subsequent use of these universal criteria offered the new internationalist imperialism of the post-Cold War world a consensus of received views that could be directed against those deemed unacceptable, such as Saddam Hussein of Iraq from 1990 to 2003.

The transnational world, indeed, can be presented as leading to a new type of empire and new forms of imperialism. Although they scarcely define or exhaust transnationalism, the North Atlantic Treaty Organization, the European Union, and the United Nations provide instances of this development. Those subject to interventionist actions by these bodies might note their use of civilisational language similar to that of boosters for imperial rule in the nineteenth and twentieth centuries. There is an emphasis on the positive, especially humanitarian, values that intervention can lead to and on the negative aspects of those subject to such intervention. In the 1990s and early twenty-first century, these negative aspects are a matter of human rights violations (a very amorphous concept), rather than the slave trade and slavery, which were the subject of international (particularly British) action from the early nineteenth century. Nevertheless, the intention is frequently similar. So also is the outrage expressed by those subject to international action, for example Serb nationalists in the 1990s or the regime of Saddam Hussein in Iraq, notably in 1990–91 and in 2003. This was a variant of a longer-term process in which ideology, intellectualism, typologies, and language served to offer definitions that created hierarchies of acceptability and in analysis. For example, conventionally, there was a division between sociology and ethnology enabling commentators to think one way about metropolitan populations, on sociological grounds, and another about colonial subjects, on ethnological criteria. In doing so, intellectuals took forward earlier distinctions between 'peoples' based on religion and race.

A presentation of humanitarian interventionism as a cutting-edge of modern-day transnationalism and its supposed values, offers a way, albeit one that will be contested, to look at the motivation and cartography of the new imperialism. The League of Nations' mandates after World War One, and the United Nations' trusteeships after World War Two, can be seen as intermediary steps; with traditional imperial power politics and defences of rule linked in these cases to supervision by new international agencies. Their role does not compare with the very harsh character of late nineteenth- and early twentieth-century imperialism, notably that of Germany in what ultimately became Namibia and of Japan in Korea. However, the idea of the modern period as an age of empire appears more plausible if imperialism is treated not as an essential state with one particularly true manifestation in a given period, but, instead, as in this book, as a shifting practice. Moreover, imperialism was, and is, a practice that is far from uniform even for one given period. Such an approach displaces attention from the classic age of 'high imperialism' in the late nineteenth century.[32]

This is the period that commonly dominates discussion, and establishes the basic images and assumptions, both for empire as a whole and for the British empire. In contrast to the Atlantic empire of the seventeenth and eighteenth centuries, the nineteenth is sometimes referred to as the second British empire. While that description captures an important difference, it is also necessary, as this book indicates in Chapter 2, to consider earlier ages of empire in, and by, Britain. It can be argued, in opposition, that any focus on the shifting practice of imperialism risks having imperialism become another term for rule; but such a focus is not overly flawed, as the range of types of rule described and criticised, or described through criticism, as imperial or imperialism is, in fact, very extensive. Indeed, there is often a marked looseness of language in the way imperialism is used in academic as well as common parlance; a sort of catch-all phrase for the external imposition of power.

To provide a prime instance of this range, the range and rationale of commercial imperialism were different to those of territorial rule. At the same time, there was the overlap captured in the 1930s' advertisement sporting the Union Jack, the British flag: 'Wherever flies the flag that's braved a thousand

32 For a parallel approach, see the treatment in J. Black, *Slavery: A New Global History* (London, 2011). For a treatment focused on the classic age, J. Darwin, *The Empire Project: The Rise and Fall of the British World-System, 1830–1970* (Cambridge, 2009).

years the battle and the breeze, there Beecham's Pills will triumph o'er disease'. This was an instance of a whole strand of advertising. Commerce was a key element in empire, and the use of the concept of informal empire, to describe, for example, British commercial (and other) influence in Latin America during the nineteenth century, expands the vocabulary and range of empire. This concept directs attention away from sovereignty as central to imperialism; an approach that may be unsatisfactory to some readers, however.

If informal empire can be used in the case of the nineteenth century, notably in the discussion of the British empire, it is unclear why the term should not also be used for the twenty-first century to discuss, for example, the spreading economic and military power of China, or the interventionist conduct of Russia and India in neighbouring states, or the attempts by Brazil, Nigeria, and South Africa to act as regional powers. In some lights, Myanmar, Cambodia, or Sri Lanka appear, to at least a degree, as parts of a Chinese informal empire, and North Korea as a very independent part. Similar and other aspects of Chinese imperialism can be seen further afield as China establishes control over resources, notably in Africa, for example the oil of Equatorial Guinea, but also elsewhere, for example copper in Afghanistan. Chinese economic control contrasts with that of the British in Latin America in the nineteenth century, as both economic and cultural attraction were at work in the latter case. Such cultural attraction is less prominent in the case of China, although there can be, with Chinese investment and assistance, a model of can-do utilitarianism, for example in the provision of hospitals in areas of influence such as Tanzania, a provision that has proved attractive to some states. Economic dominance is linked to geopolitical competition, with China competing with Vietnam for influence in Cambodia, a competition that was prominent from the 1970s, while China's strategic role in Myanmar (Burma) is directed against India. Naval bases become a key instance and means of Chinese imperial power.

Comparisons can be qualified by reference to the specific circumstances of particular periods and individual imperialisms. Nevertheless, comparisons serve to underline, if not the universality of imperialism, at least the extent to which it is a lasting theme in international assumptions and political organisation. The latter point is also made in the presentation of American policy as imperial.

Alongside imposition and coercion, many empires relied heavily on co-operation by local people, and were quite prepared to acknowledge this. In the Gulf, building on the far larger and more complex system already developed in India, British influence depended on working through existing political arrangements. The choice as agents of locally established, affluent, and influential merchants with whom the rulers were financially and politically interdependent encouraged the rulers to co-operate.[33]

The significance of co-operation ensured that the indigenous contexts of imperial activity were very significant. These contexts, whether provided by Indian princes, African chiefs, Latin American élites, or other groups, were far from fixed, which underlined the dynamism of empire and the repeated need for skill and adaptability on the part of British policymakers and administrators. Empire was endlessly renegotiated. Co-operation, which had a functional as well as an ideological basis and expression, might not be on the basis of equality; indeed generally was far from it. However, the criterion of equality was less central to governmental values prior to the twentieth century than subsequently became the case. Moreover, the terms of co-operation (or indeed coercion) were rarely those in which imperialists and subjects formed coherent and exclusive blocs. Instead, there was an intermixing, compromise, co-existence, and negotiation, defined as the 'middle ground' of power;[34] as well as hostility and conflict. As such, the character of imperialism is again open to a type of debate, focusing on overlapping categories and shifting characteristics. This is a debate, however, that does not generally match modern polemical engagement.

This point is true, for example, of the recent controversy over British rule in Kenya and other colonies. Some of the public discussion is apt to underplay the extent to which the Mau Mau uprising in the 1950s involved, alongside the brutal treatment by the British of much of the Kenyan population in pursuit of a harsh 'pacification', attacks by the rebels on other Africans, who indeed made up the bulk of the victims. In addition, the British were reliant on African police and troops who, while under British command, were responsible for much of the violence against detainees. At the time, many of the abuses were blamed on Africans getting 'out of control' or being inadequately supervised: the Africans did the bulk of the dirty work and then received the blame for the excesses.[35]

---

33 C.A. Bayly, *Empire and Information: Intelligence Gathering and Social Communication in India, 1780–1870* (Cambridge, 1997); J. Onley, *The Arabian Frontier of the British Raj: Merchants, Rulers, and the British in the Nineteenth Century Gulf* (Oxford, 2007).

34 R. White, *The Middle Ground: Indians, Empires and Republics in the Great Lakes Region, 1650–1815* (Cambridge, 1981).

35 For different emphases, read first C. Elkins, *Imperial Reckoning: The Untold Story of Britain's Gulag in Kenya* (London, 2005) and D. Anderson, *Histories of the Hanged: The Dirty War in Kenya and the End of Empire* (London, 2005), and then J. Paget, *Counter-Insurgency Operations: Techniques of Guerrilla Warfare* (London, 1967); A. Clayton, *Counter-Insurgency in Kenya* (Nairobi, 1976); R.W. Heather, 'Intelligence

Such a level of complexity or shared responsibility is lost when counter-insurgency operations are referred to simply in terms of the British. The same point is true, for example, of the killing of demonstrators at Amritsar in the Punjab in 1919. The majority of the troops involved in that episode were Indian, again under British command, and Britain's rule there was always dependent on large-scale Indian participation. This observation is not made in order to extenuate the action, and General Reginald Dyer clearly had the command responsibility, and was placed on the retired list accordingly. Nevertheless, the events in Amritsar, which, in causing considerable controversy at the time in Britain as well as India, marked a major transition in the character and tone of the British empire,[36] can be explained (not extenuated or excused) at least in part in terms of the real and apparent security situation then and the related complexities of counter-insurgency. Moreover, it is important to relate individual episodes to wider strands of policy, both civilian and military.[37] These points, however, are frequently neglected when imperialism serves present-day nationalist myth-making. The same is true of the attack on imperialism as part of a critique of capitalism.

In part, any discussion of imperialism is a discussion of myth, specifically of the processes by which past power, and the related rationales, drives, negotiations, ambiguities, and visions of the then future, were, and are, seen and presented. The depiction of rule as benign (whatever the reality) was part of the way in which imperialism was presented as normative. This depiction and presentation might be seriously flawed, not least because it underplays the extent of routine, but unspectacular, forms of violence, as well as the deterrent power of collective

---

and Counter-Insurgency in Kenya, 1952–56', *Intelligence and National Security*, 5 (1990), pp. 57–83; I.F.W. Beckett, *Modern Insurgencies and Counter-Insurgencies* (London, 2001), pp. 121–30; D. Branch, *Defeating Mau Mau, Creating Kenya: Counterinsurgency, Civil War, and Decolonisation* (Cambridge, 2009); H. Bennett, *Fighting the Mau Mau: The British Army and Counter-Insurgency in the Kenya Emergency* (Cambridge, 2013). For an excellent analysis of the dynamics of bureaucracy, colonial violence and the media, N. Owen, '"Facts are Sacred": The Manchester Guardian and Colonial Violence, 1930–32', *Journal of Modern History*, 84 (2012), pp. 643–78.

36 D.G. Boyce, 'From Assaye to the Assaye: Reflections on British Government, Force, and Moral Authority in India', *Journal of Military History*, 63 (1999), pp. 643–68; M. Doyle, 'Massacre by the Book: Amritsar and the Rules of Public-Order Policing in Britain and India', *Britain and the World*, 4 (2011), pp. 247–68.

37 G. Kudaisya, '"In Aid of Civil Power": The Colonial Army in Northern India, *c.*1919–42', *Journal of Imperial and Commonwealth History*, 32 (2004), pp. 41–68; B. Grob-Fitzgibbon, *Imperial Endgame: Britain's Dirty Wars and the End of Empire* (Basingstoke, 2011).

punishment; but so also is the current tendency simply to adopt the opposite stance and present imperial rule as malign.

To oppose complexity to myth, contextualisation to ahistoricism, and relativism to universalism, may appear pointless, yet it is the purpose of this book. Some of the views I express here are unfashionable, but it is important, for pedagogic and intellectual reasons, to consider different accounts and contrasting conclusions. To do so involves the processes of debate that are central both to scholarly investigation and to public discussion in a true democracy.

Chapter 2

The British Empire to 1700

This book focuses on the British empire. However, the number of definitions offered for empire, and discussed in the previous chapter, extend to the British empire. Indeed, this variety of definitions of empire is highly relevant to the discussion of the British empire because it links to such central issues as motivation, intention, and control. For long, however, the questions of definition and motivation as far as Britain was concerned were relatively simple in that imperial rule for many centuries involved a drive for territorial control over much, or all, of Britain or the British Isles. Although the context and character were very different, this drive for control was, at least chronologically, the forerunner of Britain's trans-oceanic expansion. Contrasts and parallels between the two can be profitably considered.

Roman Britain

It is instructive to begin Britain's history as an empire with mention of its prior history as a Roman colony, because the Roman empire for long served as a key source of inspiration. British imperial rule repeatedly looked to historic and external, as well as contemporary, sources of authentication. Some Roman emperors, particularly Nero (r. 54–68 CE), were subsequently seen as examples of tyrants, and, notably, as persecutors of Christians, a practice that retrospectively helped define unacceptable rule once Constantine, by the Edict of Milan of 313 CE, brought toleration to Christians throughout the Roman empire. Nevertheless, the (Classical) Roman empire, including for the period prior to Constantine, the period when the conquest of much of Britain took place, long offered a model of civilisation and aspiration in Britain, as elsewhere across much of Europe.[1]

England, Wales, and (more briefly) southern Scotland were all united, each separately and together, for the first time as part of the Roman empire. Roman

1 J.M.H. Smith, *Europe after Rome: A New Cultural History, 500–1000* (Oxford, 2007).

control in Britain began with the Emperor Claudius' invasion in 43 CE and lasted continuously until the withdrawal of Roman troops in 409. Claudius sought to gain a military reputation to strengthen his position in Rome and invaded because Rome's protégés in southern Britain had lost control. By 78, all of England and Wales was under Roman control.

Roman rule was to be deployed by later British imperialists when looking for an appropriate backdrop, not least, in the eighteenth and nineteenth centuries in particular, by presenting contemporary Britain as the successor to Rome, an approach that no longer strikes a significant echo. Rome was seen as the model for Britain's growing empire, but, in practice, the onset of Roman rule was brutal and involved, as recent work has pointed out, conquest, expropriation, the suppression of rebellion, and military policing.[2] The emphasis in discussing Roman rule, however, can also be placed elsewhere, not only on those rulers and tribes who co-operated in the initial stages of the Roman conquest, greatly reducing the area that had to be conquered, for example the Atrebates, but also on the subsequent nature of rule of Roman Britain, most of which was internally peaceful. After the defeat of Queen Boudicca of the Iceni in 60, the history of Roman Britain did not centre on rebellions, other than those by Roman commanders seeking greater power. This was a contrast to the history of the British empire.

The nature of the Roman empire in Britain reflected, therefore, the varied, and ambiguous, character of imperial rule, one that was subsequently to be seen with British imperial rule. Roman rule in what was later called Wales is a prime example. Military operations probably began there in 48, ending in the late '70s. The emphasis for Wales can be placed on coercion and exploitation. An extensive network of about 35 fortresses was constructed, and they were linked by roads to legionary bases at Caerleon and Deva (Chester). This system was designed to enforce pacification in what was a military zone. Moreover, whereas pre-Roman exploitation of mineral resources had been limited, there was major expansion in mining under the Romans, and this made Wales important to the Roman state. At the same time, the security presence was rapidly reduced, with some forts abandoned, in part because the country became quiet. In addition, the Celtic leadership was deliberately Romanised – urged to follow Roman ways and, in many cases, live in towns that were established on the Roman pattern.

More generally, the largely peaceful nature of Roman society encouraged a process of Romanisation. Roman citizenship was restricted neither to Romans

---

2 D. Mattingly, *An Imperial Possession: Britain in the Roman Empire, 54 BC–AD 409* (London, 2006).

nor to Italians. Roman religious cults were introduced, but assimilation with native Celtic beliefs was important. A valuable source of mineral exports, notably silver, lead, gold, and iron, Britain made a major contribution to the economics and finances of the empire.

A Medieval Millennium, 410–1458

A key theme in this book is the relationship between England's 'inner' empire in Britain and its 'outer' or overseas empire. This theme was present from the consolidation of a major state in Britain, but that consolidation was the work of many centuries. Once Roman rule of Britain within the continuing power of the Roman empire had ended in 409–10, Britain fragmented anew. This was not to be a general experience of former colonies of the later British empire. Instead, partly due to the role of nationalism, and to continuity with colonial-period administrative structures, post-colonial territories in the nineteenth and twentieth centuries have not usually proved fissiparous, and if, in some cases, this has been an element, that was not commonly because of their experience as colonies. In Britain, fragmentation after Roman rule owed much to conquest from abroad; although the fissiparous nature of sub-Roman Britain (Britain after the Roman troops withdrew but before the invasions) was also significant.

The invading Angles, Saxons, and Jutes of the fifth century were not imperial as the word is generally employed. It is more pertinent to regard them as conquerors, while noting that they were also settlers. The extent to which they were a ruling group, rather than a people migrating en bloc, is controversial, which again underlines the issue and problems of definition. While fighting the post-(sub-)Roman British, and subsequently, the invaders also competed. This process saw the emergence of *brytenwaldas* (overlord-kings), first Kentish, then East Anglian, Northumbrian, Mercian, and finally Wessex. Each *brytenwalda* claimed a degree of overlordship over other dynasties and regions. The nature of this overlordship varied, but it was an important feature of British politics. It can be seen as imperial in character. Oswald (r. 634–41), Oswy (r. 641–70), and Egfrith (r. 670–85) of Northumbria ruled between the Humber and the Forth in eastern Britain and the Mersey and the Ayr in the west, and were at times treated as overlords by the rulers of Mercia, Wessex, Strathclyde, and the Pict and Scottish territories. Offa of Mercia (r. 757–96) controlled such formerly independent kingdoms as Essex, Lindsey, East Anglia, Kent, and Sussex, while Wessex recognised Mercian protection in 786. In turn, Egbert of Wessex (r. 802–39) defeated the Mercians, conquered south-east England, and had his overlordship acknowledged by Northumbria. He was briefly recognised as king throughout England.

In turn, this order was overthrown by the Viking invasions of the ninth century, more seriously from the 850s. However, the successful defiance of the Vikings by the West Saxons under Alfred, King of Wessex (r. 871–99), and their subsequent conquest of England in the tenth century, defeating the Vikings, provided the basis both for their hegemony over the non-Viking peoples in England and for claims of imperial status, notably by Edgar (r. 959–75). In 973, at Bath, Edgar was the first monarch to be crowned as King of the English; although earlier monarchs, Offa of Mercia and Athelstan of Wessex (r. 924–39), had used the title. This royal identification was crucial in the formation of the unified English nation. The long witness lists to Athelstan's charters provide evidence of significant national assemblies that look towards the later development of parliament.

The empire over much of Western Europe established by the Frankish ruler Charlemagne in 800, the origins of the later (and weaker) Holy Roman Empire, provided a model of imperial behaviour and prestige and a vision of universal sovereignty, as well as a potential challenge to other contemporary rulers. Probably as a consequence of the influence of Carolingian (the Frankish dynasty of Charlemagne) ideology, specifically the idea of a Christian empire, expressed by Jonas of Orleans and Hincmar of Rheims, which influenced Athelstan and Edgar, tenth-century Wessex moved towards a notion of kingship different from that of the amalgam of kingdoms epitomised by Offa's Mercia in the eighth century. The period from Alfred to Edgar was that of the definition of an English state, one that did not require, nor was constrained by, precise ethnic, tribal, or geographical borders. Such a state can be seen as having an imperial potential. The West Saxon rulers also laid claim to the overlordship of all Britain and exercised a degree of hegemony over their British neighbours, in part by direct power, notably the use of naval action, but, more commonly, by indirect influence. In 920, the rulers of Scotland, York, English Northumbria, and Strathclyde Britons were said, by West Saxon sources, to have accepted the lordship of Alfred's son, Edward (r. 899–924). For his coins, Athelstan (r. 924–39), who fought in Scotland, chose a new image, becoming the first Anglo-Saxon king to be shown wearing a crown and described as *rex totius Britanniae*, King of all the British. He exacted tribute from the Welsh princes. The story of Edgar being rowed by other British rulers was to be used from the eighteenth century by popular historians seeking to provide a lengthy pedigree for the Union with Scotland in 1707.

If the history of English (later British) imperialism can therefore be traced to the tenth century, that was scarcely an empire to last in this form. Instead,

England was conquered by the Danish Crown, under Sveyn and, then, his son Cnut, in 1013–16. Under Cnut (r. 1016–35), England became, briefly, a part of a North Sea empire in the form of a Scandinavian multiple kingdom, with Denmark and Norway. After this inheritance was divided from 1035 by Cnut's sons, England returned to rule by the House of Wessex in the person of Edward the Confessor (r. 1042–66). He designated Earl Harold of Wessex (r. 1066) as his successor, but England was then conquered in 1066 by the Normans under William the Conqueror (r. 1066–87). This extensive experience of conquest is worth remembering alongside the usual stress on Britain over more recent centuries as an imperial power. Norman rule ensured that England could not readily serve as the basis for development of imperial claims, as it was now a subordinate part of a trans-Channel realm; one, moreover, that was a 'multiple kingship', not a united state. Such a kingship was the basic pattern of far-flung states in Western Europe. It was seen, for example, with Cnut's empire. In contrast, Byzantium, or the Eastern Roman Empire, maintained the earlier Roman pattern of the empire as a united state.

In some respects, the Norman conquest of England provided one model for imperial expansion, and was indeed to be seen in this light during the heyday of British imperialism. However, unlike the British empire, Norman feudalism accommodated transnational fiefdoms by means of suzerainty between rulers without imperial control, notably with the relationship between the Normans and the kings of France, and between the kings of Scotland and the kings of England. Moreover, the concept of empire was one that was problematic in the Middle Ages as the position and pretensions of the Holy Roman Empire, that created by Charlemagne in 800, dominated the ideology and vocabulary of empire in Western and Central Europe, while those of Byzantium had the same role further east.[3] This dominance left no role for other empires. As with the Norman conquests of Sicily from the Arabs, and of Apulia and Calabria in South Italy from the Byzantine empire, in the late eleventh century, a small group of invaders seized power in England in 1066, replacing the social élite. There was no mass displacement of the original population and much of the earlier administrative structure – Old English, Byzantine, or Arab – continued; although it was now used for the benefit of new rulers.

The Norman rulers of England had a particular territorial problem, the defence of the Duchy of Normandy against its neighbours, notably the expansionist kings of France. This problem helped determine English territorial

---

3 J. Muldoon, *Empire and Order: The Concept of Empire, 800–1800* (Basingstoke, 1999).

interests throughout the Middle Ages. The problem continued after Normandy was lost in 1204, because, by then, there were also other possessions in France. As a result of these concerns on the Continent, the composite state, of which England was a part, was concerned about land frontiers, alongside the maritime routes across the Channel that were the crucial link within the state. The continuous military effort that war on the Continent entailed was to be a central theme in domestic history, not least because it was instrumental in the development of English government.

England was not an empire. The Normans, as kings of England, followed, from the accession in 1154 of Henry II, by the Angevin dynasty, that of the Counts of Anjou, both owed fealty to the king of France for lands in France and ruled a separate realm in England. However, the kings of England and some of their leading subjects practised what, to those who experienced it, must have seemed like imperialism. This was true not only for Anglo-Saxon England (whose rulers were themselves descended from conquerors), but also for the Welsh, and, later, for Ireland and Scotland. Land was a key goal. In Wales and Ireland, Anglo-Norman aristocrats pursued their own territorial interests, exploiting divisions between the local rulers. These were lands of opportunity for the aggressive and land-hungry, notably younger sons. This was a pattern that was subsequently to be repeatedly seen with British imperialism. As later with British imperialism, there was an imposition of new patterns of control over land and people.

For example, the Anglo-Norman attitude in Wales was expropriatory and its lords introduced feudal land tenure and government to Wales. Feudalism rested on agricultural service by serfs. The existence of the unfree was not new, but it was now different because of the benefit to non-Welsh lords. The replacement of the open court-houses of Welsh rulers by Anglo-Norman castles was symptomatic of a major change of attitude. In addition, the authority of the Archbishop of Canterbury was extended over the Welsh Bishoprics of St David's and Llandaff. Gwynedd, the remaining area of Welsh independence, was conquered by Edward I in 1277 and, after a rebellion, in 1282–83. As with later episodes of British imperialism, however, this conquest was in part also a civil war, an element that subsequent public history tends to ignore completely. The expansionism of the Princes of Gwynedd had affected Welsh rivals, while more Welshmen fought for Edward than against him. The conquest was secured by a new military order, with a very expensive system of castles. The dimension of force was very much to the fore in this instance of imperialism. The castles provided Edward I (r. 1272–1307) and his successors with military bases, centres of government, and visual demonstrations of power. The latter included the echo of another empire as Caernarvon castle symbolically made reference to the fortifications of Constantinople.[4] Alongside the castles, the English system of shires and criminal law was introduced. Partly as a result, there was resentment at the dominance of administration and Church by Englishmen, and at the commercial privileges granted to the inhabitants of the new towns. In contrast, the Welsh remained overwhelmingly rural. The political, administrative, and legal system worked to the benefit of the English, who had the necessary patrons at the royal court, which was crucial in the administration of justice.

At the same time, in Wales, there was scant change at the local level where the same families, the traditional leaders of the community, remained in charge. This was to be true of much of the experience of empire when areas with significant populations were taken over, as opposed in particular to those areas inhabited by hunter–gatherers. The ambiguous nature of English control was seen with the rising of Owain Glyn Dŵr (Owen Glendower) in 1400–08. He has served as a potent symbol of Welsh nationalism over the last half century, including providing the name of a new university. The rising was certainly an indication of disaffection and of the survival of separatist feeling. The wider pattern of English rule was challenged by the prevalence of bardic myths that saw the Welsh as different and as destined to regain Wales. Yet, there was also strong opposition to Glyn Dŵr from within Wales, notably from native gentry who regarded alliance with the Crown as the best way to maintain their privileges. Opposition to Glyn Dŵr was strongest in South and East Wales, in both of which there was long experience of English control and practices of co-operation that retained considerable vitality. This example is more generally useful as an introduction to the nature of imperialism.[5]

In the case of Ireland, as of Wales, the English Crown sought to impose its authority after the Anglo-Norman aristocrats had seized territories. Henry II, the first of the Angevins (r. 1154–89), invaded Ireland in 1171, taking authority there both from Anglo-Norman barons, who had established an independent position in 1170, and from the Irish rulers. The Treaty of Windsor of 1175 recognised Henry as Lord of Ireland, a title implying overlordship over

---

4 J. Richard, *The Castle Community: The Personnel of English and Welsh Castles, 1272–1422* (Woodbridge, 2002), p. 25.

5 R. Davies, *Conquest, Coexistence and Change: Wales, 1063–1415* (London, 1987) and *The Revolt of Owain Glyn Dŵr* (Oxford, 1985); J. Given, *State and Society in Medieval Europe: Gwynedd and Languedoc under Outside Rule* (Ithaca, New York, 1990); R. Griffiths, *Conquerors and Conquered in Medieval Wales* (Stroud, 1994); A.D. Carr, *Medieval Wales* (London, 1995).

the petty kings. The kings of England only became kings of Ireland in the sixteenth century.

In Scotland, when the native Canmore dynasty ran out of male heirs, English political expansion was initiated by the monarch, in this case Edward I. This role was symbolised when, in 1292, Edward adjudicated between the claimants to the Scottish throne, and John Balliol, his choice, swore fealty and did homage.[6] The hegemony of the king of England over the British Isles seemed established by Edward, but was rapidly rejected in Scotland. Edward's interventionism, not least his encouragement of appeals by Scots to English courts, was unacceptable to many Scots. Edward and his successors proved unable to sustain control, Edward II being badly beaten in 1314 at Bannockburn, a battle still resonant in modern Scottish politics. This failure, and also that of English control over much of fourteenth-century Ireland, throws light on the limitations of imperial expansion. The Edwards relied in Scotland, and in most of Ireland, not on colonisation, but on collaboration, yet it proved impossible to maintain the necessary level. Furthermore, military intervention faced formidable logistical problems. More seriously, from the late 1330s, Edward III (r. 1327–77) was most concerned about his ambitions in France. The resulting commitment was also of great importance to his successors. In contrast, Scotland generally took a minor role for the kings of England from the late 1330s, other than as an ally to France. This is a reminder of the common problem, for empires as for other states, of multiple challenges, and therefore of prioritisation.

At the same time, there was in England a degree of public, national engagement with territorial expansion. The development of a public politics in England ensured that policymaking was not simply a case of the Crown but, instead, from the early thirteenth century, involved the 'community of the realm', an entity that was to be represented in parliament. As a result, what would later be termed the public sphere played a role in the discussion of policy, both directly and, via the impact on the raising of resources, notably troops and taxes, indirectly. A similar process occurred in Ireland, where the conflicts played out in the Dublin parliament, England's first colonial legislature, helped crystallise a distinctive colonial identity.[7] However, the extent to which English public opinion supported the longlasting intervention in France, which became more insistent once the Hundred Years' War had broken out in the 1330s, is unclear.

---

6 R. Davies, *Domination and Conquest: The Experience of Ireland, Scotland, and Wales, 1100–1300* (Oxford, 1990).

7 P. Crooks, 'Representation and Dissent: "Parliamentarianism" and the Structure of Politics in Colonial Ireland, *c.*1370–1420', *English Historical Review*, 125 (2010), p. 34.

In part, the issue of the 'ownership' of imperialism occurs, an issue that was to be of recurring importance. Parliamentary hostility to the cost of the war could be related to a stress on Englishness, as opposed to the wider-ranging territorial controls of the dynasty. This stress was also seen in opposition to foreign advisers of the Crown and to money from the Church going abroad. Each issue became of considerable significance, the first from the thirteenth century, notably during the reign of Henry III (r. 1216–72), and the second from the fourteenth.

The complete failure in the early 1450s of the longstanding attempt on France and the French throne was important to the development of English nationhood and government, and thus provided a backdrop to later trans-oceanic ambitions. The earlier cross-border interests and nobility that had resulted from the Norman Conquest, and, subsequently, from England's place within the Angevins' amalgamation of distinctive territories, had inhibited the political consequences of an increasingly apparent national consciousness. However, the relationship was more complex because the war with France that stemmed from the links, also encouraged this national consciousness. It did so not least by leading to xenophobia, royal war-propaganda, military service (and also resistance to it), national taxation, and the enhanced role of parliament. As a result of the demands of war finance in the particular circumstances of English politics, the need for parliamentary consent for taxation was confirmed. Thereby, the role of parliament was enhanced. In turn, rulers, notably Henry V (r. 1413–22), emphasised their English character, although, in practice, Henry V devoted most of his reign to the pursuit of French conquests and, subsequently, the French throne.

After a counter-offensive was crushed at Castillon in 1453, the English Crown was shut out from the Continent, at least in so far as a major territorial presence was concerned. Although Calais, originally conquered by Edward III, was held until lost by Mary in 1558, and the Channel Isles, the last of the Norman legacy, are still held by the Crown, France was lost. This was one of the crucial political legacies of the medieval period, but not a legacy that monarchs were keen to accept. The claim to the French throne was only abandoned in the reign of George III (1760–1820). Moreover, Edward IV in 1475, Henry VII in 1492, and Henry VIII campaigned there, the last waging a series of wars, the first in 1511–14, with conflict resuming in 1522, and the final war, which started in 1544, only finishing in 1550, in the reign of his son, Edward VI. Nevertheless, these campaigns had no lasting success: the Norman duchy, the Angevin empire, and Lancastrian France, had all gone. Moreover, the consolidation of France meant that these could not be revived. The more insular, even, at times, and, in some aspects, isolationist character of England and its politics after 1453 was one of the keys to its subsequent domestic and international development. However, although linked in the case of Britain, a loss of Continental empire was not a necessary precondition for trans-oceanic expansion and the creation of a new empire. Instead, Spain gained both an Italian and an American empire in 1492–1559. This example indicates the value of comparisons.

Tudor Empire

If the Anglicisation of the English monarchy after the failure of the Hundred Years' War with France represented a check for dynasticism as a form of transnationalism, it also helped look towards what would long be a characteristic of English (later British) imperialism, its anchoring in a degree of public support, and the formulation of royal goals accordingly. Henry VIII's use of parliament for pursuing his ecclesiastical agenda in the 1530s was a major advance for this tendency. Henry's acquisition, as 'Supreme Head', of jurisdiction over the Church was accompanied by the statement that England was an empire, and thus jurisdictionally self-sufficient, with an imperial Crown allegedly descended from that of the Roman Emperor Constantine, who was a figure of great symbolic potency because of his central role in converting the Roman empire to Christianity. For Britain, to avoid being seen as subordinate, actually or potentially, it was important to claim imperial status, which, indeed, helped to explain Henry's assertion of it in 1533. That was a time of grave tension over relations with the Papacy and when the Holy Roman Emperor, Charles V, the uncle of Henry's divorced wife, Katherine of Aragon, and the ruler of Spain, the Low Countries, Austria, and much of Italy, was a threat. In the preamble to the Act in Restraint of Appeals [to Rome], a major legislative step in the Henrician Reformation, the break with Papal authority and thus the international Catholic Church, it was claimed that,

> by divers sundry old authentic histories and chronicles it is manifestly declared and expressed that this realm of England is an empire, and so hath been accepted in the world, governed by one supreme head and king, having the dignity and royal estate of the imperial crown of the same.

This assertion by Henry looked back to the House of Wessex's claims of overlordship in Britain in the tenth and eleventh centuries, and to the post-1066 pursuit of a territorial sway on both sides of the English Channel by the rulers of the Norman and Angevin dynasties. He wore a crown with arches and was called majesty, both symbols of imperial power. Henry saw himself as responsible for what his subjects believed, and the English Church as national and independent.

Ireland

At the same time, the Protestant Reformation, in its various iterations, made the pursuit of imperial goals at once more necessary and more problematic. More necessary, because territories in heterodox hands threatened the new religious order, a situation that led to particular concern about Ireland where Protestantism made only limited progress among the native population. More problematic, because the conquest and rule of heterodox areas made co-operation between subjects and rulers far less likely and greatly increased the possibility of conflict. A major theme in English and, later, British discussion of the empire was to be its Protestant as well as Christian identity and its consciously prudential character.[8] However, the failure of the Reformation in Ireland helped ensure that Protestantism played a seriously divisive role there for the empire in the short and long terms, and, eventually, permanently. Indeed, the definition of Ireland's past position from the perspective of the present day is hugely problematic, notably given the different Republican/Nationalist and Unionist viewpoints.

Henry VIII had sought to maintain his father's policy of increasing Tudor control in Ireland without major initiatives. The area around Dublin, the 'Pale', was under royal control, much of Ireland was dominated by Marcher Lords, the descendants of medieval English colonists, while large parts were under the Gaelic-speaking 'wild Irish'. For most of his early years, a Marcher Lord, Gerald, 9th Earl of Kildare, or his rival, Piers, Earl of Ormond, was Deputy, with two attempts at more direct control from England proving of limited success. The Reformation altered the situation in Ireland and greatly increased the range and problems of imperial co-operation there. It was necessary for Henry VIII to have Ireland renounce papal authority. However, in 1534, Thomas, 10th Earl of Kildare, rebelled, offering the overlordship of Ireland to the Pope or the Emperor Charles V, in place of the schismatic Henry. Kildare was also responding to the support of London for his Irish rivals. He was initially successful, but in 1535 an English force restored control. Kildare surrendered on promise of his life – only to be executed.

---

8 H.M. Carey, *God's Empire: Religion and Colonialism in the British World, c.1801–1908* (Cambridge, 2011).

Henry discarded the policy of rule via Marcher Lords and, instead, decided that the Deputy would need to be English and to be supported by a council under English control and by a standing (permanent) army. The Irish 'Reformation' parliament met in 1536 and passed the necessary legislation. Henry was declared 'Supreme Head' of the Irish Church. In 1541, the parliament recognised Henry as 'King' of Ireland. Attention was focused on building up control of the Pale, while Gaelic nobles were offered English law and charters for their lands, an attempt to incorporate them peacefully into the structure of governmental control. Such a relatively conciliatory policy was to be abandoned after Henry's death in 1547, but it already faced formidable difficulties given the precarious nature of royal control over much of the island and the competing commitment to the control represented by kingship. In 1544, Henry was able to enlist Irish troops, but the financial basis for royal power was weak and the English exchequer had to transfer funds each year. Under Henry VIII's successors, his policy was replaced by that of the 'plantation' of areas with English settlers. This aggressive new approach was presented as a way to make Ireland prosperous, profitable, and civil, and thus was used to justify control and its enhancement. 'Plantation' apparently increased the security of the Crown's position, but the harsh expropriation of Gaelic landowners it involved, alongside the stigmatisation of the 'wild Irish' not in these plantations, heightened the unpopularity of the policy and of the Crown.[9]

From the late 1560s, English rule in Ireland became increasingly military in character and intention, leading to fresh attempts to extend and enforce control, at the expense of Gaelic Irish opposition. These attempts received little support from the Anglo-Irish, most of whom were Catholics. This was not a conducive environment for the expansion of Protestantism, and, as Catholic energies were greatly revived by the Counter-Reformation, so religious differences became a more important feature of the situation in Ireland. They symbolised, reflected, and strengthened a political rift, and both the hatred felt, between what were increasingly seen as conquerors and a subject population, and the reasons why Ireland, and problems associated with it, frightened English commentators.[10]

In the long term, this rift was to undermine imperial rule in Ireland. In the short and medium term, religious tension helped give this rule much of its character, not least a frequently embattled sense of identity. The complex ethnic

---

9 J.P. Montaño, *The Roots of English Colonialism in Ireland* (Cambridge, 2011).

10 M. Smuts, 'Organised Violence in the Elizabethan Monarchical Republic', and B. Kane, 'Ordinary Violence? Ireland as Emergency in the Tudor State', *History*, 99 (2014), pp. 437, 464.

and sectarian politics of the late-sixteenth-century Ireland made any consensus there unlikely. The 'New English' enjoyed office and the benefits of government support; while the Catholic 'Old English' felt alienated and excluded from office, and the Gaels (natives of non-English descent) felt harshly treated by a corrupt and brutal rule. These complex politics also indicated the extent to which imperial rule could contribute to such division, within territories and between them and the imperial power, and be linked to this division. Again, this situation was to occur repeatedly in the case of the British empire.

The Development of Trans-Oceanic Imperialism

In Reformation England, not only was the monarch now head of the Church, but the Church was now depicted as representative of a chosen people with a sense of divine mandate. Protestant England was presented as God's New Israel, a Protestant people and state, with all the possibilities that this depiction entailed of defining purposes and identities separate to those of the rest of Christendom. Cultural nationalism became stronger as a result of the Reformation, not least the embrace of the English language and a greater commitment to Englishness.[11]

Moreover, the challenge to authority represented by the Reformation was to help lead to a view of the world in which it was easier to respond to new information without being constrained by existing patterns of authority. This situation looked towards the prominent English role in the Scientific Revolution of the late seventeenth century.

As usual, domestic developments, notably the reformulation of power within Britain, were linked to the fate of empire abroad. The Reformation helped ensure enmity between England (and later Britain) and the leading European imperial powers, because Spain, Portugal, and France remained Catholic. Moreover, religious tensions became more serious owing to the Counter-Reformation, which gathered pace in Catholic Europe from the 1550s. These developments lent a religious dimension to imperial competition that was to be very important to the domestic understanding of empire, both then and subsequently. The religious dimension also helped encourage the rethinking of territorial ambitions and concerns that was so important to England's changing role in the world. Thus, there is the paradox that Protestantism helped make England into an empire, but also brought her into conflict with other empires.

11 P. Collinson, *This England: Essays on the English Nation and Commonwealth in the Sixteenth Century* (Manchester, 2011).

In the sixteenth century, the playing out of the Reformation in terms of dynastic and political agendas, both international and domestic, ensured that the pursuit of international interests by England and Scotland largely took place in the British Isles, and in nearby areas of Western Europe. Already prior to the Reformation, England and Scotland had done badly from the first burst of European trans-oceanic activity at the cusp of the fifteenth and sixteenth centuries. Despite ascertaining the fishing wealth of the waters off Newfoundland, John Cabot's voyages in 1497–98 were very much on the margins of profitable trans-Atlantic activity, although there was later to be the claim that Britain's imperial identity owed its origins to Henry's reign, notably an abortive link with Columbus.[12]

Later, in the sixteenth century, English expeditions failed to discover the direct route to Asia they sought through a north-west passage to the north of America or a north-east passage north of Asia, and also missed out on the compensation of American bullion (gold and silver) that Hernán Cortés and Francisco Pizarro had seized for Spain in Mexico and Peru respectively. Moreover, in contrast to the major effort expended by England in Ireland, there was only limited interest in England in trans-oceanic activity. At the same time, the effort put into imperial activity in any individual state was not necessarily commensurate to its impact on other societies. What is limited war (or imperialism) for one society may be total war (or conquest) for another, for example for the Native Americans subject to English expansion from the seventeenth century.

In the sixteenth century, Spain devoted more governmental attention to the European commitments of the Habsburg dynasty, rather than to its extensive new overseas territories. Nevertheless, Spain, under Charles V and Philip II, gained the most far-flung empire in the world, that of Philip (r. 1556–98), being, thanks to the establishment of a presence in the Philippines, the first empire in the world on which the sun never set. Given that England had no such territories outside the British Isles, it is scarcely surprising that this focus on Europe was even more the case for her. Arguably, more benefit could have been gained from trans-oceanic expansion, but security concerns for England, as for Spain, all came from nearby. In England's case, this meant Scotland, Ireland, the Spanish possessions in the Low Countries, and nearby areas in France: English forces operated in the last three in the 1590s.

The focus on domestic and European concerns, however, did not preclude an interest in the trans-oceanic world. Indeed, the opportunities the latter offered

12 R. Johnson, *Nova Britannia* (London, 1609).

for entrepreneurialism, especially corporate and collective, but also individual, were such that the views of government were not necessarily to the fore. Long-distance seafaring became more important to England as part of a maritime world in which fishing, shipping, and trade adapted to the opportunities and problems of longer distances. Growing trans-Atlantic interests in the late sixteenth century led to an increased engagement with the idea of England as an Atlantic power, a theme in John Dee's *General and Rare Memorials Pertaining to the Perfect Art of Navigation* (1577). This idea of maritime destiny was also significant in Richard Hakluyt's *Principal Navigations, Voyages, Traffiques and Discoveries of the English Nation* (1598–1600).[13]

In turn, Elizabethan trans-oceanic exploration, trade, and warfare proved an inspiration to later consideration of empire, notably by the Victorians. Paintings of this theme such as John Everett Millais' *The Boyhood of Raleigh* were much reproduced. Millais (1829–96), a member and, eventually, President of the Royal Academy, was created a baronet in 1885. Sir Francis Drake was another iconic figure. Charles Kingsley's novel *Westward Ho!* (1855) offered a strongly biased account of the Elizabethan age. It was co-dedicated to James Brooke (1803–68), the White Rajah, who was establishing British power in northern Borneo. Brooke appeared a swashbuckler similar to the Elizabethans.

Swashbuckling was provided with opportunities in the early-modern period by attitudes toward trans-oceanic activity. Governmental views were significant for English trans-oceanic activity when it was a case of relations with other European powers, as war and power were more under state auspices in this case. However, especially prior to the eighteenth century, it was possible to pursue a policy of 'no peace beyond the line', one that entailed trans-oceanic hostilities with other European states even if both were at peace in Europe. Thus, the English could fight Spain in the Caribbean, but not in Europe, although such conflict strained relations, as it did with Spain in the 1570s and the Dutch in the early 1660s. Trans-oceanic and colonial warfare served as a proxy for direct warfare.

Even the idea of 'no peace beyond the line', which still entailed a measure of restraint, did not pertain with non-European powers. In the latter cases, there was far more room for independent initiatives on the part of colonists and non-governmental organisations, such as the East India Company. In 1600,

13 A. Alexander, 'The Imperialist Space of Elizabethan Mathematics', *Studies in the History and Philosophy of Science*, 26 (1995), pp. 559–91; L. Cormack, *Charting an Empire: Geography at the English Universities, 1580–1620* (Chicago, Illinois, 1997).

this company, founded by London commercial circles, was granted by royal charter a monopoly of trade by sea with South and South-East Asia and the East Indies (modern Indonesia), principally in order to obtain spices for which there was great demand in Europe. The low-bulk, high-value, nature of spices justified their transport. Excluded, in the event, from the East Indies by Dutch competition, the company was eventually to focus on trade with India and to form the basis of Britain's Indian empire. A joint-stock concern, and thus able to raise investment from, and share risk among, a wide range of participants, the company reflected the strength and sophistication of English, especially London, commercial and financial circles, and contrasted with the far greater state direction of most Continental trading companies. This company was to enable Britain to profit from the resources of South and East Asia, and to draw on their wealth.

The role of chartered companies, such as the Muscovy, Levant, East India, and Hudson Bay Companies, serves as a reminder that, from the outset, English/British imperialism was, in part, outside state control and had a character later discussed in terms of informal empire. The state chartered these companies and could reap considerable profit from them, but control was less direct than in the case of the exploitation of Ireland. In many respects, this situation of limited state control was particularly true of England/Britain. This was because, in terms certainly of authority, if not always power, its central government was relatively weak (compared with other states with the exception of the Netherlands). Moreover, with the major exception of Ireland, British imperial expansion was, in large part, a distant activity as opposed to being in Europe. This underlines the extent to which, alongside similarities between some empires, there was no essential condition of empire, and no single developmental model.

Empire in the Seventeenth Century

The focus of successive English/British governments on the political situation within the British Isles was particularly apparent in the seventeenth century, as opposed to the eighteenth. Empire in the early seventeenth century was very much a theme focused on the possibilities for a kingdom of Great Britain created by the accession of James VI of Scotland to the thrones of England and Ireland as James I (r. 1603–25). James I frequently used the term empire in order to describe the new union. He declared that he had achieved the 'reuniting of these two mightie, famous and ancient Kingdoms of England and Scotland, under one Imperiall Crowne'.[14] Others supported this claim. In 1611, the English cartographer John Speed published a collection of maps under the title *The Theatre of the Empire of Great Britain*, an atlas dedicated to James I as the uniter of the 'British Empire'.[15]

This idea of Britishness proved particularly attractive to those who stressed a militant Protestant identity in the midst of a hostile Catholic world. At the same time, the complex and shifting relationships between Britain, England, Scotland, and Ireland indicated the compromises and nuances that were to characterise much of the subsequent history of the British empire. James' hopes of a 'union of love' or, at least, a measure of administrative and economic union between England and Scotland, were not realised, and separate parliamentary, ecclesiastical, and legal systems continued. There were fears in England about the legal and constitutional implications of any union, and the Westminster parliament rejected a parliamentary or legal bond with Scotland.

Ireland

There were more immediate changes in Ireland. For the first time, in the 1590s–1600s, the entire island was conquered, and this conquest was followed by the imposition of English law and custom, and by the confiscation of much of Ulster. Whereas, in the sixteenth century, due to the costs of conflict and expenditure, Ireland was a cause of expenditure, rather than profit, for the English Crown, in the early seventeenth century there were significant gains, although little of the benefit went to the Crown. Instead, the gains were principally in the form of land, and, as also later with imperial settlement policies, that had to be made attractive to settlers. Some of the less fertile portion of Ulster was granted to the native Irish, but the rest was allocated to English and Scottish settlers, Crown officials, the Established (Protestant) Church, and, in return for financial support for the plantation, the City of London. Indeed, London's financial resources, enterprising energy, and political connections were to be crucial to much of the dynamic of empire. Large portions of Antrim and Down in Ulster were granted as private plantations, and also settled largely by Scots, for whom Ireland was more important as a sphere for expansion than it had been

14 J.F. Larkin and L.P. Hughes (ed.), *Stuart Royal Proclamations I: Royal Proclamations of King James I, 1603–1625* (Oxford, 1973), pp. 95–6. See, more generally, T.J. Dandelet, *The Renaissance of Empire in Early Modern Europe* (Cambridge, 2014).

15 B.P. Levack, 'Britain's First Global Century: England, Scotland and Empire, 1603–1707', *Britain and the World*, 6 (2013), pp. 101–2.

in the sixteenth century; and, by 1618, there were about 40,000 Scots in Ulster. Other plantations were established further south, in, for example, Wexford, Leitrim, Westmeath, and Longford.

This was one of the most significant instances of the role of migration and of force in Britain's early imperial experience, as native Catholics were transplanted to the west of Ireland in order to make space for the plantations. Across much of Ireland, while some Irish chiefs successfully transformed themselves into English-style landlords, the British empire in large part became a matter of the dispossession of native landowners, while, in Ulster, the native population as a whole saw their position deteriorate as large numbers of Protestants were settled.[16] Moreover, expansion in Ireland was an important background to trans-oceanic colonisation, helping to mould attitudes towards territorial control and non-Protestants; and, in some cases, similar groups were involved in sponsoring activity in Ireland and across the oceans.

In the seventeenth century, Ireland was, at once, a part of the British multiple polity and a British colony, a religious battlefield, and a site of complex politico-cultural identities and alignments. Co-operation with the thrust of government policy was made problematic by abrupt shifts in the latter, notably between pro-Catholic policies and the violent anti-Catholicism of the Cromwellian conquest and order in 1648–60. The degree to which the Irish, including the power-brokers there, could only influence policy from London to a limited extent was an aspect of the colonial relationship. At the same time, as a reminder of the danger of simplistic labelling, this situation was also a facet of political relationships within multiple polities/kingdoms, and, indeed, of governance within individual states in the absence of a democratic culture.

The subjugation of Ireland was a key element of British imperial expansion in the period, one in which force on land was supported by naval strength.[17] This subjugation was to be repeated as control over Ireland was challenged in successive crises, first, from 1641 linked to the breakdown of Stuart control, then from 1688 linked to the overthrow of James II, and lastly in the 1790s in the turmoil touched off by the French Revolution. However, looked at differently, these challenges in part reflected, not only Irish separatism, which was important, but also the extent to which the 'metropole', or government of Britain as a whole, was divided. Charles I during and after the Civil War in

16 N. Canny, *Making Ireland British, 1580–1650* (Oxford, 2001); J. Lyttleton and C. Rynne (eds), *Plantation Ireland: Settlement and Material Culture,* c.*1550*–c.*1730* (Dublin, 2009).

17 E. Murphy, *Ireland and the War at Sea, 1641–1653* (Woodbridge, 2012).

the 1640s, Charles II as claimant to the throne in the 1650s, and James II after expulsion in the 'Glorious Revolution' of 1688–89 provided legitimacy, context, and, less securely, leadership for resistance to policy from London.

Separately, as an aspect of a wider overlap of politics within the British Isles, there was no united Irish opposition to the British connection. Indeed, the collapse in 1603 of the rebellion of Hugh O'Neill, Earl of Tyrone against English rule launched in 1594 indicated not only (eventual) English military capability, but also the extent to which Elizabeth I was not faced by opposition from across the entire island. Subsequently, under James I (r. 1603–25), as later under both Oliver Cromwell and William III (r. 1689–1702), the new order was consolidated with the large-scale redistribution of lands to supportive interests, and with measures to back Protestantism and the use of the English language (as opposed to Gaelic). These bland remarks do not give due weight to the harshness and disruption involved, harshness and disruption that have played, and continue to play, a major role in the subsequent account not only of Ireland's history, but also of its identity. Expropriation was the key element of the redistribution of land.

Empire, more generally, represented and reflected choices. If, in the early seventeenth century, they included the response to the problematic relationship between England and Scotland, as well as the treatment of Ireland, there was also the question of the emphasis between Europe and the trans-oceanic world. The circles of James's eldest son, Prince Henry, included men with an interest in geography and imperial expansion, but, in 1612, he predeceased his father. In the 1620s, James and his second son and successor, Charles I (r. 1625–49), instead, focused their attention on European power politics and devoted little attention to colonial expansion.

North America

In the seventeenth century, the century of the Civil War (1642–46) and the 'Glorious Revolution' (1688–89), much English expansion was driven from the imperial periphery, as it also was in the eighteenth and nineteenth centuries and even in the early twentieth. This was notably the case in North America. It was not until a base was established by the Virginia Company at Jamestown in the Chesapeake in 1607 that a permanent English colony was founded on the eastern seaboard of North America. Spain regarded this colony as an invasion of its rights and protested about its foundation. However, although the defences at Jamestown were prepared to resist Spanish attack, it did not come: Virginia was too distant from the centres of Spanish power. Despite heavy initial losses of settlers, largely due to the impact of disease in a unfamiliar environment,[18] the Virginia colony expanded as a result of the continued arrival of new settlers and the willingness to put an emphasis on growing food. After much bloodshed, native resistance was overcome in 1622–24 and 1644. No gold or silver was found in Virginia. Nor was it possible to trade with the Spanish colonies in order to obtain sugar and tobacco that could be profitably sold in England, as Spain was determined to exclude foreign traders. The bankrupt Virginia Company failed in 1624, but the colony was continued with a royal governor.

Further north, the establishment, in 1602 by Bartholomew Gosnold, of a settlement on an island near what he had named Cape Cod was rendered redundant by Gosnold's failure to develop initial trading contacts with the natives. Moreover, in the face of the latter's hostility, the settlement had to be abandoned,[19] a pattern similar to that which had probably ended the Viking settlement of Greenland in the Middle Ages. In 1620, however, the Pilgrim Fathers, a group of Protestant nonconformist separatists who had leased a concession from the New England Company, sailed from Plymouth on the *Mayflower*, made a landing at Cape Cod, and established a settlement at New Plymouth, beginning the development of a colony in New England. This was a term first used in 1614 by Captain John Smith when he described the coastline north of the River Hudson; it was popularised by his *Description of New England* (1616). The naming of the new land was significant for a process of appropriation.

The settlers sought to create a godly agrarian world, and they believed that their righteousness made them more entitled to the land than the natives; although it was not only Protestant nonconformist settlers who saw natives as savages.[20] The settlers benefited from the impact on the natives of (probably) the plague in 1616–18 and of smallpox in 1634. The effects of disease were highly significant for the contours, and indeed character, of colonial settlement, both in creating opportunities and in thwarting others. The separatists were followed to New England by settlers who were not separatists, but who were also zealous for a godly commonwealth. These more mainstream Protestants, sponsored by the Massachusetts Bay Company established in 1629, founded Boston in 1630.

18 K. Kupperman, 'Apathy and Death in Early Jamestown', *Journal of American History*, 66 (1979), pp. 24–40.

19 N. Salisbury, *Manitou and Providence: Indians, Europeans, and the Making of New England, 1500–1643* (New York, 1980).

20 H.C. Porter, *The Inconstant Savage: England and the North American Indian, 1500–1660* (Cambridge, 1979).

This colony expanded rapidly, and the natives were unable to confront the growth of the English presence. The settlers' brutal defeat of the native Pequots in a brief war in 1637 confirmed the Puritans' position and their conviction of divine support. English settlement spread, for example in the Connecticut River Valley from 1634, and, with it, a new English-style landscape was created. Land use was a major aspect of control. Like other aspects, it was not one restricted to empires, but it was generally greatly accentuated by imperial control.[21] By 1642, there were over 15,000 English settlers in New England, and by 1650 nearly 23,000, although some Puritans returned to England during the republican Interregnum in the 1650s, a period of Puritan rule, raising the prospect of possible early decolonisation if sufficient numbers had done so. However, the Interregnum was cut short with the return of Charles II in 1660.

These colonies remained closely focused on England. An emphasis on spreading settlement can lead to an underrating of the major role of ports in the colonies, especially of Boston, and, more particularly, the importance of the beginning of the annual sailing season and the arrival of ships that brought immigrants, products, money, and news from England. Their likely arrival was the focus of continual discussion and concern in the colonies.

West Indies

Further south, English colonies were also established on some of the Caribbean islands that the Spaniards had not colonised; although this was not an easy process while there was also colonisation by France and the Dutch. English settlements were founded on St Lucia in 1605 and Grenada in 1609, but opposition from native Caribs helped lead to their failure. Bermuda, an island in the Atlantic that was remote from other islands, was discovered in 1609, possibly helping inspire Shakespeare's play *The Tempest*. However, it has also been argued that *The Tempest* refers to the island nation of Great Britain as recreated by the Union of the Crowns in 1603, and not to America.[22] Settled in 1612, Bermuda became a successful colony where tobacco cultivation was swiftly introduced. Bermuda, which was taken over by the Crown when the Virginia Company failed, was followed by the establishment of colonies in the West Indies: St Christopher

21 W. Cronon, *Changes in the Land: Indians, Colonists, and the Ecology of New England* (New York, 1983).

22 T. Marshall, 'The Tempest and the British Imperium in 1611', *Historical Journal*, 41 (1998), pp. 375–400.

(Kitts, 1624), Barbados (1627), Nevis (1628), and Antigua and Montserrat (1632), although an attempt upon the Spaniards on Trinidad in 1626 failed, and the Puritan-run colony on Providence Island off the coast of Nicaragua did not last. It remains as an atmospheric fragment of the extensive mosaic of the might-have-beens of empire. As England was, unsuccessfully, at war with Spain and, then, also France in the 1620s, there was a congruence of bellicosity with schemes for new colonies.

The colonies established were to be important bases for subsequent expansion. Without these, it would have been far more difficult to make subsequent gains at the expense of Spain and, later, France. Colonies also helped in a transfer of English energy in the Caribbean from buccaneering to a more regulated process of activity and expansion. However, buccaneering continued to be important to the established colonial authorities in the second half of the century.[23] Indeed, the threat from buccaneering to English trade helped lead the Royal Navy to stamp it out in the 1710s and 1720s. The opportunities of, and profits derived from, colonies made their development, and the acquisition of new ones, normative and important. In addition, although disease hit hard, the presence of settlers permitted a process of acclimatisation and the development, among survivors, of a degree of immunity to tropical diseases that provided an important local resource for future aggression and growth. New settlers provided the colonies with a vital assistance against the inroads of war and disease. These were not the only problems facing the colonies, although the settlers were not fully aware of their responsibility for deleterious change. The troubling impact of the rats that were unwittingly introduced by the English to Bermuda was an instance of a wider devastating ecological impact: European diseases ravaged native societies, while hunting and the introduction of new species hit indigenous animals.

The Caribbean islands were no mere adjunct to North America, and, indeed, until the 1660s, they attracted more English settlers. Barbados proved the most popular destination while the Church of England divided Antigua up into parishes in the 1670s. These islands were rapidly used for commercial agriculture, and the labour-intensive nature of the resulting plantation economies led to a need for settlers, at this stage largely English labourers provided by contracts of indenture. This was a practice of labour provision and control transplanted from England.[24] Tobacco and cotton were the initial crops, but, from the 1640s,

23 C. and R. Bridenbaugh, *No Peace beyond the Line: The English in the Caribbean, 1624–1690* (New York, 1972).

24 H. McD. Beckles, '"Black Men in White Skins": The Formation of a White Proletariat in West Indian Slave Society', *Journal of Imperial and Commonwealth History,*

there was a shift to sugar, particularly on Barbados. The profitability of sugar was rapidly recognised, a profitability that reflected the opportunities for capital investment and economies of scale in light of major demand in Britain, notably when the cost of sugar fell. Sugar was to lead to slaves, but it is important not to see this as the inevitable economic and social pattern of the colonies in the West Indies. Instead, a more mixed economic pattern that was less capital intensive was initially dominant, and it continued to be important even after there was an emphasis on sugar. Tobacco, which was also worked by slaves, became the major crop around Chesapeake Bay, in the colonies of Virginia and Maryland, and its limited capital requirements (compared with sugar) and high profitability encouraged settlers and investment.

Assessing Imperialism

With the agents of English central government generally weak or distracted, colonists were able to pursue the search for land, trade, and other resources, for example Native Americans for enslavement. The colonists extended their power into the interior. In a parallel process, control spread in the West Indies into, and in, islands where there was no European presence already. As with other discussion of imperialism, it is appropriate to emphasise themes of expropriation, notably what is now known as the use of the doctrine of discovery.[25] The cruelty and violence of English, later British, imperialism and settlement can be stressed. It is also possible to consider the extent to which Native American society itself saw imperialism, with powerful tribes and confederations, notably the Iroquois in the east, and later the Comanche in the west, despoiling Native opponents and victims and subsequently being described in terms of empire.[26] This was a process that had not begun with European arrival, however much the European role may subsequently have accentuated the rivalry between Native Americans. From one perspective, as repeatedly with imperialism, the outside power fed into local rivalries and was manipulated accordingly, as much as it manipulated them. This situation pertained with the English use, in clashing with Native Americans, of the support of other tribes, and, also, of this use while competing

---

15 (1986), pp. 5–21, and *White Servitude and Black Slavery in Barbados, 1627–1715* (Knoxville, 1989).

25 R.J. Miller, J. Ruru, L. Behrendt, and T. Lindberg, *Discovering Indigenous Lands: The Doctrine of English Colonies* (Oxford, 2010).

26 P. Hämäläinen, *The Comanche Empire* (New Haven, Connecticut, 2008).

with other European powers, the Dutch, French, and Spaniards.[27] The European colonists could bring specific advantages to this manipulation, notably the superior firepower stemming from a distinctive weapons technology, that of gunpowder, which gives commentators the view that this was an 'unfair' fight. These advantages, at times, could transform the situation, but, more commonly, they provided the Europeans with an entry to the contest, and not with an ability to determine its course or consequences. Such a comment can, more generally, be made about the course of imperialism, down to its close.

In terms of the current politics of imperial contention, however, the degree of assistance received by imperial powers can be a matter of controversy. Critics of imperialism, notably in the public arena, tend to underplay this assistance, and to argue that, in so far as it occurred, it should be labelled collaboration or was obtained under some degree or other of coercion or duress. In the case of the slave trade, which is frequently treated as an aspect of empire, the degree of local co-operation in Africa in the slave trade, indeed of African activity or agency, is frequently underplayed outside academic circles.[28] This process contributes to the presentation of imperialism in terms of foreign oppressors and domestic agents, a process that denies agency to the latter and thus, paradoxically (or not), contributes to their presentation as weak and vulnerable. Given the role of the slave trade and slavery in the assessment of empire, it is important to understand the number and range of the interests involved. While in the British empire there was a close relationship between slavery and the imperial economy in the New World, this was less the case for Spain.

With territorial control, the key issues in co-operation, are those in the stages of territorial acquisition (whether or not conquest is involved), subsequent imperial governance, and resistance to pressure for decolonisation. These stages are not necessarily separate, and frequently overlapped, but there was also a degree of separation. Co-operation, both passive and active, non-violent and violent, existed in all three stages, and, without it, empire would not have been viable. That assertion, a simple statement, reflects not only the burden of much empirical work, but also theoretical developments. The reworking of military history to put an emphasis both on winning co-operation, rather than simply lethality, and on the capabilities of non-Western military systems, has been highly significant.[29] So also has been the development of transnational

---

27 G. Harvard, *The Great Peace of Montreal of 1701: French-Native Diplomacy in the Seventeenth Century* (Montreal, 2001).

28 J. Thornton, *Africa and Africans in the Making of the Atlantic World, 1400–1800* (2nd edn, Cambridge, 1998).

29 J. Thornton, *Warfare in Atlantic Africa, 1500–1800* (London, 1999).

perspectives. Indeed, empire, in both whole and part, has increasingly been presented as a transnational project, an account that very much puts the emphasis on co-operation and on shared roles. Such co-operation, however, varied greatly in cause, type, and result, which was a key aspect of the history of empire.

Government and Empire

Government support for trade and colonies was important, but not invariable. In the 1620s, war with, first, Spain and, then, France led to conflict outside Europe, including the capture of Québec in 1629 by the Scots captain David Kirke. Competition with the French added a new dimension to the English Atlantic world, for it meant that it was no longer centred on hostility with Spain. However, neither James I nor Charles I was particularly interested in Québec, and it was returned to France in 1632 as part of the peace settlement. In contrast, the Dutch were able to benefit from their resumption of war with Spain in 1621, a conflict that lasted until 1648 (longer with Portugal), in order to make a major effort to seize Spanish and Portuguese colonies. England was unable to grasp a similar opportunity, although, in 1622, the East India Company helped Shah Abbas I of Persia capture the Portuguese base of Hormuz in the Gulf and, in return, gained favourable terms in trade with Persia.

Charles I dissociated himself in the 1630s from the idea of maritime expansion at the expense of Spain, preferring to align himself with her. Partly as a result, disputes over financing the navy accentuated distrust of Charles. This was particularly the case with the extension from 1634 of Ship Money, a form of taxation. Meanwhile, the idea of a Protestant foreign policy and a triumphant naval war with Spain remained potent.[30] This idea was both an inheritance from the reign of Elizabeth I and a subsequent presentation of what had been in practice an often difficult and disappointing, as well as costly, conflict. The Providence Island Company, from its base off the coast of modern Nicaragua (where there are still remains to be seen), kept alive the idea of profitable piratical opposition to Spain.[31] Charles, however, was not interested. This contrast underlines the extent to which the course and contours

30 K. Andrews, *Ships, Money and Politics: Seafaring and Naval Enterprise in the Reign of Charles I* (Cambridge, 1991), p. 5.

31 W.F. Craven, 'The Earl of Warwick, a Speculator in Piracy', *Hispanic American Historical Review*, 10 (1930), pp. 457–79; K.O. Kupperman, *Providence Island, 1630–1641: The Other Puritan Colony* (Cambridge, 1993).

of imperialism involved both the issue of commitment and, as a consequence, political contention.

By the 1630s, the imperial community had developed a powerful momentum of its own in the English world, with the East India Company and the North American colonies owing relatively little to the Crown. James I sent Sir Thomas Roe as ambassador to the Mughal Emperor of India, and he was there from 1615 to 1618. However, the East India Company's position in Asia depended on its own resources and efforts, and, after initial difficulties, it raised nearly £3 million in its first 30 years. Thanks to the autonomous structure of the Company, it was able to use the profits of its trade to support a forceful stance, as when it repelled Portuguese attacks off Surat in West India in 1612 and 1615 and, in co-operation with Abbas I of Persia, attacked the Portugal at Hormuz, these the most prominent of a series of clashes.[32]

Alongside conflict, the Company had to establish relations with local powers, not least in order to benefit from the 'country trade' between Asian ports. This benefit reflected the extent to which it was necessary to plug into non-Western commercial networks in order to profit from trade. This was a key instance of the processes of co-operation and compromise already referred to.

Whereas considerable profits had been made by the East India Company in the 1600s, the situation in the 1620s and 1630s was less favourable, and a failure to live up to expectations led to the abandonment of trading bases in Japan, Siam (Thailand), and what is now Malaysia in 1623. Dutch competition over the spice trade from the East Indies affected profits, and the position did not improve until the 1660s. In 1623, ten English merchants on the spice island of Amboyna in the Moluccas were massacred by the Dutch, but the Company had already decided to withdraw from the Moluccas, although it maintained an important role in the East Indies spice trade, especially through Macassar in the Celebes (Sulawesi), Bantam on Java, and bases on Sumatra. At the same time, the Company developed its interests in India, especially in the import of cotton textiles, initially from Gujarat, and subsequently from the Coromandel Coast, at first from Masulipatam and, from 1639, from Madras (Chennai), where a fortified position was established. Activity in the Indian Ocean included an unsuccessful effort in mid-century to colonise Madagascar. In West Africa, the Company of Merchants Trading to Guinea was given a monopoly in 1631. It established factories on the Gold Coast in the 1630s, initially at Komenda and subsequently at Kormantin, which was fortified from 1638, and Winneba.

32 G.V. Scammell, 'England, Portugal and the Estado da India, *c.*1500–1635', *Modern Asian Studies*, 16 (1982), pp. 177–92, esp. pp. 187–8.

Although the Crown did not direct overseas enterprise, it did play a role in the granting of monopoly rights through charters. This role was useful in raising finance from mercantile sources. However, opportunities were frequently judged in terms of short-term gain, so that unprofitable trades, such as that to the Gambia in 1618–21 launched by the Company of Adventurers of London Trading to the Parts of Africa (the Guinea Company), which was granted a monopoly by James I in 1618, were abandoned. Monopolies could be a form of extortion. In the 1630s there was considerable anger in England about the extent to which royal pressure created problems for the chartered companies, such as the East India and Levant Companies. Monopolies, moreover, were unwelcome to other economic interests, as well as to consumers.

The limited role of the Crown in supporting trans-oceanic activity helped lessen the impact on Britain's overseas position of the civil wars in Scotland, Ireland, and England that broke out in 1639 lasting until 1652. However, this impact was still serious. Moreover, the challenge to established assumptions about the conduct of government posed both by Charles I, and by some of his critics, manifested itself in the colonies as well as in the British Isles. In 1638, Massachusetts refused an order to submit its charter for scrutiny and slighted the condemnation of the charter by the Privy Council. Charles was considering a forceful response when the crisis of authority in Scotland gathered pace. Within New England, there were also tensions over authority, with Connecticut and Rhode Island being founded as breakaway settlements from Massachusetts in response to differences over church government. Eventual parliamentary success in the civil wars, however, ensured that the empire held together; and this uniformity in outcome was continued during the subsequent turmoil of the seventeenth century.

Expansion from 1650

Oliver Cromwell, Lord Protector from 1653 to 1658, and Charles II (r. 1660–85) each saw England as a maritime and commercial power and actively backed naval developments. The Navigation Acts of 1650 and 1651, which excluded other powers from the trade of the English colonies, and restricted most of the trade of England, Wales, and Ireland to nationals, were reprised in the Navigation Act of 1660 and the Staple Act of 1663. Customs revenues were helped by the prohibition of exports direct from the colonies to foreign markets, and, instead, by the requirement they be exported to England or one of its colonies. It was laid down in 1660 that all foreign-built ships in English ownership should be registered. Two years later, the purchase of Dutch ships was hindered when an Act decreed that ships of foreign build not registered by that date were to be deemed alien and to be subject to alien duties.[33]

Union with Scotland in 1707 ended its exclusion from what had been an English empire, as the Navigation Acts now encompassed Scotland, and this incorporation was to be important to the dynamic of the British empire. Local tariffs were not an issue in Britain; in contrast, on the national scale, the mercantilism of the Navigation Acts provided an important degree of protectionism. This represented the origin of a new stage in the use of colonies, a use that can be regarded as exploitation by Britain, or as a sharing and allocation of inputs and benefits between Britain and the colonies, a sharing that included the provision of capital and protection by Britain.

Aside from measures to encourage shipping, there was also assistance for exports, as trade took precedence over short-term financial considerations. In 1722, the export duties on most British manufactured products were abolished; while import duties on foreign raw materials required for these products were reduced or abolished. Exports to the colonies rose, average annual British exports to North America rising from £0.27 million in 1701–05 to £1.3 million in 1751–55.[34] The British West Indies remained as important a market for most of the period, reflecting their profitability as a plantation economy, as well as their role as entrepots for a contraband trade with Spanish America. This trade, which helped lead to war with Spain in 1739–48, the War of Jenkins' Ear, provided an infusion of bullion into the British trading system, as well as contrasting with the British determination to use navigation laws to prevent Europeans from challenging their own monopolistic claims.[35]

Trade protection was a crucial goal, but it entailed policy choices and different levels of commitment. Naval protection became more regular and consistent with time, with convoys for defence, and squadrons for attacking opposing naval forces including privateers. In the Mediterranean, this tasking was fully operational by the time of the Second Anglo-Dutch War (1665–67).

33 C. Wilson, *Profit and Power: A Study of England and the Dutch Wars* (London, 1957), pp. 97–102; R. Conquest, 'The State and Commercial Expansion: England in the Years 1642–1688', *Journal of European Economic History*, 14 (1995), pp. 155–72.

34 W. Minchinton (ed.), *The Growth of English Overseas Trade in the Seventeenth and Eighteenth Centuries* (London, 1969).

35 N. Zahedieh, 'The Merchants of Port Royal, Jamaica, and the Spanish Contraband Trade, 1655–1692', *William and Mary Quarterly*, 3rd ser., 43 (1986), pp. 570–93; G.V. Scammell, '"A Very Profitable and Advantageous Trade": British Smuggling in the Iberian Americas, *c.*1500–1750', *Itinerario*, 24 (2000), p. 167.

This protection cut shipping losses, as well as increasing the efficiency of the commercial system by creating a clear distinction between mercantile and military functions, and thus increasing the appeal of investing in trade.[36] A stress on trade protection represents an emphasis on the role of government policy. That was certainly important and captures a shift from the situation under Charles I when the focus had been on a foreign policy centred on Continental power politics. Moreover, this emphasis on the role of government policy captures the degree to which the trans-national and autonomous elements of maritime activity and empire were subordinated to a greater degree of cohesion in terms of an imperial policy. However, this emphasis underplays the extent to which these elements continued to be prominent, notably economic and financial links with the Dutch. Within England, the key roles were taken by entrepreneurs able to provide and use capital. London finance and institutions played the central role in this provision, helping provide the capital that permitted economies of scale in the supply of trans-Atlantic goods, notably sugar, as well as the credit that made a workable system reliant on delayed payment.[37]

A different instance of co-operation was provided by voyages of exploration. William Dampier, a one-time buccaneer, was placed by the government in command of an expedition in 1699 that was intended to acquire knowledge about Australia. He found nothing of apparent value but left a legacy in the shape of books including his *New Voyage round the World* (1697), *A Discourse of Winds* (1699), and *A Voyage to New Holland* (1703–09). All published in London, these works reflected the degree to which there was a strong interest in information about the world. Similarly, in 1699–1700, the astronomer Edmund Halley explored the South Atlantic in the *Paramour*, a naval sloop of which he had been given command by William III. This led to the production of a chart of terrestrial magnetism, an important tool for navigators.

The expansion of trade assisted shipping, justifying investment, and English shipping tonnage rose from 162,000 in 1660, to 340,000 in 1686, and 421,000 in 1751. The focus on more distant trades played a major role in this expansion. Furthermore, long-distance trade entailed particular requirements for shipbuilding, both in Britain, where most large ships were built on the Thames, and in the colonies, especially Boston. Britain's first commercial wet dock, the Howland Great Dock, built on the banks of the River Thames at Rotherhithe

36 G. Pagano de Divitiis, *English Merchants in Seventeenth-Century Italy* (Cambridge, 1997), pp. 62, 184.

37 C.J. Koot, *Empire at the Periphery: British Colonists, Anglo-Dutch Trade and the Development of the British Atlantic* (New York, 2009); N. Zahedieh, *The Capital and the Colonies: London and the Atlantic Economy, 1660–1700* (Cambridge, 2010).

in 1695–98, was used by the East India Company, initially as a safe anchorage and ship repair facility. London's first dry dock had been built at Rotherhithe in 1599, followed by another, for the East India Company, at Blackwall, in 1614–17. The Union with Scotland in 1707 created opportunities for Scottish shipbuilding: the number of Glasgow's ships rose from 30 in the late 1680s to 70 by the 1730s. Overseas, shipbuilding also began in North America, and, to a lesser extent, Bermuda, Barbados, and Jamaica.[38]

The increase in the range, as well as the volume, of exports to the colonies helped spread the benefits of empire throughout different areas of British industry, and was particularly important to the development of the iron and textile industries. Aside from advantages in terms of sales, there were also important qualitative changes, not least those that flowed from the economies of scale made possible by exports.[39] Such production and trade brought turnover and profit that provided crucial investment capital. As a result, although colonial trade might be an enclave activity centred on ports, such as Whitehaven, the profits gained as a result acted as stimuli for other economic sectors, providing both liquidity for bankers and investment capital. This point is directly relevant to the question of the wider economic impact of slave-produced plantation goods.

Trade affected diet and health in Britain. Sugar and tobacco came from the colonies, and were seen as beneficial as they helped to finance their import of British manufactured goods. Although sugar was initially a luxury item, the average retail price fell considerably in the second half of the seventeenth century, and sugar came to be important to the British diet, partly replacing honey as a sweetener for food and drink. In 1702, John Evelyn had at Falmouth, 'a small bowl of punch made with Brazil sugar'. The addition of sugar to hot drinks increased their popularity: chocolate was altered by sugar, making it a sweet, rather than a bitter, drink, and leading to the growth in the import of chocolate's main ingredient, cacao. Cacao plantations were established on Jamaica in the 1660s, and this production encouraged consumption, although, by the 1680s, the place of cacao on the island had been superseded by sugar. As the consumption of caffeine drinks rose, so demand for sugar increased, while, in Britain, the new drinks led to the production, purchase, and use of new goods,

---

38 R. Davis, *The Rise of the English Shipping Industry in the Seventeenth and Eighteenth Centuries* (Newton Abbot, 1962); G.V. Scammell, 'British Merchant Shipbuilding *c.*1500–1750', *International Journal of Maritime History*, 11 (1999), pp. 27–52, esp. 41–2.

39 P.K. O'Brien and S.L. Engerman, 'Exports and the Growth of the British Economy from the Glorious Revolution to the Peace of Amiens', in B.L. Solow (ed.), *Slavery and the Rise of the Atlantic System* (Cambridge, 1991), pp. 177–209.

such as teapots and sugar-tongs. The consequences for health of greater sugar and tobacco consumption were very serious.

New colonies were founded in the late seventeenth century: Connecticut in 1662, Carolina (named after Charles II) in 1663, New Jersey in 1664, Pennsylvania (named after the Quaker William Penn) in 1681, and New York in 1689. In 1663, Charles II granted to eight supporters the proprietorship of a colony from the Atlantic to the Pacific, between 31° and 36°N, 'and that the country ... may be dignified by us ... we of our grace ... call it the Province of Carolina'. Two years later, the bounds were extended to 29° to 36°30'N. The assertion of claims rested in part on a conviction that the Native inability or unwillingness to settle and develop lands, at least apparently, left them free for imperial acquisition and improvement.[40] This was a self-serving belief, but it stemmed from a powerful conviction of human responsibility to make the best use of the gifts and opportunities given by God. This was a religious conviction that helped condition moral, judicial, and social assumptions within Britain and her colonies. Applied in the colonies, in a Christian context that was determined by British norms, these attitudes provided ready guidelines by which most commentators judged Native mores and practices inadequate. A similar harsh stance was adopted towards those mores regarded as inherent to slave society. Thus, religion helped provide a ranking of peoples and a justification for settlement that prefigured what has been referred to as the Social Darwinism seen in the late-nineteenth-century heyday of imperialism.

Although the creation of the colony of Carolina was intended to free the area from dependence on the colony of Virginia, as much as to deny Native interests, it indicated the extent to which British territorial claims bore no relation to the frontier of settlement but vastly exceeded it. This was also the case with expansion in North America in the eighteenth century. Partly a matter of initiatives by colonists, this expansion saw extravagant land claims by speculative interests. Slave-raiding at the expense of Native Americans was important to the labour needs of the new colony of Carolina. This raiding involved brutal coercion as well as purchase from allied Native Americans who raided for slaves. In terms of scale, however, such raiding was far less significant than the trans-Atlantic slave trade.

A very different form of co-operation, but one that also rested on force, was provided by the extent to which, once conquered in the 1660s, the Dutch

40 W.E. Washburn, 'The Moral and Legal Justifications for Dispossessing the Indians', in J.M. Smith (ed.), *Seventeenth Century America: Essays in Colonial History* (Chapel Hill, North Carolina, 1959), pp. 24–32; B. Arneil, *John Locke and America* (Oxford, 1996).

population of New Netherland provided a support for the English position in the middle colonies. This support provided a key imperial component of the eventual alliance between the two powers, an alliance developed, in the crucible of successive wars with France, from the 'Glorious Revolution' of 1688–89.

Narratives of Imperial Expansion

One pattern of imperial narrative presents the practices and attitudes developed by imperial power in Ireland as important to contemporary and subsequent British conduct in the trans-oceanic sphere, notably in the New World. The emphasis is on expropriation and harshness, and connections are drawn, notably by Christopher Bayly,[41] to the subsequent role of the Protestant Anglo-Irish aristocracy in British imperialism, and particularly the central role in India in the 1800s of Arthur Wellesley, later Duke of Wellington, the victor over the Marathas at Assaye and Argaum in 1803, and of his elder brother, Richard, Marquess Wellesley, the Governor-General. A parallel argument, advanced by Geoffrey Plank, focuses on the practices and attitudes arising from the suppression of Jacobitism in Scotland from 1689 to the mid-eighteenth century, and, as in Ireland, would direct attention to the new governmental policies developed to administer the conquered region.[42] Again, the link to the subsequent commitment of Scots to imperialism attracts attention. As an instructive instance of how modern views provide different accounts, the commitment of Scots to British imperialism is downplayed by some Scottish nationalists. Instead, there is often a misleading tendency to present Scotland as the victim of England.

An approach to the empire focused on the military, on officials, and on landowners offers an account that is different to the more commercial focus of much of the work on maritime empire, with its emphasis on mercantile networks and their significance for naval strength. This contrast, which was to be pertinent throughout the course of empire, reflects the multiplicity of imperial narratives offered by empire, alongside the obvious one of the contrast between the imperialists and those who suffered from their activity. This multiplicity is not only one of choice in analysis, but also reflects the extent to which there were

---

41 C.A. Bayly, *Imperial Meridian: The British Empire and the World 1780–1830* (Harlow, 1989).

42 G. Plank, *An Unsettled Conquest: The British Campaign against the Peoples of Acadia* (Philadelphia, Pennsylvania, 2001).

indeed several tendencies at play at any time. That was certainly the case at the close of the seventeenth century. The English (in fact, with its numerous Scottish components, British) territorial empire that was readily apparent in Ireland was different to the variety of British territorial empires in the New World, a variety that stretched from Hudson Bay and Newfoundland to the Caribbean, and let alone to the commercial empire in the Indian Ocean.[43] This variety leads to an emphasis on a complexity of development and causation that makes judgement difficult. If this point is valid for subsequent scholarship, it was also the case for contemporary discussion about imperial issues. These issues themselves were not a separate category to other aspects of politics for contemporary discussion. The same was to be true throughout the course of empire.

Migration

Empire was dynamic, not static, with its dynamism provided, not only by shifting relationships between imperial power and native peoples, but also by a British energy expressed in particular in trade and migration. The pace of migration was such that, by 1700, despite Britain's population only being about a quarter that of France, the European population of English North America was considerably greater than that in French North America by about 210,000 to 10,000. This growing contrast was important in the struggle between the two powers for dominance in North America, one apparently settled in favour of Britain in 1760, because this population provided important local sources of manpower and a stronger local infrastructure to support military activities. Both were to be highly significant in British campaigning against (French) Canada and (Spanish) Florida, and notably in the conquest of Canada in 1758–60, especially the successful advance on Fort Duquesne in 1759.

Much of the French population was ready to migrate within France. In contrast, in Britain, there was a greater willingness to emigrate to, or act as an entrepreneur in, distant areas. Compared with France and Spain, the British population, on average, lived closer to the sea, a function of Britain's island nature. For those in port-cities and coastal regions, maritime activity played a role in the popular consciousness that was very different to the situation today. However, whereas large numbers went to the West Indies and North America,

43 For a questioning of the standard argument that the imperial experience in Ireland acted as a basis for policy in America, A. Games, *The Web of Empire: English Cosmopolitans in an Age of Expansion, 1560–1660* (Oxford, 2008).

there was no settlement migration to India or West Africa. Emigration followed possibilities created by trade and other contacts. Voluntary emigration was a cumulative process, as it made particular use of networks of family, friends, and other contacts, especially neighbourhood and religious groups. These provided the collective solidarity that helped individuals overcome the hardships and anxieties of migration and settlement. Voluntary settlement was also encouraged by particular sponsors, especially the proprietors of colonies, for example, from the 1730s, the Trustees of Georgia. All these factors combined to produce a mass of information about options concerning work and settlement overseas. However, it was difficult to distinguish fact from rumour, for empire always attracted projectors, and flourished on rumour.[44] Indeed, rumour was a key source, means, and product of the confidence that was so important to imperialism.

Growing Strength

By 1700, England was the leading naval and maritime power in the world, superseding Spain, the United Provinces and France, which had each held that position in sequence. In particular, England dominated the North Atlantic world, and was best able to deploy maritime power on both sides of the Atlantic. Moreover, England's overseas trade had risen substantially. This trade led to mercantile prosperity and crucial customs revenues. International trade, which also provided the Admiralty with a proto-intelligence network, focused on the leading port, London, accentuating its importance in the country and the empire.[45] This role helped provide a context for policy discussion that was very much dominated by mercantile values and by those that could be presented as mercantile. There was no comparison in France or Spain of a context for such policy discussion, and nor was there to be so in Germany. This discussion involved a lobbying of government that, from the 1690s, increasingly focused also on parliament. This focus, and the resulting legislation, encouraged an engagement with economic policy at the national level, as opposed to seeking the particular privileges that pursuing monopolies had led to.[46] That Ireland was represented by a separate parliament meant that, largely, it was directly excluded

44 A. Games, *Migration and the Origins of the English Atlantic World* (Cambridge, Massachusetts, 1999).

45 J. Flavell, *When London Was Capital of America* (New Haven, Connecticut, 2010).

46 P. Gauci (ed.), *Regulating the British Economy, 1660–1850* (Farnham, 2011).

politically from this economic nation. With this exception, there was a focus on the supposed interests of such a national unit, and of lobbying accordingly.

Mercantile strength underpinned effective public finances, providing a major advantage for the British in successive conflicts with France: 1689–97, 1702–13, 1754–63, 1775–83, 1793–1802, 1803–14, 1815. Thus, international competition established a context in which domestic circumstances were assessed in terms of relative international effectiveness. This concern with effectiveness led to interest in new institutions, such as the Bank of England founded in 1694, as well as to periodic reforming bursts. The same process was to be seen in the early twentieth century. The governmental response in the 1690s and 1700s was related to the 'Glorious Revolution' of 1688–89, in which the autocratic Catholic James II of England (James VII of Scotland) had been driven from Britain, and replaced by William of Orange, as well as by a system of government and politics in which parliament played a greater role. The governmental response also had a greater scope thanks to the parliamentary union with Scotland in 1707. Union owed much to the determination to prevent a Jacobite restoration on behalf of the French-supported 'James III and VIII', the son of James II and VII. The economic opportunities of empire were also important for the Scots, although, until the second half of the century, they focused on the Atlantic colonies and not, as later, India.[47] In the long term, both the Revolution Settlement that followed 1688 and war with France transformed the context in which imperial, as well as English and British, policies and identities were defined. This process was an important instance of the way in which the British empire was remade in new circumstances and for new tasks.

Politics

Politics within the colonies were also affected by the 'Glorious Revolution', the Revolution Settlement, and war with France. Tensions between colonists and government reflected a complex interaction of links and differences played out against a background of social developments and also repeating the politics of the homeland. As far as links are concerned, it can be too easy to underrate the Englishness or Britishness of early colonial history. In the case of the Thirteen Colonies, which were, in 1776, to declare independence from the British Crown,

47 S.J. Brown and C.A. Whatley (eds), *The Union of 1707: New Dimensions* (Edinburgh, 2008); A. Mackillop, 'Accessing Empire: Scotland, Europe, Britain, and the Asia Trade, 1695–*c.*1750', *Itinerario*, 29 (2005), pp. 7–30.

it is understandable both that knowledge of eventual independence colours the analysis, and that the experience of emigration and the conditions encountered in the colonies are assumed to have constituted a radical break with Britain. This assessment should be qualified. Indeed, the American colonists claimed the rights established in England in 1688. Moreover, the evolution of colonial societies was greatly affected by British society, culture, and related assumptions. However, this process should not be presented as passive, for the impact of the local environment and economy were important, not least in creating very different worlds of work, with consequent social relations. In addition, far from there being uniform views and experiences, the variety of settler communities interacted with that of British patterns of behaviour and thought.

Thus, New England, with its Puritanism, urban character, and (albeit limited) democratic practices, in part drew on different traditions to the more Episcopalian, rural, and hierarchical society that was established round the Chesapeake. To understand both, it is necessary to appreciate the varied character of English social development. In the case of seventeenth-century Maryland and Virginia, both of which then focused on the Chesapeake, most settlers were English by birth and upbringing, they established a society based on English laws, government, and economic organisation, and they brought traditional English attitudes towards the social order and religious practices. However, in the case of the Chesapeake, immigration from England greatly slackened from the 1690s, and social contrasts became more marked. This development was linked to a demographic shift in which, thanks to a decline in death rates, the percentage of native-born inhabitants rose. This led to a better balance of men and women, early marriages, and thus more children. A greater separateness from England emerged.[48] Colonies settled later, notably, from the 1730s, Georgia and, from the 1760s (East and West) Florida, did not have time to experience the same change to the same degree.

The politics of the homeland were important in the development of British colonies. Indeed, their history in the seventeenth century reflected the instability of the homeland, for, in both, this was an era of rapid change that challenged existing ideas and institutions, and that ensured that developments occurred against a background of instability and crisis. Rather than thinking primarily in terms of a tension between colonial autonomy and English (later British) authority, differing political positions, for and against royal authority, spanned the Atlantic. As a result, under Charles II (r. 1660–85), the formal authority of

48 J. Horn, *Adapting to a New World: English Society in the Seventeenth-Century Chesapeake* (Chapel Hill, North Carolina, 1994).

the Crown over the governments of Barbados and Massachusetts was increased, while, in 1677–79, abortive plans were drafted to make legislation in Virginia and Jamaica dependent on the assent of parliament. From his accession in 1685, James II of England and VII of Scotland's attempt to impose autocracy clashed, in both Britain and the colonies, with the corporate ideal of government, as well as with a Protestant suspicion of the intentions of the Catholic monarch whatever his claims to grant religious toleration. He was also brought down by his maladroit handling of people. Circumstances worked against James: he was unable to mould them or to respond adequately.

The overthrow of James in the 'Glorious Revolution' of 1688–89 was popular with colonial élites not only because it promised to roll back Stuart autocracy, but also because it provided legitimation for America's evolving politics.[49] James had created a Dominion of New England (1686–89) that had sought to give force to royal edicts and to overcome colonial autonomy, so that the Navigation Acts, which had been ignored by a number of the colonies, were enforced. As an aspect of the 'Glorious Revolution', royal governors were overthrown in Boston, New York, Maryland, and Antigua in 1689,[50] and the Dominion disintegrated as colonists restored the governments replaced by James. Thus, the 'Glorious Revolution', like subsequent defeats in Britain for Jacobitism – attempts at Stuart revival – endorsed Protestant Providentialism, and helped strengthen the community of sentiment that spanned the Atlantic. This community of sentiment rested on shared experiences and values. As with other aspects of the empire, the situation in the early eighteenth century looked towards other, but different, situations, indeed contexts, later in its history. In the specific case of the North Atlantic, the role of context was to be demonstrated by the contrasts between the trajectory of Canada and the USA. The situation in the late seventeenth century would have been very different had James held on to his position in the British Isles, but not in the New World, as the latter would then have been reconquered for James. This process would have created a very different public memory for imperial rule in British North America. Counterfactual (what if?) accounts face many methodological problems, but they are pertinent for the British empire. Counterfactuals return us, not only to the uncertainties of past decision-makers, but also to the fears and anxieties within which attitudes to imperial circumstances, processes, and decisions were developed and refracted.

49 R. Bliss, *Revolution and Empire: English Politics and the American Colonies in the Seventeenth Century* (Manchester, 1993).

50 D.S. Lovejoy, *The Glorious Revolution in America* (New York, 1972).

The 'Glorious Revolution' was followed, in both England and the colonies, by the implementation of a new order that included a measure of religious toleration as well as an extension of government based on the Westminster parliament; Ireland and Scotland still had their separate parliaments. This extension was seen with the revised Navigation Act of 1696, that authorised colonial Vice-Admiralty courts, and with the creation in 1700 of a General Post Office that had branches in the colonies. Furthermore, the spread of a measure of religious toleration (markedly so in contrast with the French and Spanish empires) led to pressure on colonial assemblies to copy the Toleration Act of 1689. This toleration also led to the Naturalization Act of 1740, which offered to foreign Protestants and Jews in the colonies the rights of British subjects.

Parliamentary assertiveness added a dimension to the relations between Crown and colonies that had, in other respects, been modified in favour of co-operation, not only by the joint and hostile reaction to James II and VII, but also because the series of wars with France and Spain between 1689 and 1763 put a major premium on colonial assistance in order to be able to attack French and Spanish colonies. The contiguity or proximity of British colonies with Bourbon possessions in North America and the West Indies was particularly important to this co-operation. In the person of Philip V (r. 1700–46), a branch of the French Bourbon dynasty came to the throne of Spain in 1700, and, generally, the two powers were allies until the French Revolution. As a result, whereas Britain and Spain had been allies in the 1690s, the Spanish colonies later became targets for British attack. In contrast, alliance between Britain and Portugal meant that the Portuguese colonies could not be targets; instead they were part of the British informal empire. In war with France and Spain, colonial military assistance was both necessary and possible, although the pressure of war also led to a more active (or at least attempted) imperial grip in colonies, or at least colonial positions, deemed of strategic importance. However, alongside respect for established rights, pressure for co-operation during a developing crisis with France helped ensure the failure of the Board of Trade's attempt in 1701–02 to bring all the remaining chartered colonies under the direct control of the Crown.

In addition to changes in authority to match those in England, there was also conflict specific to the colonies. This was especially so in 1676, when there was a serious rising among part of the settler population in Virginia: Bacon's Rebellion. When many of the militia supported the rebellion, the governor, Sir William Berkeley, a wealthy landowner who represented élite interests, turned to local loyalists. However, he was unable to hold Jamestown, and the rebellion only collapsed when Bacon died.[51] There was a parallel 'Huy and Crye' rebellion in Maryland in 1676, directed against the autocratic and pro-Catholic policies of the proprietor, Lord Baltimore. Such activity reflected the dynamic character of politics in the colonies. This character was linked to the problems of control posed by the expansion of settlement in the interior. Although English proprietors and merchants had begun the colonisation of the American seaboard, they soon lost control over the resulting colonies and over the process of new settlement. The proprietors and merchants were defeated by the enormous availability of agricultural land and the difficulty of commanding immigrant labour. The consequences were to help lead to the rebellion of the Thirteen Colonies in 1775.[52]

---

51 W.E. Washburn, *The Governor and the Rebel: A History of Bacon's Rebellion in Virginia* (Chapel Hill, North Carolina, 1957); S.S. Webb, *1676: The End of American Independence* (New York, 1984).

52 S.J. Hornsby, *British Atlantic, American Frontier: Spaces of Power in Early Modern British America* (Hanover, New Hampshire, 2005).

Chapter 3

The Eighteenth-Century Empire

The eighteenth century was the period in which key elements of the empire that were later to be highly controversial came to great prominence. This was true both of Britain's establishment of a significant territorial position in India and of its dominance of the Atlantic slave trade. These developments did not exhaust the long-term importance of the century. The cohesion of an English-, indeed London-, dominated British Isles was ensured with the defeat of Jacobite risings in Scotland and northern England in 1715–16 and 1745–46, and with the suppression of the Irish rebellion of 1798. Alongside, as a result of defeat in the American Revolution, the loss of the Thirteen Colonies that became the basis for the modern USA, these contradictory developments serve as a reminder that the empire was contested not only by foreign powers, most prominently France, but also by native as well as by settler opposition. Indeed, the response to opposition to imperial control became, with the American Revolution, an important aspect of the debate within Britain about the purpose, effectiveness, and future of the British empire. This opposition could overlap with the debate. Moreover, the aftermath of these rebellions, notably in Scotland and Ireland, is an important aspect of the contested legacy of empire.

The eighteenth century witnessed the continuation of earlier developments, but also two highly significant changes that, between them, greatly altered the character of the empire. The establishment, in mid-century, of a major British territorial position in India, notably in the prosperous region of Bengal, looked towards nineteenth-century expansion, there and in Asia as a whole. Conversely, the loss, in 1775–83, of the Thirteen Colonies represented both a major challenge and also a departure from the position that the empire included the extensive British diaspora, or, at least, the Protestant diaspora. The American Revolution was a major blow, but not a trauma equivalent to the revolution in France that began in 1789, because there was no conflict within Britain itself, as there was to be in Wales in 1797 and, more seriously, in Ireland in 1798. This loss of leading settler colonies in North America, however, looked towards the threat of the loss of Ireland in the 1790s and suggested a precariousness to empire at the very moment when it was also developing in new directions. This situation was not unique, being seen for example in the immediate aftermath of World War One (1914–18), when major territorial gains were accompanied by overstretch in the Middle East, as well as by loss of control over most of Ireland.

As empire developed in the eighteenth century in a number of directions, reflecting political, economic, social, religious, and cultural drives, it was scarcely surprising that varying, even contrasting, ideas about the empire were expressed.[1] These diverse directions and ideas reflected the variety of reasons for the development of empire, and this variety affects current perception. There is a range of scholarly emphases. A consideration of the development of empire in terms of challenge and opposition, both within the colonies and, more significantly, from other imperial powers, might seem to underplay the importance of autonomous ideological and political developments in Britain itself. A focus on the latter is relevant, but the autonomy of any individual strand in imperial history has to be queried. This point emerges in response to the active academic debate about whether Britain was primarily a European or an Atlantic power in so far as its external concerns were focused.[2]

In part, as so often with scholarly controversies, this debate revolves around the sources considered. Government was more concerned about European power politics, so that ministerial correspondence accordingly devoted much attention to foreign policy. Much of the public, conversely, became more interested in trans-oceanic issues and therefore these issues played a greater role in the press. At the same time, there was a chronological dimension, with attention in each sphere of politics moving towards a concern with trans-oceanic issues, although not at the same rate. The government remained more wedded to European issues in the 1730s, 1740s, and early 1750s than the public, in so far as the latter can be treated as an abstraction and a unity. From the outbreak of hostilities in the American interior in 1754, however, trans-Atlantic issues were also to the fore for the government, and this became even more the case after the breakdown of the Anglo-Prussian alliance in 1762 marked a move away from a major commitment to European power politics, a move that was apparent until interventionism resumed with the Dutch Crisis of 1787.

1 S.A. Reinert, *Translating Empire: Emulation and the Origins of Political Economy* (Cambridge, Massachusetts, 2011).

2 For the former, see B. Simms, *Three Victories and a Defeat: The Rise and Fall of the First British Empire* (London, 2007).

Imperial Wars

Repeatedly throughout history, much about empire was a consequence of real or apparent challenge, although this element can be insufficiently present in modern public perceptions that tend, instead, to focus on expansionism. For Britain, challenge and a sense of challenge were present aplenty during the eighteenth century. Britain was formally at war with France in 1702–13, 1744–48, 1756–63, 1778–83, and 1793–1802, as well as with Spain in 1719–20, 1739–48, 1779–83, and 1796–1802. In addition, there was a situation of conflict with France short of formal war in 1743–44 and 1754–56. There were also confrontations in which Britain prepared militarily. These included, crises with France in 1731, 1770, 1787, and 1790, and with Spain in 1726–27, 1770, and 1790. Other powers also posed challenges, notably the Dutch, Russia, and Prussia; while, outside Europe, there was conflict with the Marathas and Mysore in India, and with American rebels.

Anxiety was the prime result of all these conflicts and confrontations. This drew in particular on attempted invasions, notably by France in 1692, 1708, 1744–46, 1759, 1779, 1795, 1796, and 1798, and by Spain in 1719 and 1779. In addition, there were fears of invasion on other occasions, notably by France in 1731 and 1733, and by Spain in 1732. Anxieties could be mocked, as, on stage, in plays by Henry Fielding in 1730 (*The Coffee-House Politician*) and Richard Brinsley Sheridan in 1779 (*The Critic*). However, these anxieties were an ever-present part of British public culture. France was a formidable military power, with a far larger army. With its Catholicism and its more autocratic constitution, France also had a different and challenging political system and public culture. Moreover, the French government supported the Jacobite cause for part of the first 60 years, notably with invasion attempts, and its active backing always seemed a prospect during this period.

Fear of France drew on, and was expressed in terms of, the idea that France represented the threat of universal monarchy. Thus, in 1754, Joseph Yorke, an MP as well as a diplomat and the son of the Lord Chancellor, wrote to his MP brother Philip about 'the measures necessary to be taken to prevent France's acquiring a real universal monarchy'.[3] This idea looked back to the notion of Spain as threatening such monarchy and, beyond that, to opposition to the pretensions of the Holy Roman Empires. Thus, British imperialism was in part expressed in terms of an opposition to what was presented as universal imperialism. Instead, British imperialism was seen as more modern as a form and goal of power.

3 Joseph to Philip Yorke, 10 Dec. 1754, BL. Add. 35364 fol. 25.

Concern about France was a key aspect of the background to empire. From the perspective of today, imperial expansion appears as an aggressive process in which Britain spread its power at the expense of non-Western peoples, who were conquered or enslaved. In contrast, in the eighteenth century, the focus in Britain was on the British Isles, on existing colonial territories, on the German territory of Hanover, which provided Britain with its monarchs from 1714 to 1837, and on British relations with rival European empires, pre-eminently France. This concern did not mean that Britain simply acquired trans-oceanic empire as an adjunct to European power politics, let alone by accident, but it does put relations with other European powers at the forefront of governmental attention. At the same time, chronological change was highly significant. The focus on European territorial issues was more apparent in the first half of the century than subsequently. In contrast, in the second half, especially from the 1760s, there was a greater tendency to see European rivals, notably France, at least in part as an aspect of competing imperial systems, although that view had always been present.

Rivalry with France drew on potent ideological elements, notably anti-Catholicism and opposition to autocracy; each also central features in the response to Spain. This ideology was that of state and society, one reinforced by a recent history of conflict. Attitudes to empire did not comprise a separate sphere, but, instead, reflected these values. Indeed, the absence of a distinct set of values for imperial policy is striking. The same was true of governance and commercial policy. This lack of separateness means that empire cannot be readily separated from the rest of the national narrative, while also ensuring that it was not necessary to take particular initiatives in order to move forward an imperial project. Nor are there the records of an all-powerful imperial planning body for study; no such body existed, although the Board of Trade could advance bold plans under powerful heads, such as George, 2nd Earl of Halifax in 1748–51. The Board of Control for India was subsequently to do the same, particularly under Henry Dundas from 1784 to 1801.

Conflict with France, Spain, and the Dutch during the century produced a string of imperial gains, most lastingly Gibraltar from Spain in 1704, gains that were a symbol of victory in war and of success at peace settlements. Victory in the War of the Spanish Succession (1702–13 for Britain) indicated the difficulty of separating out imperial themes. Gains at the expense of Spain exemplified this, as Gibraltar, a new British position in the Mediterranean, proved more strategically and, in the short term, politically significant than the degree of entry into the protectionist trading system of Spanish America that was gained, an entry that was limited and subsequently contested. The Peace of Utrecht of 1713 left Britain with Gibraltar and Minorca, the latter captured from Spain in 1708. As a result,

Britain acquired naval bases to support its position as a major Mediterranean power, a position shown in subsequent conflicts and crises. Most conspicuously, Britain sank a Spanish fleet off Sicily in 1718, in the battle of Cape Passaro, affirming British naval dominance in the Mediterranean; convoyed Don Carlos, the new ruler of Parma (later, the resentful Charles III of Spain), from Spain to Italy in 1731; and used the threat of the bombardment of Naples to force a change in Neapolitan policy in 1742, a change that benefited the Austrian position in Italy. The Mediterranean also became a safe sphere for British trade.

The reconciliation of the leading Italian powers, Austria, Spain, and Savoy-Piedmont (the kingdom of Sardinia), in the early 1750s made the British position in the Mediterranean less significant, while the fall of Minorca to French attack in 1756 and (after it was returned under the Peace of Paris of 1763) in 1782 again, was a conspicuous blow to the British position. This was notably so in the former case, which constituted a national humiliation that was to be assuaged by the trial and execution of Admiral Byng, the commander of the squadron that failed to come to the relief of the besieged British garrison. Nevertheless, the British position in the Mediterranean, especially in the first half of the century, indicated the range of British imperial activity and presence, as well as the extent to which it was not dependent on wide domains, but, instead, was a matter of maritime power supported by naval bases.

The contrast with territorial expansion in North America was readily apparent. The latter attracts more attention, not least as empire tends to be defined in terms of territorial control, which provided a ready opportunity for settlement; but, as already indicated, this definition is too narrow. Moreover, as far as the British were concerned in the early eighteenth century, the Mediterranean presence was very important. This point links to two issues, first that of the emphasis on Europe as opposed to trans-oceanic interests in British foreign policy, and, secondly, the extent to which past imperial priorities are misunderstood because of hindsight, notably the habit of considering the first age of empire in terms of High Victorian practices and priorities. Whether this eighteenth-century Mediterranean presence should be seen as imperial, with the focus on Gibraltar and Minorca (and, for the following century, on Gibraltar, Malta, the Ionian Islands, Cyprus, and Egypt), or whether it is best to present it primarily in terms of European power politics, is unclear. Seeking benefit in these power politics was a traditional theme and, as Britain became more powerful in the early eighteenth century, so it became more plausible to think of such politics in terms of territorial gains.[4]

---

4 Possibly because of interest in the oceans, the Mediterranean is generally underplayed in the maritime account of empire. See, for example, H.V. Bowen, E. Mancke,

Gibraltar and Minorca were not the sole territorial issues in Europe. There was talk in 1748, as part of the peace treaty at the close of the War of the Austrian Succession (in which Britain fought from 1743 to 1748), of acquiring Ostend, an invasion port that was also a point of entry into the Low Countries, although the idea was not pursued.[5] Hanoverian acquisitions, moreover, were in part due to British power, notably the use of naval power and diplomatic weight during the Great Northern War of 1700–21. As a result of this conflict, George I, as Elector of Hanover, gained the secularised Archbishopric of Bremen and Bishopric of Verden, which expanded Hanover's presence in North-West Germany. To see these, or his son's (unsuccessful) efforts to gain the Prince-Bishoprics of Osnabrück, Hildesheim, and Paderborn, notably as a result of participation in the Seven Years' War (1756–63), as part of the British empire, might test credibility, but there is no inherent reason why they should not be considered as part of a broader consideration of the British state and its territorial and political interests. Such discussion would put a focus on the dynastic dimension of empire, which indeed was an important element in the first half of the century, notably as Bourbon princes succeeded to Spain (1700), Parma (1731), and Naples (1734). This dynastic accumulation looked back at the way in which Habsburg power had spread both in Europe and, as a result of the dynastic union with Portugal in 1580–1640, on the global scale.

The British account of empire, in contrast, discounted dynasticism and notably outside the British Isles, where dynasticism, in the shape of opposition to the Stuarts, played a major role in the explanation of why there had to be union between England and Scotland as well as a Protestant Ascendancy in Ireland. The discounting of dynasticism in the account of empire outside the British Isles was an aspect of the populist and constitutional character of this account. Moreover, this account was not only seen at the time, as the government sought to deny claims that Hanoverian interests affected British policy, but has also affected subsequent views.

Another aspect of empire that tends to be downplayed in England was that of the consolidation of control over the British Isles. Aside from the military dimension, which brought to a close a longstanding series of conflicts, there was also the constitutional one leading to the parliamentary Union with first

and J.G. Reid (eds), *Britain's Oceanic Empire: Atlantic and Indian Ocean Worlds, c.1550–1850* (Cambridge, 2012). The best study, but for the latter imperial period, is R. Holland, *Blue-Water Empire: The British in the Mediterranean since 1800* (London, 2012).

5 J. Black, 'Territorial Gain on the Continent: An Overlooked Aspect of Mid-Eighteenth Century British Foreign Policy', *Durham University Journal*, 86 (1994), pp. 43–50.

Scotland (1707) and later Ireland (1801). Britain and the United Kingdom as the product of imperialism was not a theme that was to the fore in discussion during the Victorian highpoint of empire, but it is one that has become more pronounced as separatism developed, first in Ireland and then in Scotland. In large part, this recent and current use of imperialism as an attack on British identity and links reflects the automatic hostility to the idea of empire among a significant section of modern opinion.

This use, however, is less secure as a guide to attitudes in the eighteenth century. Indeed, it is striking to note how far the Jacobite risings were not national uprisings against a hostile English/British imperial rule, but, instead, bitter civil wars. This was particularly apparent in Scotland, where, despite the claims of later Scottish nationalists, there was much hostility to the Jacobite cause, notably from Presbyterians. Indeed, a war of religion can be discerned, with Episcopalians and Catholics tending to support the Jacobites. As a result, there were more Scots on George II's side at Culloden (1746), where his forces were commanded by his second son, William, Duke of Cumberland, than on that of the Jacobites. Despite this, in Scotland, Cumberland's Army is today frequently called the English Army.

Similarly, there was a religious dimension to the American War of Independence (1775–83), with Nonconformists more prone to oppose George III, while Episcopalians were more likely to back him; although there was no automatic relationship in either case. More generally, the religious dimension joined empire at home to the situation abroad, with hostility to Catholicism providing a key element in opposition to France and Spain. Linda Colley's perceptive account, in *Britons: Forging the Nation 1707–1837* (1992), of the role of Protestantism in British national identity, by extension covers the empire. Religious concerns help explain not only the logic of empire but also the artificiality of treating it separately to domestic and foreign policies. Missionary activity was a product of this aspect of empire and one that linked congregations in Britain to an exalted sense of imperial purpose.[6]

The Peace of Utrecht (1713) had strengthened Britain's position in North America. The acquisition of conquered Nova Scotia from France was particularly significant, even if it was not matched by the capture of the French base of Québec, which had been unsuccessfully attacked in 1711. The British amphibious force hit rocks in St Lawrence, losing many troops as transports sank. No further attack on Québec was to be mounted until 1759, a reminder of the contingent character of opportunities. Nova Scotia strengthened the

6 R. Tennant, *Corporate Holiness* (Oxford, 2013).

British position on the eastern seaboard of North America, and also provided an important geographical margin in preparing for future attacks on New France, the basis of modern Canada. At the same time, the early years of the eighteenth century affected the geopolitics of North America by closing the British off from the Gulf of Mexico for another half-century: the French became established in Louisiana, which was named after Louis XIV, while Spain, now allied to France, retained Florida. Thus, while environmental and geopolitical factors helped frame the opportunities of, and for, empire, the possibilities offered by choice and contingency also played a role. Indeed, these factors remained especially pertinent between the War of the Spanish Succession (1702–13) and the outbreak of the War of Jenkins' Ear with Spain in 1739. This was because a range of domestic and European power-political circumstances led Britain to alliance with France from 1716 to 1731 and (less closely) Spain from 1729 to 1733, and kept Britain neutral thereafter in the War of the Polish Succession from 1733 to 1735. Moreover, Sir Robert Walpole, the dominant minister from 1720 to 1742, preferred to keep out of war and proved reluctant to fight France in 1733–35 and Spain in 1729 and 1738–39. In all of these cases, this stance entailed thwarting the views of colleagues.

Politics and Imperial Expansion

As a consequence, imperial expansion from the 1720s became a platform for critics of the Whig ministries, both opposition Whigs, such as William Pulteney, their leader in the House of Commons in the late 1720s and 1730s, and William Pitt the Elder in the late 1730s and mid-1750s, and also Tories. The accusation that the ministry was failing to defend national interests was pushed hard at the time of the agitations in 1729 and 1738–39 about Spanish depredations on British merchant shipping in the Caribbean, and again in 1754 as Anglo-French relations deteriorated in the interior of North America, and in 1756 when the relief of Minorca failed. These criticisms were but a part of a wider critique of the Whig ministries for political betrayal and cultural malaise, but the imperial theme became more central to these accusations in the late 1730s as assumptions about national identity were configured, especially by opposition commentators, in an imperial manner. The attack on the imperial issue provided a way to link Tories and opposition Whigs behind the 'Country' platform. A new identity and foreign policy suited a new would-be politics.

As with later bursts of imperial and anti-imperial sentiment, this agitation and presentation was a reminder of the extent to which empire was politicised as issue and image. The terms of this politicisation varied, but the common pattern was one in which the use of imperial arguments and language was designed to strike political echoes. That did not make this usage less important. Indeed, as the political resonance of empire grew in significance in Britain from the late 1730s, so it became easier to make arguments about rectitude and identity in imperial terms. The xenophobic assault on Spain and France was linked both to Protestantism and to migration, in the development of concepts of Britishness and the British empire as a political community encompassing England, Wales, Scotland, Protestant Ireland, and the British possessions in the New World. This development was long drawn out, in part because the conceptual language of Britishness and that of empire was used until the seventeenth century to describe more restricted communities within the British Isles: England (and Wales) and Scotland, or the three and Ireland. Notions of empire tended to be somewhat hazy in periods of peace, but rhetoric and reality proved different in wartime.

In the first half of the eighteenth century, the languages of Britishness and empire provided the idea of a larger community, that of the British Isles and the seas, with, as well, the full range of English-speaking territories in the western hemisphere, being members of a single body, the empire. This potent ideology accorded with other developments within British public culture, specifically an emphasis on the successful linkage of Protestantism, trade, maritime range, and liberty, their central role in British identity and uniqueness, and their positive synergy.[7] The vision and, increasingly, reality of a maritime commercial empire identified the success of a trading nation with the liberty of its government, and distinguished this process (in a positive fashion) from territorial conquest. This contrast was seen, by British writers, as ensuring that the corruptions and debilities discerned in Classical and modern republics, and associated with a lack of liberty and with conquest, need not destroy British liberties. Thus, the Dutch republic, the United Provinces, was presented as going the way of Venice into weakness and decadence. Asserting a British exceptionalism or uniqueness, this approach integrated the British world in terms of an imperial nationalism. At the same time, there were tensions within the British world, as the Patriot ideologies that drew on notions of Britishness and the proper operation of empire were defined differently in Ireland and, eventually, the Thirteen Colonies that were to become the USA.[8]

---

7 S. Satsuma, *Britain and Colonial Maritime War in the Early Eighteenth Century: Silver, Seapower and the Atlantic* (Woodbridge, 2013).

8 This paragraph draws heavily on D. Armitage, *The Ideological Origins of the British Empire* (Cambridge, 2000). See also, L. Colley, *Britons: Forging the Nation 1707–1837*

The British perception of their empire also led to a clear expression of superiority over other empires. Thus, in 1739, in condemning the Convention of the Pardo with Spain as ignominious and a betrayal of national interests, William Pitt the Elder, then making his name as a vigorous opposition parliamentarian, also objected to referring Britain's right to freedom of navigation to negotiators. He told the House of Commons, that this course was treating as equal two very different situations: 'On the part of Spain, an usurpation, an inhuman tyranny claimed and exercised over the American Seas; on the part of England, an undoubted right by treaties and from God and Nature, declared and asserted in the resolutions of parliament'.[9] Thus, the 'Black Legend', of criticisms of Spanish imperialism as particularly cruel, expressed in the sixteenth century, was revived for use in the eighteenth century. This moral critique, by a supporter of Britain's empire, of other empires, was directed, in this case, to a specific political target, compromise with Spain in the shape of the attempt to end commercial differences and prevent war. The government's attempt at compromise with Spain in 1738–39 only succeeded in the short term, and the controversy helped to make subsequent attempts at compromise difficult. In part, this situation helped explain why a war wanted by neither government broke out with France in the mid-1750s.

The positive presentation of empire was enhanced as trans-oceanic victories, most obviously Edward Vernon's at Porto Bello in 1739, where a Spanish Caribbean base was taken, and George Anson's success in capturing the Manila galleon with its fabulous cargo in the Pacific,[10] brought more of the world within Britain's real and imaginative grasp. In 1740–44, Anson staged the first British circumnavigation of the globe since those of Francis Drake in 1577–80, Thomas Cavendish in 1586–88, William Dampier in 1679–97, 1703–06 and 1708–11, William Funnell in 1703–06, and Woodes Rogers in 1708–11. Greater interest in empire was not restricted to mercantile and political circles, nor to the depiction of warships and other maritime themes on canvas,[11] and it was no coincidence that 'Rule Britannia' was matched by 'God Save the King', earlier a tune sung by Jacobites, but now a popular and loyal song.

(New Haven, Connecticut, 1992); K. Wilson, *The Sense of the People: Politics, Culture and Imperialism in England, 1715–1785* (Cambridge, 1995).

9 R. Chandler (ed.), *The History of Proceedings of the House of Commons from the Restoration to the Present Time* (London, 1743), XI, cols 32–3.

10 G. Williams, *'The Prize of all the Oceans': The Triumph and Tragedy of Anson's Voyage round the World* (New Haven, Connecticut, 1999).

11 G. Quilley, '"All Ocean is her Own": The Image of the Sea and the Identity of the Maritime Nation in Eighteenth-Century British Art', in G. Cubitt (ed.), *Imagining Nations* (Manchester, 1998), pp. 132–52.

The emphasis on an imperial politics looked towards the controversies over liberty and governance in the American colonies in 1765–75, and the subsequent quarrels over the governance of India in the 1780s. If Britain was to have an imperial destiny, the nature of that destiny became more controversial once territorial rule was an issue, especially at a large scale, and notably over people with a degree of representation or influence in the British system. This issue crystallised competing assumptions about empire as well as reflecting developments in the colonies, especially the settlement colonies. Indeed, governors clashed with colonial assemblies, which, on the whole, displayed more independence than the English (later) British House of Commons showed in the eighteenth century. There was a strong sense of local rights and privileges that were seen as the local and necessary encapsulation of British liberties. In addition, disputes over the power and pretensions of governors were widespread and frequent. In 1708, Nathaniel Johnson, Governor of Carolina, imprisoned Thomas Nairne, the province's first Indian agent, for complaining about his abuse of commercial links with the natives, while, two years later, Daniel Parke, the Governor of the Leeward Islands, was lynched by colonists in Antigua when he sought to overawe complaints with a display of military strength; no one was punished.

The expansion of territorial claims and settlement was a particular source of dispute in the North American colonies, as it brought questions of both authority and interest into play, and that in a context in which competition for status led to a determination to establish a right to land. One strand of imperial history was control over land, and land-grabbing was a central theme. The British empire was far from unique in this, and in some contexts there was concern over native rights, notably in North America from 1763. Yet, from the perspective of the colonists, this concern was unwelcome and an autocratic imposition. Indeed, there were to be perennial tensions during the course of empire between settlers and metropolitan authorities. From the perspective of the natives, in contrast, the experience of settlers' land-grabbing was at least of a marked deterioration in circumstances whatever the legal situation.

Financial and other support for imperial defence was also an issue in all colonies and one that rivalry with the Bourbons made acute. In 1703, when Britain was at war with France, Colonel Dudley, the Governor of Massachusetts, traced his difficulties to the character of the colony's political culture, specifically the extent of representation, claiming that as the colony's council was

> of the people's choice ... they are more careful of their election than of the Queen's service and satisfaction, in so much that I have only power to deny anything offered me that is amiss in the Assembly, but no assistance to bring to pass what

> is necessary for the service, which will be in a great measure altered when Her Majesty will please to assume her just power to name her own Council here as in all the other governments in America.[12]

Migration

By mid-century, the British empire was, while still in flux, becoming more defined and populous: Ireland seemed under secure control, and there were no rebellions there during the Wars of the Spanish (1702–13) and Austrian (1743–48 for Britain) successions or the Seven Years' War (1756–63). Maritime predominance aided in economic development,[13] in securing overseas colonies, and in making them profitable. Robert, 4th Earl of Holdernesse, one of the two Secretaries of State, wrote in 1756

> of the various services in which His Majesty's fleet must necessarily be employed; the possessions of the Crown of England are so extensive, so distant one from another, and from their mother country, and the land force of the kingdom from the particular circumstances of our constitution, so little proportioned to the defence of such extended dominions, that the marine is necessarily employed to garrison, in a manner, its extended dominions.[14]

The port-cities that anchored this predominance and were the centres of imperial activity, for example Portsmouth and Bombay (Mumbai), Kingston and Bristol, or New York and Liverpool, increased greatly in size during the century. Philadelphia's population grew from 2,500 in 1685 to about 25,000 by 1760. Through these cities, in addition, migrants moved into the colonial hinterland and to other colonies. The disparity between European migration to the British and French colonies became more marked during the eighteenth century, with important consequences when the two powers clashed in North America. Canada had only about 56,000 inhabitants of French origin in 1740, whereas, by then, British North America had nearly a million people of European

---

12 Dudley to John, 1st Duke of Marlborough, 28 Dec. 1703, BL. Add. 61306 fol. 144. See also John, 4th Earl of Loudoun to William, Duke of Cumberland, 26 Dec. 1756; S. Pargellis (ed.), *Military Affairs in North America 1748–1765* (New York, 1936), p. 273.

13 P. Parthasarthi, *Why Europe Grew Rich and Asia Did Not: Global Economic Divergence, 1600–1850* (Cambridge, 2011).

14 Holdernesse to Andrew Mitchell MP, envoy in Berlin, 25 June 1756, NA. SP. 90/65.

background, reflecting the willingness to accept both a high rate of migration from the British Isles and the number of non-British immigrants. The poverty of some settlers did not discourage others from migrating, because labour rates were higher in the New World than in the British Isles. An Act of Parliament of 1697 that allowed people to seek work outside their own parish if they carried a certificate made the poor more mobile and encouraged the migration of indentured servants to America[15] and the West Indies.

It is too easy to lose sight of migration to the West Indies both here and more generally in the history of the empire. Indeed, between 30,000 and 50,000 white migrants arrived in Jamaica in the first half of the eighteenth century. Aside from the importance of the island as an entrepot for Spanish America,[16] the cultivated area on Jamaica increased greatly; tellingly, this information refers to the land under imperial control, not that tilled by escaped slaves. But for the inroads of disease, this migration would have led to a British New World demographically dominated by the West Indies, where the British presence was expanded by the settlement of Jamaica and the Cayman Islands from 1655, the Virgin Islands from 1666, and the Bahamas from 1670, although much immigration by both white migrants and slaves was to already-established colonies, notably Barbados. If migrants in the West Indies had multiplied at the same rate as emigrants to the mainland, their population by 1760 would have been nearly 3 million, compared with only 1.7 million in British North America; and if the rate had been the same as that of migrants to the southern plantation colonies in North America, the figures would have been equal. Conversely, death rates comparable to those in the British West Indies would have left a mainland population of fewer than 200,000 in 1760, of whom only about 50,000 lived in the northern colonies. In Jamaica, white death rates were higher than those of slaves, although they also suffered grievously; and this contrast ensured that the colony could not become a settler society with a large locally born white population. Yellow fever, which first struck in 1694, was a particular scourge, and was especially virulent in those previously unexposed to the disease, while malaria was a serious problem.[17]

15 R.V. Wells, *The Population of the British Colonies in America before 1776: A Survey of Census Data* (Princeton, New Jersey, 1975); A. Gogleman, 'Migrations to the Thirteen British North American Colonies, 1700–1775: New Estimates', *Journal of Interdisciplinary History*, 22 (1992), pp. 691–709; K. Morgan, *Slavery and Servitude in North America, 1607–1800* (Edinburgh, 2000).

16 T. Burnard, 'Prodigious Riches: The Wealth of Jamaica before the American Revolution', *Economic History Review*, 54 (2001), pp. 506–24.

17 T. Burnard, '"The Countrie Continues Sicklie": White Mortality in Jamaica, 1655–1780', *Social History of Medicine*, 12 (1999), pp. 45–72.

Whereas, in the seventeenth century, English migrants dominated emigration from the British Isles to the New World, in the eighteenth there was also extensive emigration from Scotland and Ireland, especially in response to economic difficulties in both.[18] This emigration helps provide a key to the detailed patchwork of settlement, not least in religious terms, a patchwork that, in turn, directed further emigration. Much of the emigration from both Scotland and Ireland (the latter referred to today in the USA as Scots-Irish) was of Presbyterians, and they had a different religious culture to the Episcopalians, who were particularly prominent in Virginia. The Presbyterians had a strong sense of community, but they lacked the emphasis on hierarchical authority seen among Episcopalians. That the emigration from Scotland and Ireland was to new lands ensured that many of the migrants settled in the back country, for example western North Carolina, away from the coastal littoral, and this situation contributed to the degree of independence they displayed. The debts owed by these farmers to coastal merchants accentuated the tension.

Furthermore, emigration to the British colonies from outside the British Isles affected both the general character of the colonies and specific locations. Germans were particularly concentrated in Pennsylvania, but not only there. In North Carolina in 1710, a group of German and Swiss immigrants established the town of New Bern, which was so successful that it became the capital of the colony in 1770, and, by then, maybe as much as 30 per cent of the colony's population was of German descent.[19] Many had come from the Rhineland, where, in the Palatinate, there had been serious persecution of Protestants in the 1700s and 1710s. Religious refugees were especially encouraged in Georgia (where the first settlement was established in 1733), enabling the fledgling colony to anchor Britain's presence between Carolina and Florida: many of these Protestant refugees came from the Archbishopric of Salzburg, indicating the importance of colonisation in the British empire for ordinary people far distant from the Atlantic coast. More generally, this was to be a central aspect of imperial history, both for the British and for other empires. It provided an opportunity for large numbers from outside the metropoles to create a new life. That this new life was often at the expense of others, in the shape of the indigenous population of the colonies, was the other side of this story, and one that ensures that there are very different collective memories of imperialism.

---

18 A.L. Karras, *Sojourners in the Sun: Scottish Migrants in Jamaica and the Chesapeake, 1740–1800* (Ithaca, New York, 1993). For the situation in the British Isles, I.D. Whyte, *Migration and Society in Britain 1550–1830* (Basingstoke, 2000).

19 M.S. Wokeck, *Trade in Strangers: The Beginnings of Mass Migration to North America* (University Park, Pennsylvania, 1999).

Under the Plantation Act of 1745, it was possible for all, bar Catholics, to become eligible for naturalisation after seven years in a British colony. These migrants helped push forward the frontier of settlement, taking advantage of the new land made available by Native American defeats, and earlier territorial claims, for example in Carolina, were given a degree of substance by this advance. The inherently dynamic nature of the empire was represented in this process.

The dispatch of convicts to provide a labour force was also important, and was a pointed instance both of how colonies were supposed to accommodate what was seen as surplus population and of the social politics of imperialism. Concern in Britain about rising crime after the War of the Spanish Succession (1702–13), when demobilisation released large numbers of fit men trained to violence into an economy that was not growing fast and a labour market that could not cope, led to the Transportation Act of 1718. This, for the first time, allowed for transportation to the colonies, not only as part of the pardoning process in the case of capital offences, but as a penalty for a wide range of non-capital crimes, including grand larceny – the theft of property between a shilling (five new pence) and £2. Parliament went on to pass another 16 Acts between 1720 and 1763 that established transportation as a penalty for crimes from perjury to poaching, and, as a result, as many as 50,000 convicts were transported from the British Isles to America and the West Indies in 1718–75: including well over 30,000 from England and more than 13,000 from Ireland. The shipboard mortality rate was about 14 per cent, a counterpart to the cruel treatment of Africans sent as slaves: infectious disease in the crowded conditions was, again, the major problem. The majority of the convicts sent to America went to Virginia and Maryland, with most of the rest being sent to Pennsylvania. Very few were dispatched to New England,[20] reflecting, but also accentuating, the contrasting social character and political culture of the colonies, particularly the lesser role of social distinction and control in New England. Similarly, an analysis of indentured servants leaving from Liverpool in 1697 to 1707 has shown that the great majority left for Virginia or Maryland, and very few for New England.[21]

Alongside slaves, the use of convicts testified to the widespread belief that coercion was the only way to deal with the labour needs of settlement colonies,

---

20 A.R. Ekirch, *Bound for America: The Transportation of British Convicts to the Colonies, 1718–1775* (Oxford, 1987).

21 D.M. Hockedy, 'Bound for a New World: Emigration of Indentured Servants via Liverpool to America and the West Indies, 1697–1707', *Transactions of the Historic Society of Lancashire and Cheshire*, 144 (1995), pp. 124–5.

as coercion made possible the diligent and purposeful supervision required for the proper improvement of the colonies, and, possibly, both slaves and convicts. The eighteenth century saw Britain become the largest shipper of slaves in the world. The slave trade was responsible for the British presence in West Africa and was central to the prosperity of Britain's West Indian colonies and the southern ones in what became the USA. Slaves provided the labour force for Jamaica's (and many other colonies') sugar, Georgia's rice, and Virginia's tobacco. Not all the colonial cash crops and exports involved slaves. This was particularly so of timber and forest products from New England and North Carolina, fish from Newfoundland, and furs from the American interior. However, slaves were central to the economy from the Chesapeake southwards. They were also significant to aspects of the economy further north. Rhode Island provided slave-ships as well as food products for the slave plantations in the south, and processed molasses into rum. Slaves also supported the living standards of the colonists. The growth of the slave trade in the British Atlantic reflected the supply of slaves as a result of internecine conflict in Africa, Britain's dominance of the Atlantic world, and the organisational and fiscal resources of her entrepreneurs. The replacement of the Royal African Company's monopoly of the slave trade by the energy of private merchants was particularly important. Bristol, London, and Liverpool were the key slaving ports, with London playing the central role in financing the trade. Its economics rested in part on a triangular trade obtaining profit and mutually reinforcing benefits in each stage. Goods exported to West Africa such as firearms and textiles, goods important to the prosperity of manufacturing districts in Britain,[22] were used to purchase slaves who were transported to the New World. Colonial products were then shipped to Britain.

Alongside those who were compelled to travel and work in order to serve the needs of the imperial economy and state, came the voluntary migrants. In a pattern that was to be continued throughout the age of empire, the number of British emigrants to the New World far outnumbered those to South Asia and West Africa, neither of which attracted settlers. This emigration greatly accentuated the impact of earlier migration, increasing the number and percentage of non-Natives in the British New World. The pace of settlement was higher in the British than in the French North American colonies, because the opportunities in the British colonies were as much a matter of governmental attitude as of agricultural and urban possibilities. The British

22 M.D. Mitchell, 'Three English Cloth Towns and the Royal African Company', *Journal of the Historical Society*, 13 (2013), pp. 421–47.

were particularly tolerant of religious groups outside the Established Churches, although the position in individual colonies varied: in Virginia, in 1643, Puritan nonconformity was banned, whereas, six years later, Lord Baltimore, the Catholic proprietor of Maryland, had the Assembly enact a law of toleration.

Community and Empire

By the 1750s, an urban hierarchy had emerged clearly among the British settlements in North America, and economic links had developed between colonies, for example providing crops and fish for the slave plantations; while economic links between the colonies and the British Isles had strengthened and become more varied. As in Spanish America, a sense of community, separate, but not opposed, to that of Britain, was increasingly apparent; this sense superimposed on the multitude of identities that colonial life and settlement gave rise to. The foundation of a colonial press was a clear sign of this. English newspapers were shipped across the Atlantic, but, as early as 1704, Boston had the *Boston News-Letter*, the first regular newspaper in British North America published by authority, although, in 1690, the unlicensed *Publick Occurrences, Both Foreign and Domestick* had been published there; only to be swiftly suppressed. Freedom of the press in the colonies followed a chronology similar to that in Britain. The press communicated both pressures for Americanisation and those for Anglicisation: both a sense of distinction from Britain and yet being part of a trans-Atlantic world.[23] Indeed the press was part of this world, for newspapers were a major component in the trans-Atlantic information system, and both in the colonies and in Britain reported the voyages of individual ships, with predictions of arrival dates, and, sometimes, information about cargoes. In addition, many printers crossed the Atlantic to the Thirteen Colonies and the West Indies.[24] Books and pamphlets, as well as newspapers, were part of the world of print. George Whitefield's printing activities in North America and Britain meant that items published in both places were carried across the Atlantic in both directions, so that there was a strong print community.

---

23 D. Armitage and M. Braddick (eds), *The British Atlantic World, 1500–1800* (Basingstoke, 2002).

24 C.E. Clark, *The Public Prints: The Newspaper in Anglo-American Culture* (Oxford, 1994).

Imperial Politics in the 1740s

As an instance of the focus and significance of political views, concern over an alleged governmental failure to defend imperial interests was a theme that linked opinion on both sides of the Atlantic in the late 1730s. Anger over what was presented as pusillanimous governmental policy, however, was less important than the breakdown in negotiations in leading to war with Spain in 1739, a war Sir Robert Walpole, the prime minister, did not want, although some of his ministerial colleagues proved willing to agree with opposition pressure for war. The mid-century emphasis on empire that began in the late 1730s initially focused on the traditional and related topics of trade, Spain, and the West Indies, and only later on the alternative nexus of land, France, and the North American interior, a nexus that first emerged clearly in British public attention in mid-century. The war with Spain began with optimism about British capability, notably with Admiral Vernon's capture of the Caribbean port of Porto Bello in 1739, but the extravagant hopes of 'blue water' enthusiasts were cruelly disabused by the costly failure to take the more important and far better-fortified South American position in Cartagena (in modern Venezuela) in 1741. The consequences of poor British command, notably inadequate co-operation between army and navy under difficult commanders, were exacerbated by an effective Spanish defence, and the British force rotted away with tropical diseases. As so often, the balance between success and failure was narrow. It is easy to explain the failure, but, had the attack succeeded, then different factors would have been pushed to the fore. Failure at Cartagena marked the effective end of bold plans for expansion at the expense of Spain, in part because concern about French expansionism in Europe was becoming more pronounced as a result of France's entry in 1741 into the War of the Austrian Succession. When British trans-Atlantic operations resumed during that war, in 1745, they were directed at French positions. British forces did not take a major position in the Spanish New World until they captured Havana in a similarly costly expedition in 1762; it was swiftly returned as part of the peace settlement.

Yet, these bold plans for expansion at the expense of Spain are of interest because they indicated a fundamental issue in British imperialism, that of the relationship with non-British peoples. There was no way in which Spanish America could be understood as an empty land, nor one populated only by 'savages', arguments employed to justify expansion into the interior of North America. Instead, Spanish America had a non-British Catholic population that could scarcely be accommodated or handled governmentally in terms of a British settler colony. That method was possible in Ireland because, although they were a minority, there was a large number of Protestant settlers entrenched by repeated conquests, while most of the land belonged to Protestants from the late seventeenth century. The situation was different in Spanish America, but, in the discussion about its future if Britain was successful, the emphasis was not on land being owned by British landowners, but on trade with Britain. In particular, it was hoped that British control of ports and the dismantling of Spanish imperial commercial preference would lead to a trade-based relationship with Spanish America, complementing that with Portuguese America, Brazil, a relationship based on friendly relations, but also on mutual commercial advantage. Brazil was part of the British informal empire. Such a development, formal or informal, for Spanish America was regarded as a necessary basis for an empire grounded on co-operation, not coercion. Hopes were also expressed that support for Protestantism and liberty might increase in Latin America.

The credibility of this prospectus may be challenged in light of what happened after the Anglo-Spanish War of 1762–63. East and West Florida became British colonies, with a plantation economy under British landlords spreading. However, the options there for the British were limited by the departure of most of the Spanish population in 1763. A degree of naivety in British hopes, which were repeated during subsequent conflicts with Spain, is more apparent, not least because, given the chance, Spanish colonial populations proved all too willing to resist British rule, as in Buenos Aires in 1807, where the total defeat of a British expeditionary force proved a very humiliating episode. It is a disaster that most people in Britain know nothing about, but one that underlines the global range of the empire. At the same time, British trade with Spanish America rose considerably despite political differences, this rise preceding the independence of these colonies that stemmed from the Napoleonic Wars in the early nineteenth century.[25]

The prospectus proposed for Spanish colonies raises the counterfactuals, first, of what might have happened had the British been more successful when at war with Spain in 1739–48 and, secondly, what might have been the outcome if Britain, when successful, had held onto the gains it did conquer, principally Havana and Manila in 1762, but also Montevideo in 1807. As a key reminder of the role of contingency, there was nothing inevitable about the pattern of British territorial gains. Louisbourg, the key naval base of French Canada, was captured in 1745, only to be returned under the 1748 peace. In 1762–63 there was a bitter debate over whether Britain should seek to retain Canada (as it did), or Martinique and Guadeloupe in the West Indies, which, in the event, were

25 A.J. Pearce, *British Trade with Spanish America, 1763–1808* (Liverpool, 2007).

returned to France, not least because of justified fears of their competitiveness with the British West Indian sugar colonies. Similarly, in 1814–15, it was unclear what conquered colonies Britain would return to France and the Dutch, whether, for example, the Dutch East Indies would be retained. Martinique and Guadeloupe were returned anew. This reminder of differing possible trajectories, and thus identities, for imperial development has, by extension, a relevance for the twentieth-century processes of British imperial decline and withdrawal, as these potential variations demonstrate the possibility of multiple outcomes then as well.

The 1740s also underlined the interplay of European and trans-oceanic interests, a theme that was to be present throughout Britain's imperial history. The fall of the Walpole ministry in 1742, after its poor results in the 1741 general election had interacted with strong tensions within the government, led to a more positive engagement with European power politics in the form of a commitment to Austria, then under attack by France, Bavaria, and Spain. British troops were sent to the Low Countries in 1742. In 1743, they moved into Germany, defeating the French at Dettingen. In turn, a French invasion attempt on England in 1744 that was dispersed in the English Channel by bad weather led to a declaration of war. Dettingen, the last battle in which a British army was commanded by the monarch, contrasted with the trans-oceanic battles of empire in none of which was there a commander from the royal family.

Conflict in the 1740s centred on Europe, but there was also fighting with the French in North America and India. In the former, the dynamism of the imperial periphery was an issue as a force of Massachusetts militia, accompanied by a squadron from the Royal Navy, sent from the West Indies, captured the major French naval base of Louisbourg on Cape Breton Island in 1745. This position threatened the British position in the western Atlantic and on the North Atlantic seaboard, acted as an important point from France en route to the French West Indies, and, more crucially, was seen as a protection for the entrance to the St Lawrence valley, the centre of French Canada. The capture of Louisbourg led to plans for further British campaigns against Canada in 1746 and 1747, plans that anticipated a far greater commitment of British resources than had been seen in 1745. There was an upsurge in Britain of hopes of imperial expansion, with extensive discussion in the press. In some respects, these hopes represented a recentring, on Canada as opposed to the Caribbean, of those that had been aroused at the close of the 1730s by war with Spain. These ambitions showed the determination of imperial protagonists to find something with which to justify their hopes. Moreover, these hopes took on greater urgency because it was argued that imperial expansion was an answer to domestic, social, and economic problems. This theme was to be seen throughout the course of empire before, ironically, being expressed at the time of the end of empire, as a focus on Europe, instead, was held out as a panacea. The European Economic Community thus succeeded the empire as the mirage of growth and the apparent source of domestic stability.

In the event, in the late 1740s, just as events and the international conjuncture had led to the disillusionment of the earlier hopes of British gains from Spain, so the same was true of those from France. The conquest by the latter in 1745–48 of the Austrian Netherlands (Belgium), of key defensive positions in the United Provinces (Netherlands), and of Madras (Chennai), the last from the British East India Company, ensured pressure in Britain to make peace on the basis of a *status quo ante bellum* or the return to the territorial position prior to the war. This outcome, in the Treaty of Aix-la-Chapelle of 1748, entailed the return of Louisbourg, which compounded and focused the frustration and anger caused by the failure, as a result of military commitments in the sharply deteriorating position in Europe, to send expeditions against Canada in 1746 and 1747. There was much criticism in the opposition press of this return and this criticism contributed to the juxtaposition of the 'nation' with its maritime and imperial interests and the royal family with its focus on Hanover.[26]

Thus, empire as a rallying cry for opposition revived, which helped explain its political positioning at the time of William Pitt the Elder's rise to power in the mid-1750s: he became a Secretary of State in 1756. Trans-oceanic imperial expansion was juxtaposed as national destiny with an alternative and rival focus on Europe, as the politics of factional interest directed critical attention to the king's ambitions as Elector of Hanover, a theme from the accession of the Hanoverian dynasty in 1714. This contrast was important not so much as an accurate description (although a strong case can be made to that effect), but rather as a strengthening of a political impression of lasting importance. Empire was presented as national, necessary, and progressive, its denial selfish, foolish, and retrograde; and this point became part of the currency of public discussion and polemic. It continued to be an important theme in this public discussion until it rapidly ebbed and then disappeared at the close of the 1950s and in the 1960s. The political usage of empire in the mid-eighteenth century helps explain why the tension between Britain as a European state and Britain as an imperial power[27]

26 For example, memorandum by French diplomat François de Bussy – June 1748, Paris, Ministère des Relations Extérieures, Mémoires et Documents, Angleterre 40 fol. 142.

27 S. Conway, *Britain, Ireland, and Continental Europe in the Eighteenth Century* (Oxford, 2011); J. Scott, *When the Waves Ruled Britannia: Geography and Political Identities, 1500–1800* (Cambridge, 2011).

was increasingly settled in favour of the latter as far as contemporary commentators were concerned.[28] This change was linked to the reconceptualisation of empire so that it became less a matter of the British Isles with some trans-oceanic outliers, and more an understanding of Britain's destiny and position across the North Atlantic. The former conception had proved readily compatible with the idea and strategic practice of Britain as a European state; but the latter was far less so.

The Seven Years' War, 1756–63

Pitt had benefited greatly from arguments about the need to defend imperial interests in his attacks on Thomas, Duke of Newcastle's ministry in 1755–56. Ironically, he found it necessary, once in power from 1757 as an ally of Newcastle,[29] an outcome that worked surprisingly well, to support the commitment of British troops to Germany in 1758. As a result, Pitt advanced a new geopolitics of imperial power in which conflict in Europe was linked to trans-oceanic expansion by means of the argument that French resources were thereby distracted. In practice, there were grave strategic risks in this policy, which, anyway, rested on specific political needs, particularly providing a justification for assisting George II's position in Hanover. Nevertheless, however misleading and self-serving, the rationale that was offered helped again to underline the idea that imperial protection and expansion were the key goals for Britain. Accordingly, other policies were explained in terms of how far they permitted the pursuit of these goals. This legacy proved significant in the subsequent discussion of how empire developed and the lessons it held for British strategy.

The Seven Years' War led to a considerable expansion of empire. In North America, the French fortresses of Louisbourg and Québec fell to amphibious operations in 1758 and 1759 respectively, although the latter proved a hard task. The sequential nature of gains was shown with the capture of Montréal in 1760 after a brilliant and innovative campaign.[30] That was the culmination of the fall of New France. Again, a sign of changing values was shown in 2009 when the 250th anniversary of the battle of Québec was largely ignored in both Britain and Canada. Far from being an iconic character, Wolfe, the victor of

28 J. Black, *Debating Foreign Policy in Eighteenth-Century Britain* (Farnham, 2011).

29 Pitt was first Secretary of State in the short-lived Devonshire ministry of 1756–57.

30 D.R. Cubbison, *All Canada in the Hands of the British: General Jeffery Amherst and the 1760 Campaign to Conquer New France* (Norman, Oklahoma, 2014), p. 217.

the decisive battle outside Québec in 1759 and a general who was killed during the battle, is now an uncomfortable figure. This is because the high point of Anglo-American consensus this victory brought[31] was to disappear with the end of that union, while, today, the Québécois (French Canadians) see the campaigning of 1759–60 as a conquest by the British. Moreover, in Britain, there is embarrassment about emphasising past victories over fellow European Union members, notably France, or, indeed, any powers.

In the Seven Years' War, the British also made gains in the West Indies, taking the French possessions there bar St Dominique, notably Guadeloupe, Martinique, and St Lucia, as well as the French bases in West Africa. Again, there is now ambivalence as the bases in West Africa, in modern Senegal, were slaving ports, while the Caribbean islands were plantation economies using slaves. Territorial gains rested on British naval mastery, which was achieved as a result of two great victories in 1759, Lagos (off the Portuguese coast) and Quiberon Bay, and these victories thwarted French invasion plans against Britain. Spain entered the war on the French side, only to have the British successfully help protect Portugal from invasion in 1762. The same year, British amphibious forces captured Havana and Manila, two key bases in the Spanish overseas empire, prefiguring the American success at the expense of Spain in 1898. The British success is now ignored, but it was especially impressive given the technological factors affecting force projection in this period.

In India, Robert Clive, who had already established Britain through military success as the leading power in South-East India in the early 1750s, was now instrumental in doing so in Bengal. His major victory over the Nawab of Bengal at Plassey in 1757 both defended the British position in Calcutta and began the process that, in particular thanks to further victories at Patna and Buxar in 1764, left Britain as the governing force in Bengal in 1765. It is symptomatic of the change of British historical consciousness that Clive is no longer a household name. In contrast, he was a hero for the Victorians, and, later, when I was a child in the early 1960s, I had a Ladybird children's book about him. The personalities of imperial conquest, such as James Wolfe were then, as also in Victorian juvenile literature, important figures in historical memorialisation, alongside those of domestic history, for example King Alfred, and civilians, such as Florence Nightingale. Each was the subject of a Ladybird book, a short,

31 N. Rogers, 'From Vernon to Wolfe: Empire and Identity in the British Atlantic World of the Mid-Eighteenth Century', in F. De Bruyn and S. Regan (eds), *The Culture of the Seven Years' War: Empire, Identity, and the Arts in the Eighteenth-Century Atlantic World* (Toronto, 2014), p. 41.

heavily illustrated, biography designed for children. One reader of a draft of this book suggested that this reference was 'not perhaps right for a serious academic book'. In practice, the presence (or not) of empire at the level of children was very important to its lasting cultural impact.

British expansion in the mid-eighteenth century was of particular note. It was certainly more notable than the overthrow of Safavid Persia (Iran) by Afghan invasion in 1721–22, or the collapse, particularly as a consequence of Maratha opposition, of Mughal power in India in the first half of the century. This is not a matter of Euro-centric judgement, but a comment on the links between different parts of the world. The fate of Safavid Persia was important in the Gulf, as well as to Oman, Afghanistan, northern India, Central Asia, the Caucasus, and to the Ottoman empire, all of which experienced the frenetic campaigning of Nadir Shah of Persia in the 1730s and 1740s. Nevertheless, it is difficult to see this fate as playing a formative role in the nineteenth- or twentieth-century world, not least because neither the Afghan control that had briefly followed the Safavids, nor the empire of Nadir Shah, proved lasting. Indeed, the last was very much an expression of individual military drive. More generally, the states of the region between the Ottoman empire and Hindustan were unable to coalesce lastingly to provide a strength able to thwart in the nineteenth century the growing interest, power, and influence there of Britain and Russia.[32]

Furthermore, there was no comparison in range between the trans-oceanic colonisation and power projection of the Atlantic European powers, especially Britain, and the more land-based character of Eastern European and non-European powers, including those, such as China and the Ottoman empire, with a lengthy coastline. China overcame the Dzungars of Xinjiang in the 1750s, demonstrating an impressive logistical capability that was the product of a sophisticated administrative system,[33] and the Chinese subsequently (unsuccessfully) invaded Myanmar and Vietnam. However, neither China nor Japan made an impact in the Pacific, either by launching voyages of exploration or by creating settlement colonies across the Pacific or around its rim. This absence from the oceans appears a failure in Atlanticist terms, in which there is an assumption that every power should have sought to be the British empire. It is necessary, nevertheless, to note the continued importance of Asian, including Chinese, merchants in maritime trade, and, conversely, to stress the major role

32 J. Onley, 'The Raj Reconsidered: British India's Informal Empire, and Spheres of Influence in Asia and Africa', *Asian Affairs*, 20 (2009), pp. 44–62.

33 P.C. Perdue, 'Culture, History and Imperial Chinese Strategy: Legacies of the Qing Conquests', in H. van de Ven (ed.), *Warfare in Chinese History* (Leiden, 2000), p. 277.

of overland economic links that were not directly dependent on this trade. This was true of the trade from India to the Near East via Kandahar (in southern Afghanistan) in the seventeenth century, which helped account for the sustained struggle between Mughals and Safavids for control of the city.[34] Britain's rise to leading imperial status depended upon not only her position within the European power system but also the relationship of the latter to non-European systems, both commercially and politically.

Eighteenth-century Western interest in the character and strength of different political systems was a prime instance of the fashionable intellectual relativism of the period. Adopting the same interest, it is difficult to discern how far Britain's great success in 1689–1815 relative to other powers stemmed from the character of her political, social, economic, and cultural system, and, conversely, how far from the more contingent application of power in particular circumstances. Globalisation certainly brought profit to societies, such as China, with whom the Europeans traded, and there was a strong degree of mutual dependence.[35] However, it was Westerners, and especially the British, who organised the new economic systems. This role affected, indeed altered, Britain's attitude to the non-European countries with which it had relations: mutual dependence and power projection were in a dynamic tension, frequently shifting in balance. Rivalry with the Bourbons led to an emphasis in Britain on power projection, which helped reshape the terms of mutual dependence with non-European countries, notably India from the 1740s. The nature and chronology of this reshaping varied greatly, as the contrast between British relations with India and (more distantly) China in the eighteenth century, and with China and (more distantly) Japan in the nineteenth, indicated.

The 1740s began a break-out period when the British empire became potentially, and then in reality, global and exceptional. In the mid-eighteenth century, the overcoming of the French in India and North America, as well as British expansion in India, were to lead to a move away from involvement in European power politics[36] and, instead, to a closer interest both in non-Western societies and in the British colonies. This was not least because it became less pertinent to consider the rest of the world in terms of rivalry with a defeated France. After France was defeated again in the Napoleonic Wars, this British interest in non-Western society became stronger anew, only for the interest to

34 S. Chaudhury and M. Morineau (eds), *Merchants, Companies and Trade: Europe and Asia in the Early Modern Era* (Cambridge, 1999).

35 R.J. Barendse, *The Arabian Seas: The Indian Ocean World of the Seventeenth Century* (Armonk, New York, 2002), p. 454.

36 D. Baugh, *The Global Seven Years War, 1754–1763* (Harlow, 2011), p. 664.

recede as imperial challenges to Britain within the Western world in the late nineteenth century coincided with a rise in Britain of racialist attitudes and a stress on the apparent merits of Westernisation.

Imperial Crises, 1763–83

The Seven Years' War ended with the Peace of Paris in 1763. Britain made major territorial acquisitions, notably French Canada and the Spanish colonies of East and West Florida, as well as gains in the West Indies (Dominica, St Vincent, Grenada, Tobago) and West Africa (Senegal). British success in the Seven Years' War left elsewhere in Europe an anger and sense of unfair British predominance that prepared the way for French and Spanish attempts to overturn their achievement. The concept of a balance of power and the language of universal empire were now directed against Britain. In turn, victory made imperial strength seem inevitable in Britain, and the reign of the new king, George III (r. 1760–1820), was initially presented in these terms.

However, he was to face serious challenges, notably the growing crisis with the North American colonists that led to the War of American Independence (1775–83). The grave fiscal strains left by the Seven Years' War, a national debt of unprecedented size, provided the cause of the political strife of the 1760s and early 1770s, with the Stamp Act Crisis of 1763–65 the first occasion for a major political breakdown. As an aspect of the attempt to breathe life into a cohesive global empire,[37] the ministry in London sought to shift more of the burden of imperial defence to the colonies (a theme later seen with the Dominions and India). However, the legislation opened up questions of the powers of parliament in colonial administration. The rejection of the authority of parliament by the North American colonists contributed to an exacerbation of the political crisis, but, for long, the colonists did not want independence. Instead, they sought self-government within an imperial context.

Nevertheless, a serious mishandling of the situation by the British government, encouraged, and directed to a great extent, by George III, increasingly made compromise less plausible. A resort to military support for colonial administration proved particularly problematic, while the passage of the Québec Act in 1774 angered Protestant Anglo-Americans by protecting the position of Catholic *Canadiens*. At the same time, the rejection of British rule was not simply a product

---

37 H.V. Bowen, 'British Conceptions of Global Empire, 1756–83', *Journal of Imperial and Commonwealth History*, 26 (1998), pp. 1–27.

of governmental mistakes, which is an approach that exaggerates the role of the metropole as opposed to the ideas and attitudes of the colonists. Their developing autonomy and political sophistication were also important. Fighting began in 1775 when the government sought to seize arms supplies in Massachusetts.

The Jacobite uprising of 1745–46 had been more serious militarily for the empire, as the collapse of the governmental position in Scotland in 1745 was rapidly translated into a crisis in England. That did not happen in the case of North America, while the crisis in the Thirteen Colonies did not spread to the other North American colonies, notably the economically important ones in the West Indies. Indeed, despite anxieties about Ireland, a key feature of the crisis was the extent to which it was not general to the empire. This situation was to be repeated with the crisis over Ireland in the early 1920s. However, despite an unprecedented deployment of strength across the Atlantic, British forces repeatedly failed to quell the rebellion in North America, while the entry of France, Spain, and the Dutch into the war against Britain, in 1778, 1779, and 1780 respectively, ensured that the conflict spread across the empire. British positions in the Mediterranean, West Africa, the West Indies, and India were attacked, and a Franco-Spanish attempt was made to invade England in 1779. In the event, the latter was thwarted by disease, while most of the empire survived attack or threats, notably Canada, Gibraltar, and Jamaica. The American invasion of Canada in 1775 eventually, in 1776, proved a total failure, as did the lengthy Spanish siege of Gibraltar, while French plans in the Caribbean were thwarted by Admiral Rodney's conclusive victory over the French fleet at the battle of the Saintes in 1782. Yet, the war closed with the impression of serious failure. Charles, 2nd Earl Cornwallis's surrender of a besieged British army at Yorktown in October 1781 was followed by the fall of the ministry of Lord North in March 1782. Britain still held New York, Charleston, and Savannah, each a key position, but victory no longer seemed a prospect and political support for continued conflict was evaporating in Britain. In the peace negotiations in 1783, the independence of the Thirteen Colonies was accepted, while Britain ceded Florida to Spain. However, Canada, Jamaica, and Gibraltar were preserved.

The conflict that reshaped global history was the last of a sequence of wars that had begun in 1739. For that formative generation, violent struggles over loyalty defined the boundaries of empire, pushing and pulling many thousands of people around the Atlantic rim and redefining empire in the process. The nature of the empire changed in particular as a result of the loss of America, a loss that was acknowledged in the peace settlement of 1783. The extent to which the overseas subjects of the Crown, were of British or, at least, European descent, Protestant, or at least Christian, white, and run through a measure of self-government, all diminished. Instead, the empire became increasingly inhabited by people of non-European descent who were not Christians, not white, and not consulted. This tendency increased during subsequent decades, notably as the British made major gains in South Asia in the 1790s–1820s. In turn, large-scale British migration to settler colonies in the nineteenth century, combined with the creation and spread of Dominion status as a form of self-government, altered the situation.

The loss of America joined the developing British position in India to push issues of colonial governance to the fore in the 1780s. These issues were linked to disquiet about the nature and fate of the empire, and a strong sense of decline. The reception of Edward Gibbon's *Decline of the Roman Empire* (1776–88) captured this, as did the trial of Warren Hastings for corruption in India, and George III's support for moral rearmament in Britain. Gibbon's work invited attention to the theme of imperial transience and decay. Wealth, especially from India, was regarded as a key source, and expression, of political corruption and pernicious, effeminate luxury. Whereas empire was to be seen as a site and source of manliness in the High Victorian period, it was a source of intellectual and cultural anxiety and social insecurity about new wealth a century earlier.

More generally, India was increasingly the pivot of much British imperial activity, and was also highly important to the changing conception of empire. Intellectual and cultural life in Britain were also affected, notably because William Jones's retrieval of Sanskrit texts and reconstruction of India's past helped introduce a significant Oriental strand to the development of Romanticism,[38] an exotic variant to the neo-Gothic. Moreover, the gain of an Indian-based oriental empire from the 1750s encouraged comparison with imperial Rome because, unlike Britain's North American empire, but like that of imperial Rome, the new British empire in India had no ethnic underpinning and was clearly imperial. As such, it also drew on the Classical Greek construction of barbarian inferiority and Oriental despotism, the subsequent Hellenistic period, 'when civilized empires ruled over inferior Orientals', and Rome. Writers in the tradition of civic humanism and, later, Romantic writers such as Byron, Shelley, and de Quincey, searched for points of reference around which to discuss and resonate their anxieties about the effects of empire, notably a corrupting India, upon metropolitan culture; and imperial Rome was the obvious parallel. Empire appeared to threaten Britain with the creation of a hybrid state, indeed nation, and this threat led to a degree of criticism and rejection.[39]

38 M.J. Franklin, *Orientalist Jones* (Oxford, 2011), p. 359.

39 K. Vlassopoulos, 'Imperial Encounters: Discourses on Empire and the Uses of Ancient History during the Eighteenth Century', in M. Bradley (ed.), *Classics and*

Empire Renewed, 1783–92

In contrast to fears, both specific and vague, about corrupt expansion or serious collapse, in practice imperial regeneration was rapidly apparent after the loss of America. This regeneration was seen in attempts to develop trade and in a more engaged approach to colonial government. In part as a response to the loss of America, there was a major attempt to explore other trans-oceanic possibilities over the following decade. Moreover, trade with America rapidly recovered without the need to bear the 'protection cost' of defending the colonies, while social and cultural links remained strong.[40] From the 1780s, ministers in London took a more pronounced role in the rule of British India, lessening that of the East India Company; although, in the short term, the attempt by the Fox–North government to do so in 1783 triggered a political crisis and the fall of the government as the attempt was seen as a grab for power and patronage. The fate of British India also involved the British position in the China trade, as well as attempts to challenge the Dutch, especially in Sumatra and Ceylon (Sri Lanka), the possibility of Pacific expansion, and the future of the maritime route to India; all of which widened the area that came within the imperial scan.

British governmental attention was truly global from the second half of the eighteenth century. This attention encouraged new themes in imperial routes, planning, and strategy, and provided a new dynamic for Britain's maritime concerns and naval mastery.[41] The range of empire was extraordinary. The expedition that seized Manila from Spain in 1762 had been dispatched from the British base at Madras (Chennai); prefiguring, in a very different context, the strategic role intended for Singapore in the 1930s and early 1940s when Britain's Asian empire was threatened by Japan. The spreading of imperial interest was obvious with the establishment of the first British bases in Malaya (1786) and Australia (1788), as well as by greater and more far-flung interest in the Indian and Pacific oceans. In 1786, local initiative by a merchant, Francis Light, led to the occupation of the island of Penang as a base on the route to

---

Imperialism in the British Empire (Oxford, 2010), pp. 52–3; T.W. Nechtman, *Nabobs: Empire and Identity in Eighteenth-Century Britain* (Cambridge, 2010).

40 S. Haggerty, *The British-Atlantic Trading Community, 1760–1810: Men, Women and the Distribution of Goods* (Boston, Massachusetts, 2006); P.J. Marshall, *Remaking the British Atlantic: The United States and the British Empire after American Independence* (Oxford, 2012).

41 D. Cannadine (ed.), *Empire, the Sea and Global History: Britain's Maritime World,* c.*1763*–c.*1840* (Basingstoke, 2007).

China. This was a move designed, in part, to check French ambitions to the east of the Bay of Bengal. The island was renamed, after the future George IV, Prince of Wales Island when the flag was hoisted, and it was to be the basis for Britain's subsequent expansion in Malaya. Three years later, the wild, in British eyes, Andaman Islands were claimed in the Bay of Bengal, and Port Cornwallis, named after William Cornwallis, Commander-in-Chief of the navy in the East Indies (and brother of Earl Cornwallis), was established as a base.

The foundation of a settlement in Australia in 1788 owed much to the loss of America, which had brought the transportation of convicts to an end. After considering transportation to Africa, the government decided, in 1786, to found the colony of New South Wales in Australia in order to provide a penal colony, and the first settlers were landed at Botany Bay in January 1788. A range of factors motivated the government. For example, it hoped for geopolitical advantage. Aside from pre-empting the French, who indeed reached Botany Bay six days later, only to discover it occupied, the government planned a base that would project British power into the southern hemisphere and would provide naval supplies. The latter were judged necessary to the articulation of imperial power, as warships had to be refitted. Initially, the high hopes were to be disappointed, as the harsh climate and difficult ground vegetation created problems, as did scurvy. A failure to provide and produce sufficient supplies ensured that there were grave difficulties until the Second Fleet arrived in 1790. Thereafter, the situation improved. More fertile soils were cultivated and Port Jackson on Sydney Cove, the latter named after the Home Secretary, Thomas, 1st Viscount Sydney, became an important calling-place for whalers and sealers. Naming after prominent figures in British public life was significant in the colonies. Thus, in Nova Scotia, there was an Annapolis Royal (after Queen Anne, under whom the colonial capital was conquered from France), a Halifax (after George, 2nd Earl of Halifax, the President of the Board of Trade when the base was established), and a Sydney.

China's trade also appeared a more prominent prospect by the 1780s. Tea imports from China grew greatly, stimulating, in turn, exports from India to China, including opium. However, the Macartney mission of 1792–94, the first British diplomatic mission to China, failed to realise hopes for a closer commercial relationship with China due to the disinclination of the Qianlong Emperor. The geographical spread of British interest was also seen in 1790 when, in the Nootka Sound Crisis, Britain came close to war with Spain (and its ally France) over competing territorial claims on Canada's Pacific coast. In the event, with France convulsed by revolution, Spain backed down. There were high hopes in Britain about the economic possibilities of the region, especially over the long sought north-west passage from the Atlantic to the Pacific.[42] One of the major purposes of Commander George Vancouver's voyage to the north-eastern Pacific, which began in April 1791, was to discover such a passage as well as to strengthen the British position on the coast by advancing the linkage of knowledge and control.[43] Suggesting the way in which the geopolitics of North America was still open to the imagination because its geography was unknown, Robert Liston, a British diplomat, wrote of a possible north-west passage from near Nootka Sound to Hudson Bay, and of the prospect of a large inland sea like the Baltic or the Mediterranean, adding: 'if the coasts of this new Mediterranean are of a rich sort, producing ship-timber, and peopled with a race of men wishing to exchange furs for our woollens and other manufactures, we cannot give up such an extensive prospect for the increase of our trade'.[44] In fact, there was no such sea, just as hopes in the nineteenth century of a large lake in the interior of Australia proved misguided. Each, however, reflected the extent to which empire provided free rein for the imagination and thus for hopes of creation and renewal, hopes that spanned government plans and imaginative fiction.

In 1790–92, Britain, moreover, fought a war in southern India against Tipu Sultan of Mysore. In this, the British achieved more success than when they had fought Mysore in 1780–84, although the war was less successful than that which was to be waged in 1799. France did not intervene in support of Mysore as it had done in the early 1780s. As a reminder of the role and range of imperial commands, Cornwallis, the general defeated at Yorktown in 1781, was the commander of the advance on Seringapatam, the Mysore capital, in 1792.

Empire at the Close of the Century, 1793–1802

The likely direction of Britain as an imperial power seemed clearly focused on trans-oceanic interests, notably in South Asia but also, increasingly, around the Pacific. However, the situation changed in 1793 when Britain entered the

42 G. Williams, *The British Search for the Northwest Passage in the Eighteenth Century* (London, 1962), pp. 221–6, 235–45; D. Mackay, *In the Wake of Cook: Exploration, Science and Empire, 1780–1801* (London, 1985), p. 83.

43 B. Anderson, *Surveyor of the Sea* (Seattle, Washington, 1960); D. Clayton, 'On the Colonial Genealogy of George Vancouver's Chart of the North-West Coast of North America', *Ecumene*, 7 (2000), p. 392, and *Islands of Truth: The Imperial Fashioning of Vancouver Island* (Vancouver, British Columbia, 2000).

44 Liston to William, Lord Auckland (earlier William Eden), 14 Sept. 1790, BL. Add. 34433 fol. 117.

French Revolutionary War that had begun the previous year and sent troops to Belgium. With two brief exceptions, in 1802–03 and 1814–15, Britain was at war with France until Napoleon finally fell in 1815 after his defeat at Waterloo. This war contributed to a more conservative presentation of national identity in Britain. Opposition to France was in part expressed in terms of counter-revolution. A Loyalist tradition, stemming from opposition to the American revolutionaries and from the Loyalist diaspora at the close of the War of American Independence, had already contributed to a more intractable conservatism, notably, but not only, in Canada, where many Loyalists settled.[45]

As France did well militarily until 1812, conquering or overawing Western Europe, it came also to be supported by other colonial and naval powers, notably Spain and the Dutch. The latter were conquered by the French in 1795 while Spain became (intermittently) an ally of France from 1796 until 1808. This alliance greatly increased the strategic challenge to Britain. In a reprise of the Seven Years' War (1756–63), the British government, in response, sought to combine European commitments with trans-oceanic expansion. The colonies of rival powers were seized, notably in the West Indies, for example Trinidad from Spain in 1797, but also Cape Colony from the Dutch (1795), and French and Dutch bases in India and Sri Lanka, notably the major harbour at Trincomalee in 1795. These successes reflected British amphibious capability and the already-pronounced strength of the empire, which offered a network of bases from which attacks could be mounted. This potential was a key instance of the cumulative character of empire, for example in the West Indies. Once Cape Colony was captured, Cape Town became a base from which the River Plate in South America could be attacked. The disruption brought by the French Revolution to the French empire and navy was also important to British success, not least the large-scale slave-rising in France's leading colony, St Dominique, which became, in 1804, the independent state of Haiti.

As in the American War of Independence, the range of European opponents posed a major challenge to the Royal Navy, while Britain also had to face opponents in India, notably Tipu Sultan in Mysore. Nevertheless, as in their other campaigning in India, the British benefited greatly from the rivalries between the Indian rulers. Thus, Nizam Ali of Hyderabad provided help against Mysore. A similar ability on the part of Britain to fight sequentially, rather than simultaneously, was also seen in the difficult war with the Marathas of West

45 R.M. Calhoon, 'Loyalist Cosmopolitanism', in J. Bannister and L. Riordan (eds), *The Loyal Atlantic: Remaking the British Atlantic in the Revolutionary Era* (Toronto, 2012), p. 285.

India in 1803–06. Arthur Wellesley's hard-fought and very costly victories at Assaye and Argaum in 1803 reflected the extent to which the military triumph of empire was far from inevitable.

The ability, alongside conflict, to elicit support was seen in other aspects of British policy in India. In Bengal, where the East India Company gained effective authority in 1765, it can be regarded as a new force trying to define mutually beneficial commercial links, but the emphasis can also be on an exploitation that brought high taxation, deflation, and famine.[46] The administration of Bengal revealed the different attitudes of the natives and the British to authority and profit, which was shown in the implementation of the law and in financial control over markets and trade. The idea of a capitalistic market economy, it has been suggested, was more important to the British (an argument that may underrate the role and sophistication of Indian banking networks), and the entry of the East India Company into regional trade involved pressure, indeed force. The colonial confrontation was thus partly a prolonged contest over the habits, terms, and meanings of goods, markets, and people, which, together, constituted a vital link between authority, patronage, and material culture in Bengal. Once Company power was forcibly established in Bengal, there was an alteration in the political economy of trade, as control over customs was monopolised, the authority of local landed chiefs was banished from rivers, ferries, and tollways, and intermediate writs over markets were ended. As a consequence, the colonial marketplace was opened up to the freer flow of imperial commodities and investment. Long-distance trade rose, and prices became more uniform. The gathering of information was central to this policy, and published lists of prices challenged the immense variety of wholesale and retail rates that had once characterised markets where trade was subject to different political authorities.[47] It was not only local chiefs who suffered: the treatment of native labour by the Company could also be harsh.

At the same time, although the British organised/taxed/exploited trade (each of the descriptions is appropriate, but, if only one is used, a single, misleading

---

46 M.A. Ali, 'Recent Theories of Eighteenth-Century India', *Indian Historical Review*, 13 (1987), pp. 101–10; H. Hossain, *The Company Weavers of Bengal: The East India Company and the Organization of Textile Production in Bengal, 1750–1813* (Delhi, 1988); S. Chaudhuri, *From Prosperity to Decline: Eighteenth-Century Bengal* (New Delhi, 1995). The debate is reviewed in P.J. Marshall, 'Reappraisal: The Rise of British Power in Eighteenth-Century India', *South Asia*, new ser., 19 (1996), pp. 71–6.

47 P.J. Marshall, 'Britain and the World in the Eighteenth Century: IV, The Turning Outwards of Britain', *Transactions of the Royal Historical Society*, 6th ser., 11 (2001), pp. 6–7; S. Sen, *Empire of Free Trade: The East India Company and the Making of the Colonial Marketplace* (Philadelphia, Pennsylvania, 1998).

resonance is struck), this process could only work if it satisfied non-Western interests and attracted their merchants. In 1772, Dean Mahomet, an Indian in the service of an officer of the Bengal Army, wrote of Calcutta, the port that the British made the capital of Bengal: 'the greatest concourse of English, French, Dutch, Armenians, Abyssinians [Ethiopians], and Jews, assemble here; besides merchants, manufacturers, and tradesmen, from the most remote parts of India'.[48] However, mutual interest was capable of many definitions, and, as their power increased, the terms of this relationship were more slanted to the benefit of the British.

During the French Revolutionary War, opposition in the British Isles, both criticism from radicals in England and Scotland and a nationalist uprising in Ireland in May 1798, was overcome, notably at Vinegar Hill on 21 June. Britain, nevertheless, was placed under acute pressure. In August 1798, the French managed to land a small expeditionary force in Ireland, although it was defeated at Ballinamuck on 8 September. Cornwallis was the victor in 1798. The French attempt indicated the importance of Britain's naval predominance. This was also the last French invasion of Ireland, the threat particularly feared by British leaders. Unlike in 1689, when Ireland was at the forefront of the civil war that followed the 'Glorious Revolution', the British state was now in a stronger position, both at sea and in Ireland.

At the same time, areas of imperial concern spread. Fears about French plans in India helped provoke an attack on Mysore, leading, on 3 May 1799, to the fall of Seringapatam, with Tipu Sultan dying in the breach. The victors were referred to as 'the Vicegerents of Heaven' in a print produced in Britain to commemorate the success.[49] The literary overhang of empire was seen in Wilkie Collins's later novel, *The Moonstone* (1868), as the fate of a jewel seized then played a key role in the plot. Napoleon's capture of Malta in June 1798 and invasion of Egypt the following month increased British interest in the eastern Mediterranean leading, at the battle of the Nile, on 1–2 August 1798, to Nelson's total victory over a French fleet, capturing or destroying 11 ships. Three years later, a British expeditionary force defeated the forces Napoleon had left in Egypt in an impressive instance of British amphibious capability and fighting skill: the British landed under fire in Aboukir Bay on 8 March and defeated the French in the battle of Alexandria on 21 March. The French forces

---

48 M.H. Fisher (ed.), *The Travels of Dean Mahomet: An Eighteenth-Century Journey through India* (Berkeley, California, 1997), p. 58.

49 *Description of the Great Print and Picture Representing the Introduction of the Sons of Tippoo Sultan to Lord Cornwallis* (London, no date).

in Egypt surrendered on 2 September. The decision to send so many troops to Egypt was an important strategic choice that reflected the weight of imperial commitments and that was dependent on the strength of British naval power. It prefigured Winston Churchill's determination to send forces to the Middle East in 1941–42. Churchill himself had a strong historical sense of both the empire and imperial strategy, as did others. The struggle against Napoleon was deployed, for example in the popular works of Arthur Bryant, as a background to that against Hitler.

The British victories in 1798 and 1801, however, were responses to French moves. Indeed, despite repeated naval victories including the Glorious First of June (1794) over the French, Cape St Vincent (14 February 1797) over the Spaniards, and Camperdown (11 October 1797) over the Dutch, the terms of the Peace of Amiens, concluded on 25 March 1802, reflected Britain's isolation. Her principal ally, Austria, had already been driven from the war by the Peace of Lunéville on 9 February 1801, bringing the War of the Second Coalition against France to an end on the European mainland. France had triumphed. The terms of Amiens also reflected the wish for peace of the government of Henry Addington that had replaced that of William Pitt the Younger in 1801. All gains from France, Spain, and the Dutch were to be restored, except Trinidad and the Dutch bases in Sri Lanka, while Minorca was lost for good. Although France agreed to withdraw from Rome and Naples, it retained its extensive gains elsewhere in Western Europe. These terms were bitterly criticised in parliament, and were viewed by the government as little more than a truce that it had been forced to. As the new century opened, the British empire appeared in serious difficulties, and, certainly, the strength it was to manifest over the nineteenth century seemed only a distant prospect.

Chapter 4
The Nineteenth-Century Empire

The nineteenth century saw a marked expansion in the extent of the empire as well as its development into a central source of themes for British public culture and identity. Britain's impact, for what at the time was, or for what subsequently would be, seen as good and ill, increased greatly. Again, this was scarcely a process in which Britain was alone. Indeed, the number of imperial powers increased during the century, notably in its closing decades when newly unified Germany and Italy pursued colonies, while the USA spread its power across the Pacific. Yet, Britain was the exceptional empire, and was seen thus both by the British and by others. The British empire spread on every continent, although there were significant variations in the nature and pace of British imperialism.

It is the nineteenth-century empire that dominates British consciousness, not least because of the role of rule of India in the recovered memory of empire. Indeed, the British Crown achieved imperial status in the nineteenth century from 1877 as ruler of an Indian empire. This memory, however, is less than an accurate account of British imperialism as a whole. It suggests that there is a true or essential identity to empire when, in practice, there was variety. This is notably the case because an emphasis on the nineteenth century underplays the earlier English/British empires, those in the British Isles, France, and the Atlantic world, and also neglects the maritime theme in British imperialism.[1]

Ireland

A key development in the British empire and one that underlined the significance of the inner core, as well as the variety of developments there, was that in the British Isles. The British–Irish Act of Union of 1800 came into effect on 1 January 1801. The Act abolished the separate Irish parliament in Dublin in return for significant Irish representation at Westminster – 100 MPs and 32 peers in what was now a parliament of the United Kingdom. Moreover, the Churches of

1 For a stress on the latter, J. Black, *The British Seaborne Empire* (New Haven, Connecticut, 2004).

England and Ireland were united. However, William Pitt the Younger's attempt to follow parliamentary Union by admitting Catholics, both to parliament and to most public offices, was thwarted by George III. He argued that this measure would breach his promise in his coronation oath to protect the position of the Church of England. This issue led to Pitt's resignation on 16 February 1801 and also contributed to the fall of the Ministry of All the Talents on 24 March 1807 when the leading members of the government refused to promise George that they would never raise the Catholic issue anew. Catholics could not become MPs in the new parliament until 1829, and, in the long term, this delay may have undermined the Union. However, a fair share of informed British public opinion thought that the Union could go forward on that narrow basis.

In an instructive comparison, the stability of Canada had been enhanced by the adroit British handling of the Québécois. From the conquest of Québec in 1759, government-sponsored Anglicisation was tempered by sensible concern for the position of the Catholic Church. Moreover, the anti-clericalism, and then atheism, of the French Revolutionaries encouraged local support for Britain.[2]

Meanwhile, the Anglo-Irish aspect of the empire centrally related to war. Union owed much to the concerns raised in London (and among Irish Protestants) by the unsuccessful Irish rising of 1798, and was thus an aspect of the strengthening of the empire in response to war with France. There was not the dynastic dimension to Union between Britain and Ireland that had been the case with Union between England and Scotland in 1707. Thereafter, despite conspiracies in the 1800s, notably Robert Emmet's disorganised and unsuccessful rebellion in July 1803, naval success ensured that the Union with Ireland could be consolidated without disruption from France comparable to the invasion in 1798. Moreover, Irish soldiers, including Catholics, played a very important role in the British Army, and, even more, in that of the East India Company, providing nearly half the latter. Of the 56 regiments added to the line in 1794, 22 were Irish. The Interchange Act (1811) allowed Irish militia to serve on English soil.[3] In addition, food from Ireland, notably beef and butter, was crucial to the logistics of British naval and overseas power as well as to feeding Britain as a whole.

Alongside active participation in empire, including pro-empire Irish nationalism, there was also, by the late nineteenth century, rising anti-British

---

2 P. Lawson, *The Imperial Challenge: Quebec and Britain in the Age of the American Revolution* (Montreal, 1989); F.M. Greenwood, *Legacies of Fear: Law and Politics in Quebec in the Era of the French Revolution* (Toronto, 1994).

3 R. Knight, *Britain Against Napoleon: The Organization of Victory 1793–1815* (London, 2013), pp. 77, 443.

and anti-imperial Irish nationalism. It is this nationalism that has defined the collective memory of empire for the Irish and has thus greatly influenced American views. Earlier in the nineteenth century, the Fenian movement had led to violent action by Irish nationalists, not only in the British Isles but also, based in the USA, in Canada. This opposition broadened out into wider currents of cultural and economic rejection and pressure. The Gaelic Athletic Association, founded in 1884, became a political expression of difference, the Gaelic League, established in 1893, also stressed difference, and the United Irish League, founded in 1895, pressed for agrarian reform.[4]

War with Napoleonic France

After a short-lived gap following the Peace of Amiens of 1802, war with France had resumed on 18 May 1803. The aggressive policies on the Continent of Napoleon, who had seized power in France in November 1799, becoming First Consul, exacerbated British distrust. Moreover, the British refused to turn over their new naval base at Malta, which had been taken from the French in September 1800. With the resumption of war, the colonial world had to be conquered anew by Britain. This process was eased by the major victory won by Horatio Nelson over a larger Franco-Spanish fleet at Trafalgar on 21 October 1805. This victory was key to the strengthening of a definition of patriotism, empire, and identity in terms of naval power and alleged related values.[5] Maritime strength thwarted Napoleon's attempt to sever British trade with the Continent.

Moreover, the profits of trade enabled Britain to finance her war effort and to make loans and grants to European allies. This relationship of trade and finance constituted a key linkage of the trans-oceanic and Continental worlds, and one that provided the wartime logic of empire. This was an offensive as well as a defensive system. Alongside protection from invasion, a strategy of economic warfare based on the naval blockade of France and her allies became feasible for Britain, and the precariousness of the French economic system was exposed as a result. Naval power enabled Britain to protect her allies, and thus to enhance and extend the informal empire. Portugal and South America were key to the latter.

---

4 D. Lowry, 'Nationalist and Unionist Responses to the British Empire in the Age of the South African War, 1899–1902', in S.J. Potter (ed.), *Newspapers and Empire in Britain and Ireland* (Dublin, 2004), pp. 159–76.

5 T. Jenks, *Naval Engagements: Patriotism, Cultural Politics, and the Royal Navy* (Oxford, 2006).

Support for Portugal was not new, and, indeed, demonstrated the long-term character of the geopolitics of English/British power. Aside from in the Middle Ages, when assistance was given first to help conquer Lisbon from the Moors in 1147 and later against attacks by Castile in the fourteenth century, the English provided key help against Spain in the 1660s during the last stages of the War of Portuguese Independence, an alliance consolidated by Charles II's marriage to Catherine of Braganza with her dowry of Bombay (Mumbai) and Tangier. Britain was allied to Portugal against a Franco-Spanish alliance from 1703 during the War of the Spanish Succession, dispatched a fleet to the Tagus in 1735 to provide support against a possible Spanish invasion, sent troops to help Portugal against a Franco-Spanish invasion in 1762, and was to act on Portugal's behalf from 1808 and, again, in the 1820s. This list is a reminder of the continuity of links that was so significant however foreign policy, indeed empire, was conceptualised. Looked at differently, empire was a matter not only of territorial control but also of the continuity of such links. Portugal was a key element in the British maritime economy, its importance greatly enhanced by the role of its colony of Brazil, from the early eighteenth century, as the major source of gold for the Western world, and that at a time very much of metallic currency systems. Naval strength was the basis of this exercise in British informal empire, as naval strength ensured protection for British and Portuguese trading systems, protected Lisbon, the centre of Portuguese power, from Spanish maritime assault, which had successfully occurred in 1580, and offered the opportunity to deploy British troops to Portugal.

These advantages were multiplied as far as more distant South America was concerned. Naval power served to secure and define national interests there and elsewhere; although tensions among policymakers arose from the very capability that enabled the British to operate on both sides of the Atlantic. Issues of prioritisation led to controversy, both governmental and popular, but British trade benefited greatly from this intervention in South America. In 1806–08, when Britain stood largely alone, South America became a central consideration in the British ability to remain fiscally sound and thus to keep going as an economic and military power.[6] This ability helped support the dispatch of British troops to Iberia, as it provided a capacity to purchase stores locally: Britain could send specie with its troops. There was not the organised extortion of supplies seen with the French. The infrastructure of British naval power was imperial and effective, capable of mobilising, protecting, and directing resources

6 M. Robson, *Britain, Portugal and South America in the Napoleonic Wars: Alliances and Diplomacy in Economic Maritime Conflict* (London, 2011).

and forces towards victory.[7] Cape Town, Madras (Chennai), Bombay (Mumbai), Trincomalee, Malta, Bermuda, Halifax, and Barbados, were all developed as naval bases, as, more briefly, were Ajaccio, Martinique, Alexandria, and Lisbon. These bases helped in force projection, the protection of trade, and the pursuit of colonial gains, while naval superiority also ensured that the British could defend far-flung positions with relatively few troops and could readily move troops between them.

During the Napoleonic Wars, the range and list of British gains was global and imperial to an unprecedented and remarkable level. Moreover, these gains helped condition rising expectations about Britain's power. For example, Cape Town was captured anew from the Dutch in January 1806, being followed, in 1807, by the Caribbean islands of St Croix, St Thomas, and St John. Martinique, Cayenne (French Guiana), and the major slaving base of Fort Louis on the Senegal River followed in 1809; the French positions in Santo Domingo, Guadeloupe, Réunion, and Mauritius, and the Dutch bases on the Moluccas and Sulawesi and of Aceh (in Sumatra) in 1810. Batavia (now Djakarta), the leading Dutch position in the East Indies, and Timor followed in 1811, and Bali in 1814. Although after Trafalgar (1805), the Royal Navy had to continue to blockade French naval bases, making a major effort, in particular, to contain the French Mediterranean fleet in Toulon, there was increased confidence in Britain's naval position, and thus in mounting amphibious operations. This confidence was enhanced after the Danish fleet was taken out of the equation with an attack on Copenhagen on 7 September 1807 and when Napoleon's invasion of Spain in February 1808 ensured that the Spanish fleet no longer co-operated with France.

Trans-oceanic British successes transformed the geopolitics of the European world. Moreover, conquest was the prequel to the introduction of British government, the integration of new ports and productive capacities into the British maritime and economic systems, and cultural developments. The last, which included the establishment of the Church of England, and missionary societies, and the launching of English-language newspapers, strengthened the British position and made it normative to British commentators. In turn, the infrastructure of empire developed in Britain, notably with the construction of new docks, such as the West India Dock (1802), the London Dock (1805), and the East India Dock (1806), all in London. Nowhere else in the world matched this capacity.

7 R. Knight, *Britain against Napoleon: The Organization of Victory 1793–1815* (London, 2013).

The British were not successful everywhere, being defeated at Buenos Aires in 1807, Rosetta (in Egypt) in 1807, and, by the Americans under Andrew Jackson, at New Orleans on 8 January 1815. However, after Trafalgar, it was only Britain that could mount such attacks. Moreover, failures make successive British triumphs in India and elsewhere more impressive. In India and round the Indian Ocean, the fusion of European training and Indian manpower was an opportunity grasped, while Arthur Wellesley, later Duke of Wellington, exemplified the need for a combination of determination, ability, and organisation. He won two key victories over the Marathas in 1803.[8] Supported by the resources of the fertile areas of India, notably Bengal and the Carnatic, British power in India served to underpin expansion. Forces from India were deployed far afield: from the East Indies to Africa. This capability was to help ensure that no European power could match Britain, which, at the same time, was the world's leading naval power and also the strongest Western empire in the part of the world where population was concentrated.

The Treaty of Paris, signed on 30 May 1814, and the International Peace Congress of Vienna (1814–15), which led to the Treaty of Vienna signed on 9 June 1815 and the Second Treaty of Paris of 20 November 1815, set the seal on Britain's triumph over France, and marked the beginning of a period in which the British empire was faced with no effective threats. British control of a host of wartime gains, including Cape Colony, the Seychelles, Mauritius, Trinidad, Tobago, St Lucia, Malta, the Ionian Islands, the Dutch bases in coastal Sri Lanka, Essequibo, and Demerara (the last two the basis of British Guiana, now Guyana), were all recognised. Britain's gains ensured that she had a system of bases to protect her trade while denying positions that would be a threat in hostile hands. The Continental settlement was also linked to Britain's imperial position. The territorial strengthening of Piedmont, Prussia, and the Netherlands along the French border was designed to restrain France, and thus to lessen the chance that France might act in an unwelcome fashion. More particularly, British anxieties that France might gain control over the major dockyard at Antwerp were assuaged when Antwerp, as part of Belgium, became part of the new kingdom of the Netherlands, which was ruled by the pro-British House of Orange. These anxieties had been significant as Britain had followed Austro-French negotiations in 1813–14 for a compromise peace. The Dutch East Indies were also returned by Britain. This was an aspect of the degree to

8 H. Davies and R. Muir, *Wellington's Wars: The Making of a Military Genius* (New Haven, Connecticut, 2012) and *Wellington: The Path to Victory, 1769–1814* (New Haven, Connecticut, 2013).

which the Netherlands in effect was part of the informal British empire. Belgium, which became independent in 1830, elected as King Leopold I (r. 1831–65), the widower of Charlotte, daughter of George IV, and the uncle of Queen Victoria. In 1839, Britain also guaranteed Belgium's neutrality, which led to war with Germany when it invaded in 1914.

Empire after 1815

Britain played the central role in the developing global political and economic system. Turning away from close involvement in most of Europe's conflicts after 1815 gave Britain a greater opportunity to expand subsequently elsewhere, as did British naval dominance. There was no overall plan for colonial conquest, but the British scarcely gained empire without thinking about it, as at one stage was suggested. In a continuation of a pattern seen in 1783–93, when Britain had lost the Thirteen Colonies in North America, Florida, and several islands in the West Indies, while expanding power in India and establishing a base in Australia, there was a further growth of empire in the east: the British made major gains in South Asia. In 1815, the kingdom of Kandy in Sri Lanka was conquered, the first time it had been overthrown by a European power, and a marked contrast with Dutch failures against Kandy in the 1760s and the earlier British failure in 1803. Moreover, victories in 1815 and 1816 brought the war with the Gurkhas of Nepal, declared in 1814, to a successful conclusion. In addition, in India, the Marathas were rapidly crushed in a new war in 1817–18 and, aside from British territorial gains, the remaining Maratha leaders had to accept terms that brought them under British protection.

Imperial growth did not always take the form of expansion at the expense of other states. There was in some areas a stress on commercial activity, and notably, as in the Pacific, where trading advantage, not territorial control, was the key issue. It is instructive to contrast such areas with Ireland and India. For example, Anglo-American frontier differences over the border of Canada were postponed in 1818 when, by the Anglo-American Convention, the status of the Oregon Country was left for future decision. This vast area, now the American states of Oregon and Washington and the Canadian province of British Columbia, offered enticing possibilities. George Canning, successively British Foreign Secretary (1807–09, 1822–27) and prime minister (1827), saw the Oregon Country as a key advantage for the British empire, opening the way for the economic development of Canada as a springboard for trans-Pacific trade with China. Rival ambitions were held by American politicians and commentators, with self-interested prudence never far from their pursuit of the gains and prospects temptingly offered by Manifest Destiny. A similar assessment can be offered for the British. The dominant role in the region in the early decades of the nineteenth century was taken by the British Hudson's Bay Company, which founded trading posts across the region in pursuit of furs, notably beaver. These positions were linked to trading vessels, and thus became part of a commercial system in which Britain was the centre. As with other centres in the British global economy, the economic base diversified from the 1830s as the Hudson's Bay Company took an interest in timber, agriculture, and fish: salmon, in particular, was exported.

Thus, a dynamic economy underwrote a presence that increasingly seemed a strategic challenge to American commentators concerned about the West and tempted by the Pacific. Reflecting, however, a difference in the character of the two imperialisms, one that was to be of growing importance, the crucial element that the British lacked in the Oregon Country was people. Yet, growing British commercial links with San Francisco created the danger for American commentators that California would look to Britain, whether as a province of a weak Mexico (of which it was a part from independence from Spain until 1846), or as an independent state, or, indeed, as a colony. Uncertainties about developments were readily apparent.

The development of American society in Oregon from the late 1830s forced the pace. Against the background of threats of war, which Britain wished to avoid, a compromise along the line of what is the current frontier, was reached in 1845. Britain was subsequently to show restraint as America greatly expanded at the expense of Mexico in 1846–48 and pressed hard on British interests in Central America, particularly, with violence, on the Caribbean coast of Nicaragua, in the 1850s. Alongside competition with America, there was large-scale investment there, notably in American railways, for example the Baltimore and Ohio, a key means for developing the American hinterland and linking it to the coastal centres of power.[9] Thus, rather like China and America today, there was both imperial competition and a shared investment in success.

Relations with America underlay the extent that the sustained burst of imperial warfare by Britain in the 1810s was not to last. Instead, although great care is necessary in suggesting coherence, let alone central direction, in imperial policy, Britain, both ministries and public opinion, was cautious about expanding its overseas territorial power in the years after the Congress of Vienna ended in 1815, and certainly in comparison with the situation later in the century. The

---

9 C. Dakers, *A Genius for Money: Business, Art and the Morrisons* (New Haven, Connecticut, 2011).

cost of the long period of war since 1793 had led to a massive rise in the national debt, the consequences of which were exacerbated by post-war depression and by a reluctance to pay taxes. Indeed, the wartime expedient of income tax was abandoned in 1816 under parliamentary pressure, even though Prime Minister Robert, 2nd Earl of Liverpool, judged it essential in order to reduce the national debt. The army and navy were dramatically reduced in size.

The fiscal situation alone was not responsible for this more cautious position, for, after 1815, there was far less reason to fear competition from France. In that respect, the situation was very different to those in 1918 and 1945 as it rapidly became clear, in both cases, that Soviet expansionism was a serious problem. Instead, a more apt comparison with 1815 is that of 1991, as the end of the Cold War and the rapid defeat of Iraq created more optimistic attitudes in the USA (and Britain) about a hoped-for 'peace dividend'. After 1815, as with Iraq and Serbia in the 1990s, there was no foreign power able, if it wished, to provide large-scale support to non-Western opponents of Britain, such as Myanmar (Burma) in the 1820s. As a reminder that it was not only Britain, or Western powers, that were an apparent threat to the *status quo*, Myanmar expansion was regarded as a challenge both to the East India Company position in Bengal and to its determination to support protectorates over nearby Indian states. As frequently with imperial expansion, Western and non-Western, differing notions of sovereignty and borders created a serious problem between the two powers, leading to the First Burmese War of 1824–26. In the subsequent peace, Britain was ceded the regions of Arakan and Tenasserim, which helped ensure that the subsequent development of an independent Myanmar was limited. These gains eased the path for later British expansion in Myanmar, in the 1850s and 1880s, and Malaysia, not least blocking opportunities for other Western powers, specifically France. The cumulative nature of British imperialism was important to its success, but also ensures that it is not always helpful to separate out individual episodes for examination or opprobrium.

Imperial Expansion

China's serious defeat by Britain in the First Opium War of 1839–42 was particularly important in the shifting balance of global power represented in, and underlined by, the rise of the British empire. This was because of the size of China as the most populous non-Western society, as well as that which was most self-confident in its strength. It is significant that it was Britain that defeated China, and not another Western empire, or a non-Western power, such as Japan, or the fragmented remains of the nomadic forces that had once challenged China. In these and other tasks, Britain benefited considerably from economic and fiscal development, specifically commercial strength, economic capability, and financial viability; and from a geopolitical position enhanced by naval power that enabled Britain to limit its role in European power politics. Comparisons of British and Chinese development have been made, but leave it unclear whether a particular type of state structure was necessary to the combination of large-scale coal mining, industrial change, and global trade that Britain, unlike China, pursued, or, more generally, to the modernisation of Britain. This modernisation proved crucial to the ability of the West, and first of Britain, to become central to global economic links and, therefore, to the process and profits of globalisation. Trade was central to the energy of British imperialism; and the growth of world trade in the nineteenth century made Britain's maritime and naval capability particularly important and, in comparison, placed non-Western powers at a greater disadvantage. Trade was the key element in Britain's war with China, notably the British determination to sell opium from India in order to finance the purchase of goods from China.[10]

Having consolidated its position in India in the 1840s, by victories in two difficult wars with the Sikhs (1845–46, 1848–49) and, more easily, in Sind in 1843, Britain went to war again in the 1850s. This proved an important decade because of the number of opponents that had to be confronted. Fortunately, unlike in World War Two, the key conflicts remained both separate and at a very different scale. In 1854–56, in the sole war with another European power between the Napoleonic Wars and World War One, Britain fought Russia in the Crimean War. However, despite the fears of the British government and commentators, the Russians did not really pose a threat to the route to India. The Russian advance in the Balkans and Central Asia was regarded as a challenge to British interests in the Mediterranean, Persia (Iran), and Afghanistan, and, thus, albeit indirectly to the British position in India. These fears underrated the difficulties faced by the Russians in applying their power in the region and at such a distance. The defence of the British position in India opened up what would subsequently be described as a geopolitics of empire. This geopolitics was to be dominated by a note of vulnerability, a note that underplayed the resources of the empire, and the major problems facing Britain's real or potential opponents. Alongside confidence and arrogance, there was anxiety.

---

10 P.W. Fay, *The Opium War, 1840–1842: Barbarians in the Celestial Empire in the Early Part of the Nineteenth Century and the War by which They Forced Her Gates Ajar* (Chapel Hill, North Carolina, 1998).

With regard to the long-term development of the empire, the Crimean War did not prove too difficult. There was serious mismanagement and humiliating failure, but these were followed by eventual success and settlement, the pattern of some other conflicts. The Crimean War did show the global reach of British power, with the Royal Navy operating not only in the Baltic, Black, and White Seas, but also in the Pacific, where it was able to put pressure on the Russian presence in the Far East.[11] At the same time, the British effort in the Crimean War served as a reminder of the inherently unstable nature of imperial hegemony for it encouraged the Russians to press ahead with their power in the Far East.

The situation with regard to the long-term reputation of empire was very varied in the late 1850s as, aside from the Crimean War, Britain was involved in war in what today are the two most populous states in the world. The Indian Mutiny (1857–59), which, in India, is widely referred to as the Rebellion or the First War of Independence, was a serious challenge in what was, militarily, the most important British colony. This was not a setback on the frontiers of empire, as the British encountered in Afghanistan in 1842, and were to encounter at the hands of the South African Boers (Afrikaners) in 1881 and 1899. At the same time, much of India did not support the Mutiny. Moreover, Indian forces, particularly the Bombay and Madras units, as well as forces raised by loyal Indian rulers, notably those of Hyderabad, Nepal, and Kashmir, greatly helped in its suppression, both actively and by not rebelling. Once the Mutiny was suppressed after bitter fighting, India returned to its former role as a key support for British power elsewhere, including China, where the Second Opium War began in 1856. In 1860, Beijing was captured, the role of Sikh cavalry supported by Armstrong artillery showing the combination of imperial manpower and home industry in the spread of British power. This was the first time that Beijing fell to a Western army, as opposed to an Asian force, and helped lead to Britain strengthening its position in the Chinese overseas economy. Alongside American power projection into Japanese waters in the 1850s, this British success encouraged the Japanese modernisation of state and military that, from the 1920s, was to challenge the British position in the Far East. Thus, the new order in the Far East represented by British power was, in a broader perspective, rapidly challenged by developments from the same period. This was an aspect both of competition between empires and of the process by which empire was created and dissolved at the same time.

---

11 J.D. Grainger, *The First Pacific War: Britain and Russia, 1854–1856* (Woodbridge, 2008).

Attitudes to Empire

The support the British empire received in, and from, India serves as a reminder of the capacity of empire to integrate interests and, at the same time, of its significant dependence on co-operation as well as consent. Both rested on practices and senses of interest that were ideological and political as much as material. This point was true for support for empire in the metropole as well as on the periphery in what was an increasingly interconnected world. The extent of the commitment of British public opinion to imperialism has been much debated. At any rate, it was greater than the strong, but more episodic, British interest in Continental wars and politics, and certainly after 1871, the end of the Franco-Prussian War.

The nature of British commitments, interests, and naval strength ensured that the alliances that counted for Britain after the Anglo-French entente during the Crimean War of 1854–56 were not so much in Europe, but those within the imperial system as local assistance was pursued. In military terms, this factor was crucial, in part, because of the difficulties of deploying large numbers of troops overseas, difficulties that reflected the detrimental ecological impact of operating in the Tropics, as well as cost and the need to retain regular forces within the West in order to cope with rivalries there. As a consequence, there was a need to recruit forces locally. Furthermore, these units were crucial in grounding and sustaining control of already-conquered regions. The suppression of the Indian Mutiny thus proved a key instance of the co-operation that was very important to the general process of imperial rule, an inclusiveness seen in Britain as well as overseas. However, allowing for the complexity of the empire and the imperial presence and the diversity of developments, the nature and terms of this co-operation shifted as Westerners became the dominant partners, both as settlers and as rulers.[12] This shift was linked to a metropolitan turn towards more racist attitudes from mid-century.

This was true not only of the position in colonies and protectorates, but also of that in other states, such as China. There was a shift there from Westerners' presentation of themselves as merchants and as suppliants for favour and, instead, an emphasis on state representation from a superior background. This shift was central to a more assertive British position in China from the outbreak of the Opium War in 1839. This position is still treated in China as a key cause of a long period of national abasement and shame. The Opium Wars, the very

---

12 R. Price, *Making Empire: Colonial Encounters and the Creation of Imperial Rule in Nineteenth-Century Africa* (Cambridge, 2008).

title of which reflected a pejorative account of British motivation that is less than complete, were seen both as a national humiliation for China and as the cause of a far greater subsequent foreign intervention that gravely weakened China. The issue has been presented on screen with Xie Jin's film *The Opium War* (1997). Despite its assertiveness, the British position in China was not essentially that of a territorial power, although maritime and commercial strength had a political edge and territorial presence.[13] This underlines the varied nature, purpose, and form of empire.

In India, in contrast, in the century from the 1750s, force played a crucial role in ensuring that Britain became a major Asian territorial power. Yet, far more than force was involved. In what was the most populous part of the British empire, there was also a careful attempt to incorporate existing hierarchies, interests, and rituals within a patron–client relationship. The princely dynasties that had gained effective independence with the decline of the Mughal empire in the early eighteenth century, only to be overawed by the British, were wooed from the 1870s by the creation of an Anglicised princely hierarchy that gave them rules and honours, such as the Orders of the Star of India and Indian Empire, in accordance with British interests and models. *The Golden Book of India* (1893) listed the various honours and awards given to Indian princes. This process was also to be followed elsewhere in the empire, for example in Malaya and northern Nigeria. Moreover, the extent to which the empire was a monarchy, presided over, once Victoria became Empress of India in 1877, by a Queen-Empress, later King-Emperor, made it easier to fit other rulers into the system as subordinate players. This was true of those who retained independence or a degree of autonomy, for example rulers in the (Persian) Gulf, northern Borneo, and southern Africa.

The emphasis for India, and elsewhere, on an Anglicised hierarchy, led to a stress on status, not race, that can be regarded as an unhelpful brake on inculcating values of economic, social, and political development. However, this policy reflected the extent to which a key division was that not of Britons and Indians, but of rulers and subjects. British policy in India was a response to the large amount of the empire that was left under princely rule. As a result, the wooing of support helped to strengthen the British position and, crucially, to consolidate the 'internal frontier'[14] of imperialism. Status proved an intermediary and expression of imperial rule and co-operation. Furthermore, alongside this

13 D. Brunero, *Britain's Imperial Cornerstone in China: The Chinese Maritime Customs Service, 1854–1949* (London, 2006).

14 J. Gommans, *Mughal Warfare* (London, 2002).

process, which has been referred to as Ornamentalism, the search for support in India and elsewhere was a multi-layered one, extending to the co-option or creation of professional and administrative groups able to meet local as well as imperial needs.

Such co-operation can also be seen in the economic sphere, and this element needs to be considered alongside the understandable tendency to present imperialism as a system of rapacity, as in part it was. It is true that the terms of economic exchange were greatly directed by Britain, its colonial representatives and settler populations. Moreover, in areas judged primitive or not yet settled, such as Australia, there was an emphasis on force, as well as the large-scale seizure of land and the appropriation of other economic assets and benefits, such as water and anchorages. Nevertheless, there was also a need to work with local providers of capital, labour, materials, and markets. This local provision became part of the imperial system, not only indirectly, but also in terms of long-range movements, as with those of Indian indentured labourers to much of the empire, for example the Caribbean (notably Trinidad), Guyana, South Africa, Malaya, and Fiji.

It was not a case of Britain, which, by 1900, had an empire covering a fifth of the world's land surface and including, mostly in South Asia, 400 million people, expanding into a passive void of decrepit states and undeveloped societies, but rather of the British as a major element in the dynamic Western and non-Western world. As part of the empire, albeit a subordinate part, India became more significant, both in the Indian Ocean world and further afield, within the empire and beyond, for example in California as well as British Columbia.[15] India also came to play a major role in the markedly growing presentation of empire in British literature.

The Economics of Empire

Imperial expansion was a matter of informal as well as formal empire. Thus, in economic terms, Latin America was largely part of the British informal empire, one in which economic, financial, and maritime influence, while considerable, did not lead to political control. In his *Just So Stories* (1902), Rudyard Kipling (1865–1936), the poet of empire, or rather of empire in the 1890s and 1900s wrote:

---

15 T.R. Metcalf, *Imperial Connections: India in the Indian Ocean Arena 1860–1920* (London, 2007).

weekly from Southampton,
Great steamers white and gold,
Go rolling down to Rio.

Although independent, Brazil was part of Britain's informal empire in South America. Due to its linkage to Britain's industrial heartland, Liverpool played an even more prominent role than Southampton as the imperial port. Commercial dominance became more significant as the flow of goods and funds in the growing world economy markedly increased. Methods of profit and systems of influence were intertwined, not separate. Alongside protectionism, the global economy was characterised, certainly in comparison with the situation between 1914 and 1945, by free trade and international capital flows; and Britain played the leading role in both. Mission, confidence, and self-interest were linked in the development of the ideal of free trade, which was presented in moral as well as economic terms. Economic liberalism was seen as the best way to improve relations between peoples, and protectionism as an unnatural restraint. Economic liberalism, which entailed an openness to British ideas as well as products, was presented as a corollary to an openness to best practice in all respects.

The pressure for free trade focused from the 1810s until the 1840s on repealing the Corn Laws passed in 1815. These protectionist measures, to safeguard British agriculture, were significantly reduced in 1842 and repealed in 1846, in response to pressure, particularly from industrial interests, for cheaper food for the workers. This outcome was seen as a way both to secure domestic peace, by restraining radicalism, and to restrain industrial wages, even though repeal adversely affected British agriculture, and thus landowners. Sir Robert Peel, the Tory prime minister during 1834–35 and 1841–46, also believed that Free Trade offered moral benefits by ending interference with the workings of Providence. The abolition of the Corn Laws seriously divided the Tory party and created a furore that led to the general collapse of protectionism, with the repeal of most of the Navigation Acts in 1849. In turn, the leading industrial producer, Britain, needed other states to open their markets to British manufactured goods. Vulnerable foreign powers were persuaded, or forced, into accepting free-trade agreements that did so. For example, Britain negotiated free-trade agreements with Turkey in 1838, Egypt, Persia (Iran), and Showa (as part of Ethiopia) in 1841, and, at the end of the Opium War, China in 1842. A treaty of amity and commerce with Texas was ratified by Britain in 1842. In addition, growing dependence on London's financial markets increased the role of trade with Britain, with the local agencies of British firms proving vital intermediaries.

Free Trade and a belief in Providence can also be linked to the unsuccessful governmental response to the appalling Irish Famine in 1846–48. Indeed, the famine was cited by the Anti-Corn Law League to argue for cheap grain exports. There was no murderous intent on the part of the government, but the horrible suffering and subsequent large-scale emigration of much of the population of Ireland left a lasting cause of, and subject for, anger. As a result of the Famine and the emigration, Ireland experienced a demographic revolution. As a consequence, the Irish population as a percentage of that of the British Isles fell significantly. In many respects, the hardships of the mid-seventeenth century, notably the Cromwellian conquest, were recreated in a new form and for a different age. The Famine was to be used by Irish nationalists in a seriously misleading fashion to characterise British imperial rule and, in particular, to give it an edge of alleged ethnic hatred to complement a marked sectarian bias against Catholics.

Imperial trade was responsible for less than half of Britain's exports and imports, but it was still of great economic importance under both categories. Indeed, the bulk of the rise in exports in 1816–42 was obtained from markets in Africa, Asia, and Latin America. A major difference between Britain and Continental countries was that Britain traded abroad far more than they did, and far more widely. Having applied new technology to industrial production more successfully than other European states, the British were producing more goods, and more efficiently than their rivals. As a result, Britain was best placed to benefit from the major expansion of the global economy. This expansion owed much to Britain and was encouraged by its forceful advancing of free trade. Continental economies were more self-sufficient than Britain. What foreign trade they conducted was mainly with other European countries, including Britain. This was related to other aspects of Britain's distinctiveness: her outward-lookingness and internationalism; her interest in peace, which was believed to create the best conditions for trade; and her opposition to a large and expensive army, and therefore to conscription. The last contrasted with other European states, and helped to reflect and define British freedom, at least for the British.

Dramatically growing international trade was largely financed by international investments, and Britain played the leading role in such investment. As an aspect of close economic, social, and cultural ties, the USA was a major recipient of investment income.[16] This serves as a reminder of the

16 A.G. Hopkins, 'The United States, 1783–1861: Britain's Honorary Dominion?', *Britain and the World*, 4 (2011), pp. 232–46.

extent to which economic flows are often between major powers, rather than between such a power and weaker and less prosperous powers. There were also important transfers of technology, particularly from Britain, France, Germany, and the USA. Furthermore, these countries organised the world economy, controlling trade, currency payments, insurance, and shipping. Improvements in communications and financial infrastructure increased the efficiency of the global economic system, and led to a convergence of prices. In turn, widespread migration, a product of marked differences in opportunities, helped wages to converge.

By modern standards, a key aspect of the liberal society of the period, and one that represented a free market, was the large-scale voluntary movement of people. Migration was a central experience of the British empire, and one of its definitions. The scale of migration in the nineteenth century was far greater than in former centuries. In part, this scale reflected increased numbers of people in Britain (and the world) as well as improved technology, in the shape of steamships in particular. There was also a comforting sense of migration as contributing to a web of Britishness, one in which the extent of loss and discontinuity represented by emigration was limited. Empire offered opportunity as well as providing pay. Networks of people, news, goods, and capital, networks heavily dependent on maritime links and activity, helped extend and define a British world as a key aspect of this global system. These networks proved very important to the creation and sustaining of identities,[17] and to the advancing of particular interests, notably those of an empire-wide middle class.[18] A far less attractive dimension of imperial migration was that of indentured labour. While not as harsh as slavery, this was not a labour system in which the emphasis was on freedom. It contributed greatly to a major Indian diaspora within the empire.[19] Substantial Indian communities today, for example in the South African city of Durban, reflect this diaspora.

The products of empire were shipped to empire, helping, alongside industrialisation, to transform the world of things there. This was a major aspect of the impact of the empire in the popular consciousness and culture.

---

17 G.B. Magee and A.S. Thompson, *Empire and Globalisation: Networks of People, Goods and Capital in the British World,* c.*1850–1914* (Cambridge, 2010); A. Lester, *Imperial Networks: Creating Identities in Nineteenth-Century South Africa and Britain* (London, 2001).

18 J.M. Mackenzie, 'Cultural, Intellectual and Religious Networks: Britain's Maritime Exchanges in the Nineteenth and Twentieth Centuries', in M. Taylor (ed.), *The Victorian Empire and Britain's Maritime World, 1837–1901* (Basingstoke, 2013), pp. 78–9.

19 D. Northrup, *Indentured Labour in the Age of Imperialism, 1834–1922* (Cambridge, 1995); J.M. Brown, *Global South Asians: Introducing the Modern Diaspora* (Cambridge, 2006).

Advertising played a significant role, notably by encouraging demand for, and recognition of, imperial products. This advertising was part of the culture of print and image through which imperial assumptions were spread. News and adventure stories were significant, as was statuary.

Imperial Missions

Missionary activity was an important aspect of British commitment to the trans-oceanic world, and most, although not all, of this activity focused on the empire. The long-established Societies for Promotion of Christian Knowledge (founded in 1698), and for the Propagation of the Gospel in Foreign Parts (1701), were joined by the Baptist Missionary Society (1792), the London Missionary Society (1795), the Anglican Church Missionary Society (1795), the Scottish Missionary Society (1799), the Society for Missions to Africa and the East (1799; from 1812 the Church Missionary Society), and the Wesleyan Missionary Society (1813). The British and Foreign Bible Society, established in 1804, spread the word in another way. From the 1860s, female missionaries became important, while the role of nuns ensured that women were always highly significant for the Catholic presence.[20] The separate missionary societies indicated the extent to which empire was a sphere for competitive proselytisation. The Church of England would not even co-operate with the Scottish Episcopal Church in India in the early nineteenth century. Moreover, a stress on Protestantism continued the theme of rivalry with Catholicism. Nevertheless, Catholicism appeared a less present threat after Britain's victories in the Napoleonic Wars. The ending of legal disabilities for Nonconformists and Catholics was highly significant for this partial reconceptualisation of the religious character of the British empire. The emphasis was on a Christian presence and ethos, rather than simply a Protestant one.

Missionary activity led to a range of links between families, communities, and congregations in Britain and the empire, although it was also seen outside empire. For example, coastal, rather than inland, China would qualify as an important part of the British informal empire, but missionaries were determined to get inland. Missionary activity contributed to a sense of superiority that appeared

20 J. Cox, *The British Missionary Enterprise since 1700* (London, 2008); H.M. Carey, *God's Empire: Religion and Colonialism in the British World, c.1801–1908* (Cambridge, 2011); R.A. Semple, *Missionary Women: Gender, Professionalism and the Victorian Idea of Christian Mission* (Woodbridge, 2003); E.E. Prevost, *The Communion of Women: Missions and Gender in Colonial Africa and the British Metropole* (Oxford, 2010).

entirely appropriate in the most powerful empire the world had hitherto seen, and that stemmed in large part from the powerful evangelical theme in British society. There was intellectual, cultural, and personal interest in the non-Christian religions that were encountered and had to be assessed,[21] but there was nothing to compare with the cultural relativism and multi-culturalism that were to follow in the twentieth century. During the age of empire, non-Christian religions were treated very differently depending on the political context, the percentage of settlers, the already-established relationship with these religions, and the extent to which they were regarded as primitive. Combined with the role of settler governments, the last encouraged an attitude of necessary control in Canada and, even more, Australia that, however, was not matched in New Zealand, where the Maori were treated with greater circumspection.[22]

Proselytisation was not only a matter of religious evangelicalism. There was also a liberal entrepreneurial ethos centred on a commitment to free trade. The hostile response to slavery had linked cultural developments to the new field of liberal political economy. This linkage helped create the basis for a liberal colonial ideology in which a doctrine of benevolent colonialism aligned the creation of new consumers with the tenets of the civilising mission. Economic sentiment was thus important to the imperial ethos.[23] The commitment to free trade was to be of great importance for economic growth across the world, as well as in Britain. Trade, rather than costly expansion on land, was the source of Britain's status as the world's wealthiest nation, and thus of her power, more particularly the resources that were to underwrite government revenues. However, the 'globalisation', or, at least, openness to markets, this commitment fostered also caused major problems of adjustment. Adopting free trade proved a major success in economic terms, but a huge problem for wartime strategy, as it accentuated Britain's vulnerability to any interruption in the supply of food and raw materials. Moreover, the benefits brought by free trade were spread very unequally.

The leading naval power by far, Britain was also the state in which navalism was strongest as an expression of identity. Celebrations such as the 1902 Coronation Naval Review provided opportunities to express both identity and power. The identity and power of British imperialism were different to the general pattern of imperial image and strength for most states as navalism led in

21 J.J. Franklin, *The Lotus and the Lion: Buddhism and the British Empire* (Ithaca, New York, 2008).

22 S. Neylan, *The Heavens are Changing: Nineteenth-Century Protestant Missions and Tsimshian Christianity* (Montreal, 2003).

23 M. Dobie, *Trading Places: Colonization and Slavery in Eighteenth-Century French Culture* (Ithaca, New York, 2010).

contrasting directions to those of land power. In part, this contrast reflected the strength of business interests, politically as well as economically, in Britain, as opposed to the landed orders so powerful in most societies.

More generally, a sense of mission was important in the British empire, alongside triumphalism, racialism, and cultural arrogance. These, together, contributed to a view that Britain was bringing civilisation to a benighted world, and was therefore fulfilling a Providential purpose. The result was a commitment, varied but insistent, to the imperial mission, a commitment that encouraged persistence in the face of adversity. This commitment drew on the experience of the Napoleonic Wars. Nelson and Wellington were presented to the public by the press as military heroes of the empire. These and other assumptions and values of empire were repeatedly disseminated thanks to the global character of the culture of the British empire. Settlers and others were bound together by the spread of educational, literary, and other activities organised on a British model. Values were diffused by the publication and distribution of literature across the empire.

Cultural values were positioned atop a series of discriminatory beliefs and practices. Racial and religious discrimination were widespread, institutionalised, and eventually helped encourage critical political associations among the colonial population. Racism drew on the notion of sharply distinguished races, and supposed differences between them, that could be classified in a hierarchy whose genesis was traced back to the sons of Adam. Racial considerations played a role in the geography of British expansion. Whereas British policy towards the USA in the 1840s and 1850s was so accommodating that it has been described in terms of appeasement,[24] such compromise was far less in evidence in British policy in Asia and Africa. Although prudence in the face of American power played a role, this contrast underlines the racist inflection of the Providential destiny affecting British attitudes towards imperial expansion. Race was seen in physical attributes, particularly skin colour, but was linked also by commentators to alleged moral and intellectual characteristics, and to stages in sociological development. These beliefs helped justify concepts of necessary control and improvement. The idea of colonies as estates ripe for development represented a move away from the more trade-centred and oceanic account of empire that had been dominant in the eighteenth century. The efficiency of the settlers helped justify their sway.[25] Life as a trust from and for God, was a supportive attitude.

---

24 G.L. Bernstein, 'Special Relationship and Appeasement: Liberal Policy Towards America in the Age of Palmerston', *Historical Journal*, 41 (1998), p. 727.

25 R. Drayton, *Nature's Government: Science, Imperial Britain, and the 'Improvement' of the World* (New Haven, Connecticut, 2000); J.M. Hodge, *Triumph of the Expert: Agrarian Doctrines of Development and the Legacies of British Colonialism* (Athens, Ohio, 2007).

As so often with empires, control focused in large part on land ownership and use, with the concept of improvement playing a particular role in the nineteenth century. The commodification of land was part of a process that lessened non-Western rights to it, while earlier spatial configurations were downplayed.[26] Surveying was designed to allocate land so that it did not lead to legal disputes, and thus justified investment. The empire was imposed on the landscape. Thus, in Ceylon (Sri Lanka), the surveying of land that was, from the 1820s, to be sold for coffee cultivation, became the key function of the Ceylon Survey Department established in 1800. This function followed, and was related to, an initial emphasis on surveying linked to the road construction designed to overawe and open up the interior.[27] Such attitudes could encourage duplicity and even atrocities, and certainly affected policy. It is difficult to know where to put the emphasis in discussing changes. For example, in Canada, treaties with Natives led to the creation of reserves that provided them with security, but limited their hunting and seasonal movement. As a result, fatalities from starvation became frequent among Natives in the Maritime Provinces (Nova Scotia, New Brunswick), while winter food shortages were more generally a problem in what became Québec and Ontario. The relatively low numbers of Natives in these colonies, compared with the situation in America, made control easier, but the expansion of European settlement in Canada posed questions including issues of purpose in history. Visiting Halifax, Nova Scotia in 1822, Henry Addington, a diplomat, wrote:

> The Indians are fast disappearing, as uncivilised tribes must always yield to the tide of civilisation. This is a necessary consequence and according to nature, no less desirable than necessary. Sentimentalists weep over deserted wigwams and the mouldering tombs of barbarian ancestry, but the man of sense hails the substitution of comfort and contentment and Christianity, flocks, cornfields, the sound of the hammer, the shuttle and the Church-bell for the scalping knife, war-whoop, and the idolatry of the savage.[28]

This was similar to the approach of Thomas Jefferson, America's President from 1801 to 1809. However, American attitudes towards the Native population proved more uncompromising than those of the British and the consequences were far more bloody.

---

26 J.H. Casid, *Sowing Empire: Landscape and Colonization* (Minneapolis, Minnesota, 2005).

27 I.J. Barlow, 'Surveying in Ceylon during the Nineteenth Century', *Imago Mundi*, 55 (2003), pp. 81–96.

28 Exeter, Devon Record Office, 152M/Box 38/Diaries vol. 7.

Aside from the assessment of the supposed inherent characteristics of the other peoples, a belief in progress, and in the association of reason with European, if not, British, culture, necessarily encouraged ideas of a hierarchy dominated by the British. Such a hierarchy was implicitly present in the Great Exhibition held in London in 1851, the first great world exhibition.[29] Related to that view came a treatment of others as inferior and in need of enlightenment. These assumptions were greatly encouraged by Britain's leading role in technological advance and scientific understanding. The latter included a conviction of the extent and role of racial difference and differences. The idea of permanent, biologically based, differences between the races was rephrased in terms of ideas of more evolved and successful races that drew on the race science that became more significant from mid-century. This approach replaced the earlier stress on comparative philology, which had emphasised the shared linguistic roots of Europeans and Asians, with a new focus on physical contrasts.

This change led to a more critical approach to India, with Indians seen in terms of degeneration through interbreeding with darker peoples, who were presented as 'lower' in a developmental racial schema. Author of *The Tribes and Castes of Bengal* (1891) and *The People of India* (1908), Sir Herbert Risley (1851–1911), the Census Commissioner, as well as Secretary in the Home Department of the Government of India, produced cranial and nasal indices to measure this process, notably by the width of nasal bridges. In place of a stress on chance and natural selection in accordance with Darwinian thought, there was an argument from design that was conducive to a sense of inevitable superiority.[30] In India, the Mutiny had encouraged a drive for classification. At the same time, the development of Indian economy and society, and the major growth in India's population and administration, led to the foundation of universities and to activity by Indian scientists. Illustrating the problems for modern assessment, and the difficulties of value-free discussion, themes of racial discrimination and stultifying imperial control can be brought forward in the discussion of British India, as can the seemingly contradictory one of a degree of encouragement for Indians. The counterfactual of how Indian science would have developed but

29 J.A. Auerbach, *The Great Exhibition of 1851: A Nation on Display* (New Haven, Connecticut, 1999); P. Young, *Globalization and the Great Exhibition: The Victorian New World Order* (Basingstoke, 2009).

30 P. Robb (ed.), *The Concept of Race in South Asia* (Delhi, 1995); T. Trautmann, *Aryans and British India* (Berkeley, California, 1997); E. Beasley, *The Victorian Reinvention of Race: New Racisms and the Problem of Grouping in the Human Sciences* (Abingdon, 2010). For racism from Thomas Macaulay (1800–1859), a figure classically seen as liberal, C. Hall, *Macaulay and Son: Architects of Imperial Britain* (New Haven, Connecticut, 2012).

for empire is problematic.[31] The British certainly brought standardisation. They unified weights, measures, and currency in India, as well as greatly improving its transport system. As with the example of the Natives in Canada, it is apparent that assessment is problematic, and that both blame and praise have to be handled with care.

In Britain and the settler colonies, the characteristics and development of other people were understood in terms of the suppositions of British culture. This approach led to, and supported, the process of hierarchisation, which was true also of the developing idea of cultural relativism. This belief was linked to the idea that the British empire was both apogee and conclusion of the historical process, an empire and project of value to the entire world,[32] and the product of both Classical and Christian impulses and purposes. There was a fascination with Classical Rome, seen, for example, in paintings and novels; and Classical Rome and modern Britain were often compared directly. Classical works with prophetic and providential tones, such as Virgil's *Aeneid*, proved particularly attractive in Britain.[33] The neo-Classical architecture that was seen as an appropriate backdrop for power in modern Britain was repeated across imperial centres, most obviously in Calcutta.

At the same time, the inheritance of other cultures was seized for ethnological and other museums. For example, the 'Benin Bronzes' were taken for the British Museum in 1897.[34] A different form of appropriation was seen with naming. In place of local names, legitimacy came from imposing the names of the colonisers, while places were ranked in terms of the names chosen. The belief that Sir George Everest (1790–1866), Welsh-born Surveyor General of the Grand Trigonometric Survey of India established in 1817, embodied the principles of mathematical and geological science, and that his name could be recognised as a symbol of the triumph of British science, helped secure the naming of Mount Everest, the world's highest mountain, in 1865.

The spread of British law and legal practice was an aspect of a moral utilitarianism that was important to the sense of mission and superiority. The British held their empire to equate with civilisation. Proponents of a rise of

---

31 D. Kumar, *Science and the Raj, 1857–1905* (Oxford, 1995).

32 D. Bell, *The Idea of Greater Britain: Empire and the Future of World Order, 1860–1900* (Princeton, New Jersey, 2007).

33 M. Bradley (ed.), *Classics and Imperialism in the British Empire* (Oxford, 2010). For an archaeological dimension, V. Hoselitz, *Imagining Roman Britain: Victorian Responses to a Roman Past* (Woodbridge, 2007).

34 A.E. Coombs, *Reinventing Africa: Museums, Material Culture and Popular Imagination in Late Victorian and Edwardian England* (London, 1994).

science linked to imperial destiny, such as Sir Roderick Murchison (1792–1871), a key figure in the Royal Geographical Society, saw exploration as a prelude to the settlement and profitable use of colonies. A keen geologist and self-promoter, Murchison claimed credit for the Victoria gold rush in Australia. Murchison Falls in Uganda and Murchison River in Western Australia were named after this Scot.[35]

The sense of national and imperial distinctiveness, purpose, and mission was also expressed in the export of the British constitution. This export was symbolised by the construction of parliament buildings, such as that for Canada in Ottawa which drew on the neo-Gothic example of the new Houses of Parliament in Westminster. Constitutional institutions and practices were only one aspect of a more general export of aspects of British culture. A prime pattern was that of the academic networks that developed. Far from universities being part of a pattern of control, they were aspects of a more shared and varied pattern of academic development. In concert with, but also often in the face of, stated university policies, expansive personal networks shaped the composition and character of academic bodies. The results reflected themes of gender, race, and class. Very few women benefited from these networks. Moreover, there was a preference for those seen as gentlemen. Other factors also played a role. In 1911, Lewis Namier, a Jew originally from Austrian-ruled Poland, was twice rejected by the University of Toronto. Despite his evident ability and good Oxford connections, the combination of anti-Semitism, British race patriotism, and the weight given to personal assessments, led Toronto to reject Namier's applications.

In a fashion seen with other aspects of activity across the empire, cultural patterns of inclusion and exclusion made the fraternal relationships between scholars work. The forms of academic association of the period gave official recognition to the web of informal ties being built by the empire's scholars. These forms and ties placed colonial universities alongside the institutions developing in provincial England, creating particular forms of recognition and providing preferential routes of access that, alongside travelling scholarships and leave of absence programmes, in turn, shaped the directions in which settler scholars travelled. The nature of the organisations, for example the 1903 Allied Colonial Universities' Conference and the Universities' Bureau of the British Empire established in 1912, also reflected the views and interests of the settler empire; imperial recognition was balanced against universities' desire to maintain their independence.[36]

---

35 R.A. Stafford, *Scientist of Empire: Sir Roderick Murchison, Scientific Exploration and Victorian Imperialism* (Cambridge, 1989).

36 T. Pietsch, *Empire of Scholars: Universities, Networks and the British Academic World 1850–1939* (Manchester, 2013).

Canada

Developments in Canada offer an account of empire from the perspective of a settler colony; although each of these colonies had a distinctive character. Canada became well grounded as a viable entity within the British empire notwithstanding the absence of large native forces that could be called upon, as in India, to provide assistance to the imperial power, and despite the presence, unlike with Australia and New Zealand, of a threatening neighbour in the shape of America. The absence of conflict with America over Canada and Latin America greatly helped British imperialism at the global level, as well as the regional one, by aiding concentration on the possibilities and problems elsewhere, notably those posed by South and East Asia. As so often, demographic factors were crucial, for, between 1815 and 1850, nearly a million immigrants arrived in Canada from the British Isles. In large part, this migration was due to demobilisation after the Napoleonic War, economic depressions, and the social disruption linked to large-scale urbanisation and economic transformation.[37] This migration strengthened the British presence by enhancing the importance of Upper Canada (Ontario). By 1851, it had 38 per cent of the population of the area of modern Canada, compared with only 4 per cent in 1800. Correspondingly, the dominance of Lower Canada (Québec) was lessened. There was high natural growth in Lower Canada, but nearly no immigration from France: the respective percentages of the population of what is now Canada in Lower Canada were 60 in 1800 and 35 in 1851.

The migration to Canada of well-connected British individuals was also significant in helping provide a group that was trusted by the metropole. This was an important aspect of the political cohesion of empire, of the attempt to propagate British culture, and of the character of the settler colonies, not least their difference to the USA. The emigration of army officers to Australia was also significant in this context.[38] A considerable measure of domestic self-government was the case for the long-established colonies of white settlement, notably with the Canada Act of 1791. Internal self-government was expanded from the mid-nineteenth century with the development of an extended form of self-government known as responsible government. Reflecting population growth in the settlement colonies, this development meant that colonial

37 H.I. Cowan, *British Immigration to British North America: The First Hundred Years* (Toronto, 1961).

38 C. Wright, *Wellington's Men in Australia: Peninsular War Veterans and the Making of Empire c.1820–40* (Basingstoke, 2011).

governors were henceforth to become politically responsible to locally elected legislatures, rather than to London. This process matched the institutionalising of a comparable parliamentary arrangement in Victorian Britain. Responsible government was first applied when Lower (Québec) and Upper (Ontario) Canada were joined together in the Province of Canada in 1840. Dominion status took this forward, the Dominions of Canada and Australia being established in 1867 and 1900 respectively.

The establishment of the Dominion of Canada provided a classic instance of the interaction of materialist and idealist considerations and notably, in the case of the first, of the importance to imperial development of war or the threat of war. The role of conjunctures and circumstances was highly significant, as was the importance of external threats. There was the dominating threat of American strength and expansion in the aftermath of the Civil War (1861–65). Anxieties about the extent to which Canada could be defended were important to the government's encouragement of Confederation. The Act of Union of 1840 creating the Province of Canada had in large part been taken in response to the revolts of 1837 within Canada. Similarly, the tension linked to the American Civil War encouraged Canadian Confederation in 1867, which brought together Canada and the Provinces of New Brunswick and Nova Scotia. Confederation linked the economically weak Maritimes to the more dynamic interior and, in strengthening an east–west axis of mutual dependency, provided a key basis for the new state. As in the USA, an economic dynamic was provided by the export of agricultural goods from the prairie west, a process enhanced by the development of rail and steamship links, and a key element of the role of agricultural settlement in the nineteenth-century empire.[39] Confederation was also a response to the rival possibilities created by trade with America.

Confederation was not the full extent of the changes in British North America. The following year, Rupert's Land Act authorised the acquisition of Rupert's Land and the Northern-Western Territory, and, in 1870, an Order in Council transferred these lands to Canada and renamed them the North-West Territories. Also in 1870, an Act of Dominion established Manitoba as a fifth province, British Columbia following in 1871, and Prince Edward Island in 1873. Alberta, Saskatchewan, and Newfoundland were to follow. Similarly, the Dominion of Australia acted as the basis for defining and organising the British settler presence.[40]

---

39 J. Belich, *Replenishing the Earth: The Settler Revolution and the Rise of the Anglo-World, 1783–1939* (Oxford, 2009).

40 P. Buckner (ed.), *Canada and the British Empire* (Oxford, 2010); D. Schreuder and S. Ward (eds), *Australia's Empire* (Oxford, 2010).

Imperial Expansion, 1861–1913

In the 1860s and 1870s, the pace of imperial expansion increased, for Britain as for other powers. None of the conflicts in which Britain was involved was a war of survival (for Britain), and none transformed British society. However, the cumulative impact of these wars for Britain was important, and their individual impact on other societies was often formative. The speed and articulation offered to British power by an existing network of bases, technological developments, maritime strength, organisational methods, notably naval coaling stations, and by financial flexibility, gave it a hitherto-unsurpassed global reach, and provided an unprecedented basis for planning and executing expansion. As a result, it became increasingly feasible to think about a global polity, with the British empire depicted as spanning the world. There were serious defeats along the way to imperial expansion, especially the retreat from Kabul in 1842, Isandhlwana (1879), and Maiwand (1880); at the hands of Afghans, Zulus, and Afghans respectively. However, the British were usually successful in battle, notably over the Zulus in 1879, in particular at Ulundi. Victory at Tel el Kebir in 1882 left Britain dominant in Egypt. The fate of Sudan was settled at Omdurman in 1898, when artillery, machine guns, and rifles devastated the attacking Mahdists, with 31,000 casualties for the latter, and only 430 for the Anglo-Egyptian force.

The strategic as well as the technological dimension was dynamic. The opening of the Suez Canal in 1869, which greatly cut the steaming distance to India and the Far East, transformed the geopolitics of British power, encouraging interest in the eastern Mediterranean, the Middle East, and Sudan as a wide-ranging forward defence zone for India. The Chief of the Imperial General Staff told the Committee of Imperial Defence on 9 November 1933 that, 'from the Army point of view, the defence of our position in the Far East began at Port Said',[41] in other words at the Suez Canal. Much British imperial expansion, especially in 1880–1914, arose directly from the response to the real or apparent plans of other powers, notably France and Russia. This was particularly seen with the Route to India and the 'Scramble for Africa'. The search for markets for British industry was also important against a background of a resurgence of protectionism in Europe and the USA, a resurgence that encouraged widespread support for an imperial, protectionist Greater Britain.[42] Thus, both economic and political

41 NA. CAB. 24/244 fol. 146.

42 M.W. Palen, 'Protection, Federation and Union: The Global Impact of the McKinley Tariff upon the British Empire, 1890–94', *Journal of Imperial and Commonwealth History*, 38 (2010), pp. 395–418 and 'Adam Smith as Advocate of Empire, *c*.1870–1932', *Historical Journal*, 57 (2014), pp. 179–98.

security were at stake. As a consequence, the imperialist surge of activity at the close of the nineteenth century can also be seen as marking the beginning of a long decline from the zenith of British power, indeed of the imperial position starting to fray under pressure at the same time as it continued to expand. This concurrence highlights the problem of where to put the emphasis.

The nature of empire also changed. Sovereignty and territorial control became crucial goals. Their acquisition replaced the pursuit of influence and of island and port possessions that had been the characteristic features of much, although by no means all, British expansion earlier in the nineteenth century. Suspicion of Russian designs on the Ottoman (Turkish) empire, and of French schemes in North Africa, led the British to move into Cyprus (1878) and to conquer Egypt (1882), although Egypt was not annexed. Concern about French ambitions in South-East Asia resulted in the conquest of Mandalay (1885) and the annexation of Upper Burma (1886). The conquest of Burma (Myanmar) in 1885–86 was in part an instance of commercial interest, with 'gentlemanly capitalists' greatly influencing government policy, not least by controlling the channels of the intelligence the government required.[43]

Russia's advance across Central Asia led to rival attempts to strengthen and move forward the North-West Frontier of British India, and also to the development of British influence in southern Persia (Iran) and the Gulf, through which the British routed their telegraph to India. An attempt to create a submarine telegraph link to India failed in 1860, but it was followed in 1865 by an overland link and in 1870 by a successful submarine cable. Similarly, French and German expansion in Africa resulted in Britain taking counter-measures, notably in Gambia, Sierra Leone, the Gold Coast (Ghana), Nigeria, and Uganda, all moves in the 'Scramble for Africa' by the European powers.

Prior to this, British interest in expansion into the interiors of West and East Africa had been limited. Scientific exploration was important to the stepping up in activity, notably in overcoming tropical disease. This exploration linked the empire to British activity elsewhere. A mission to Peru in 1859, commissioned by the India Office, led to the collection of seeds and young specimens of varieties of the cinchona tree (from which quinine is made). Once established in southern India, this production resulted in a marked fall in the price of quinine, which encouraged its use by Britain. Malaria rates fell. Thus, the empire encouraged the process by which knowledge was linked to global range in an aspect of the more general process of establishing efficiencies of production on a global scale. Britain

43 A. Webster, 'Business and Empire: A Reassessment of the British Conquest of Burma in 1885', *Historical Journal*, 43 (2000), p. 1005.

became the centre of research on tropical medicine and prevention, including in the identification of the mosquito in the transmission of malaria. The London School of Tropical Medicine gave institutional form to this activity,[44] which had direct imperial consequences, as with the Royal Society expedition to Uganda in response to the sleeping sickness (trypanosomiasis) epidemic there in the 1890s. This expedition was related to issues of wider colonial utility that were particularly present as the benefits that were to be gained from this colony were unclear, and there had been political controversy as to whether to expand there. In 1903, David Bruce identified the cause of the disease.

Overstretch?

Specific clashes over colonial influence with other European powers increasingly interacted from the late 1870s with a more general sense of imperial insecurity, as British confidence was put under pressure by the growing strength of other states. Already, in 1816, Napoleon had told Lieutenant-General Sir Hudson Lowe, the Governor of the British colony of St Helena, where he was being held prisoner: 'the high price of all articles of prime necessity is a great disadvantage in the export of your manufactures ... your manufacturers are emigrating fast to America ... In a century or perhaps half a century more, it [America] will give a new character to the affairs of the world. It has thriven upon our follies'.[45] While British strategic overstretch can be seen as latent in the 1860s and 1870s, with other states, notably Germany and the USA, growing in relative power, there was no power then mounting a sustained challenge to Britain. As a result, after the Crimean War (1854–56), Britain did not fight another European power until World War One broke out in 1914.

There was repeated concern, however, about the danger of conflict with France and Russia. Fears of invasion from France led to a naval race and to the construction of expensive defensive positions on the south coast of England. A response to the French development of ironclads, the naval race led the First Secretary to the Admiralty to tell the Commons in July 1861 that he sought 'to engender a proper confidence that we are determined to maintain our maritime position in its integrity'.[46] In the event, competition stopped short of war, and

---

44 D.M. Haynes, *Imperial Medicine: Patrick Manson and the Conquest of Tropical Disease* (Philadelphia, Pennsylvania, 2001).

45 BL. Add. 57315 fol. 39.

46 *Hansard*, 26 July 1861, vol. 164, cc. 1629–40.

only encouraged the drive to empire. As yet, the USA, Germany, Italy, and Japan were not mounting a serious naval or imperial challenge, and certainly not on a world scale, as opposed to a regional level. Nevertheless, there were significant limits to British power. Given the strength of its possible opponents and the limits to what could be achieved by the navy when up against a Continental power, it would have been unwise to intervene in the American Civil War[47] or the German unification driven by Prussia that had led, in 1866, to the annexation of Hanover, which was ruled by Queen Victoria's first cousin. However, the strength of other powers did not yet pose a serious challenge to British interests. There was repeated concern about Russia's advance into Central Asia, and the apparent threat it posed to the security of India, but the international situation appeared relatively benign. The acquisition of Cyprus (1878), the seizure of Egypt (1882), the opening of the Suez Canal (1869), and the development of telegraph systems, greatly strengthened Britain's naval position as well as facilitating maritime trade.

Yet, Britain's naval dominance was not without serious problems. If put to the test, the Royal Navy was not up to Britain's global commitments. Such an assessment was most pertinent if the commitments were all tested at the same time. This, in practice, was an excessively high bar that was not to be faced until 1941. Until then, despite threats, notably from the Russo-French alignment during the 1890s, there was no recurrence of the situation of facing other major naval powers simultaneously, as had occurred in 1744–48, 1762, 1779–83, and 1795–1814. Partly as a result, Britain in the post-Napoleonic century, with its rapidly growing economy, could act as a major power without too great an impact on its public finances or society. Britain indeed was a great power on the cheap. This was a situation that was not sustainable. It was also one that looked towards the later cheap hawkery, of seeking a major role but being unwilling to accept the fiscal and other consequences, a situation very much seen with the USA and Britain in the 2000s and 2010s.

Britain's strategic pre-eminence was reflected in its role as the centre of the communication system, not only of shipping, but also of telegraph routes. These routes sped not only political and military instructions and economic news, but also reports of imperial conflicts to British newspapers.[48] At the same time, the telegraph system had major limitations, and it did not become significantly less expensive and more effective until the 1920s when 'loaded' cables were used to

---

47 F.M. Carroll, 'The American Civil War and British Intervention: The Threat of Anglo-American Conflict', *Canadian Journal of History*, 47 (2012), pp. 87–115.

48 R. Wenzlhuemer, *Connecting the Nineteenth-Century World: The Telegraph and Globalisation* (Cambridge, 2013); S.J. Potter, *News and the British World* (Oxford, 2003).

ensure a sharper signal. In addition, there was a strategic dimension to Britain's financial position, and it cannot be separated from imperial capability, potential, and status, a linkage represented in the role of sterling and the existence of the Sterling Area. Like the American dollar today, the pound sterling was the international reserve currency in a global financial system that, unlike the present-day one, relied on a fixed exchange-rate regime and a gold standard for most significant currencies. Financial strength gave Britain a key position of influence across the world, and was linked to Britain's investment position. In 1913, a third of Britain's wealth was invested abroad, while 14.7 per cent of Britain's gross national product was exported, compared with 12.2 for Germany.

A major form of economic exchange was of manufactured products for raw materials, and this process strengthened the empire. Products included tin from Malaya, palm oil from Nigeria, rubber from Brazil and Malaya, and copper and timber from Canada. There was also important trade in manufactured products between the key industrial powers, with Germany being one of Britain's leading trading partners. In addition, Britain produced raw materials, notably coal, which was the major world source of fuel, especially for shipping in which Britain was the leading power throughout the century. Industrialisation, advances in communications, and scientific and technological developments, all accentuated the economic impact of Britain in the empire. In addition to trades focused on the imperial metropole, major commercial links developed within imperial systems, as an aspect of the significance of regionalised forms of globalisation. These trade links included the export of rice from Burma (Myanmar) to India, which led to a substantial expansion in the acreage under rice in Burma.

The industrial situation was one of flux, a flux that indicated the significance for the empire of developments in the metropole as well as in the colonies. Whereas cultural or political factors attract the attention of most modern commentators, economic realities were of great importance. Towards the close of the nineteenth century, new or newly presented resources became especially important in Western industry, notably in the shape of chemicals, particularly those based on coal and oil by-products, and of electricity. Moreover, new products, such as cars, pharmaceuticals, and telephones, provided opportunities for existing and developing industrial sectors, and also posed problems of adaptability. The balance of industrial power altered with the rise of Germany. By 1914, Germany had forged ahead of Britain in iron and steel production and was also especially successful in chemicals, electrical engineering, and optical goods. American industrial growth surpassed that of both states.

Aside from success or, relative, failure in particular industrial spheres, Britain remained the key commercial nation. This situation is important in the analysis of economic strength, as it counters an emphasis on industrial indices. The emphasis was significant for the discussion of economic policy and politics. The Conservatives, once the party of land, became increasingly that of trade and money, while the Left, both radical Liberals and Labour, came to focus on manufacturing, not least because of its wish to secure workers' support in a period when the male franchise increased notably as a result of the 1884 and 1918 Reform Acts. The strength of industry as well as the profits of trade were important to naval strength. Shipbuilding required significant investment, while the skill base of the world's leading shipbuilding industry was important to that of the world's leading naval shipbuilder. The wherewithal to pay for it depended heavily on a benign relationship between trade, finance, taxation, and borrowing. Britain had beaten France in nineteenth-century naval races, notably after 1805 and in 1858–62; and was to do the same to Germany in 1906–12. Although Britain, by 1870 and, even more, 1900, had suffered a relative decline in its economic position, that did not mean that the question of the British imperial succession – which power, and by what means, was to take Britain's leading position – was yet a leading theme, nor one that was inevitable.

Criticisms of Nineteenth-Century Empire

The nineteenth century has consistently attracted far more attention from critics of empire and British imperialism, than previous ages. In part, this is because the modern process of nation-building can be traced back to the nineteenth century, notably with India where the Indian National Congress was formed in 1885. Moreover, the nationalist account of self-determination and liberation was brought towards fruition in the first half of the twentieth century, with India itself gaining independence in 1947. From this perspective, the late nineteenth century appeared very close. As a result, the rewriting of the colonial past focused far more on that period than on the eighteenth century. This emphasis has been furthered since, because more recent interest in cultural and ideological narratives of oppression, notably of race and gender, have readily found material in the Victorian age. The processes by which Britain had gained, sustained, and expressed power were viewed far more critically than had been the case during colonial rule, and both in former colonies and Britain.

This criticism, for example, entailed an understandable rewriting of Indian atrocities that had been discussed by the imperial British in order to show their greater claim to civilisation. The key episodes were the Black Hole of Calcutta, in which Sīraj-ud-daula, the Nawab of Bengal, had imprisoned British captives with fatal results in 1756, and the murderous treatment of British women, children, and prisoners during the Indian Mutiny, notably at the captured town of Cawnpore in 1857. Colin Campbell's ability to lead a column to the relief of the besieged town of Lucknow later that year became a totemic occasion of Victorian soldiering and served as a model for subsequent actions, while Henry Havelock and other commanders demonstrated successful Christian militarism. As Mayor of London, Ken Livingstone was to complain about the plinths in Trafalgar Square occupied by statues to such heroes of empire. His ahistorical posturing also underlined the extent to which these men, unlike Nelson, who was presented as the defender of the nation against invasion, were heroes no longer, but, instead, unknown figures. Famous remarks such as the joke that Sir Charles Napier had said 'Peccavi', literally, in Latin, 'I have sinned', but referring to his conquest of Sind in 1843, are from a culture that has totally passed. Sind, indeed, means nothing to most modern Britons, for the geography of knowledge and reference has been transformed. It is the region round the Indus delta. Napier was an example of what Benjamin Disraeli called 'prancing proconsuls', who sucked British governments reluctantly into conflicts entailing further territorial expansion.

As far as atrocities are concerned, the emphasis now is on the cruelty of the British treatment of captured sepoys (mutinous soldiers) in 1857–58. Some were blown to pieces from across the muzzles of cannon during the suppression of the rebellion. Lieutenant Hugh Pearson wrote in August 1857 that the British forces had taken very heavy casualties, adding:

> village fighting ... desperate ... we took two sepoy prisoners the other day and they were blown away from the guns: the stink of fresh flesh was sickening in the extreme, but I have seen so many disgusting sights and so much bloodshed that I have grown quite callous.[49]

There was also much destruction of sites linked to the rebellion, for example, in Delhi, the Red Fort of the Mughal Emperor. This scarcely matched the idea of the British as benevolent rulers, governing in the interest of Indians. The Indians prefer the term First War of Independence (not Mutiny), and this looks towards the struggle for independence from Britain prior to 1947. The idea of successive wars of independence plays up the Indian role in obtaining independence then, as opposed to emphasising the British willingness to cede control and, earlier,

49 Pearson to his parents, 1 Aug. 1857, BL. India Office papers, MSS. Eur. C 231, p. 56.

to seek to conciliate Indian concerns by granting a considerable degree of autonomy. In practice, there was no second war of independence, even though Indian public history might prefer the idea of a Second War of Independence.

More generally, empire has been presented as an economic burden to India, and as a vehicle for British plunder and economic exploitation that gravely delayed the development of the country, and thus seriously harmed India's long-term prospects. Thus, instead of the British emphasis on progress towards modernity under colonial rule, comes a depiction of the latter as a distorting force. For centuries, Indian looms had provided cotton cloth to markets across Asia, and the arrival of the East India Company had been followed by the extension of this to Western European markets. However, between 1813 and 1830, there was a major shift in the terms of trade, with India, by 1830, importing about £2 million of cotton cloth annually from Britain. The British government put high import duties on Indian cloth entering Britain, and kept duties low on British cloth that was sent to India. Indian textile workers found themselves without employment and the economy shifted to the export of cash crops, including opium.

Other factors, however, also played a role. India lacked a significant coal-mining industry; while stability and greater Indian access to long-distance international trade were gained through Britain's rule and global position. Furthermore, the degree to which India was a British creation was downplayed, not least by neglecting the ephemeral nature of earlier Mughal control in southern India in the late seventeenth century. Other India rulers had not controlled the far south.

Criticism of nineteenth-century empire was not restricted to countries that subsequently experienced liberation struggles. Instead, what was presented as the expropriating racialism of nineteenth-century imperialism also came in for considerable criticism in former settler colonies, notably Australia, but also New Zealand. In Australia, which received 1.5 million Britons during the century, left-wing politicians tended to side with what was termed by its critics, notably John Howard, the conservative prime minister from 1996 to 2007, the 'black arm-band historical view', namely claims that the British colonisers acted in a brutal and genocidal fashion, and that this was the unacceptable foundation of modern Australia. In the 2000s, there was a bitter controversy over whether academics had exaggerated the numbers of Aborigines killed by the early British colonists. The debate still simmers, but historians of all hues are now much more wary of using the term genocide in connection with colonial Australia.

Aboriginal politicians played a role in the debate, which, as with the Maori in New Zealand, was directly linked to their calls for land rights and self-determination. The impact of changing views of empire and their centrality in public history can be seen by comparing the centenary of the beginning of British settlement in the Australian state of Tasmania with the bicentenary. On 22 February 1904, the centenary, in front of several thousand spectators, the governor unveiled a monument to the founder and praised the settlers. No Aborigines are known to have been present, and no mention was made of the subsequent massacre of Aborigines on 3 May 1804. In contrast, in 2004, no formal ceremony was held to mark the landing on 22 February 1804 and, instead, on 3 May, the massacre was commemorated from the Aboriginal perspective. The monument erected in 1904 was covered with a white sheet splattered with blood as a mark of respect to the victims of the massacre, and the Secretary of the Tasmanian Aboriginal Centre declared: 'They killed us off in this place 200 years ago, stole our land, took away our people and imposed their religion on us. But our presence here today shows they have not destroyed us'. After Aboriginal pressure, including the disruption of a re-enactment of the 1804 landing held in 1988 to celebrate the Australian bicentenary, Risdon Cove, the site of both landing and massacre, was declared an Aboriginal Historic Site and transferred to the Tasmanian Aboriginal Land Council. This, however, was challenged in the early 2000s by Reg Watson, a leading member of the Anglo-Keltic Society, who claimed that the government was bowing unnecessarily to Aboriginal pressure. Similar charges were made by Pauline Hanson, the leading right-wing populist Australian politician of the 2000s.

A related controversy led in 2004 to the replacement of the Director of the National Museum of Australia because the Howard government saw the contents of the museum as overly devoted to the Aborigines, not least in the First Australians Gallery, the largest of the museum's permanent exhibitions. This was a public controversy, not one conducted simply in the corridors of power. Howard, who argued that history had been central to the entire project of educating a nation of Australians, opposed what he saw as an excessive tendency to apologise for the fate of the Aborigines. Conversely, in the academic world, settler narratives no longer dominate the account of national history.[50]

A very different type of British imperialism is debated in the case of China, and the modern context is also far removed from that in Australia. British imperialism in China is presented there in terms of opium and coercion. This is the case in governmental and pedagogic discussion. More broadly, it is also echoed

50 T. Taylor, 'Under Siege from Right and Left: A Tale of the Australian School History Wars', in Taylor and R. Guyver (eds), *History Wars and the Classroom: Global Perspectives* (Charlotte, North Carolina, 2012), pp. 25–50.

in fiction. Thus, the Indian novelist Amitav Ghosh, who had treated Myanmar history under British rule in *The Glass Palace* (2000), turned to the Opium Wars in *Sea of Poppies* (2008) and *River of Smoke* (2011). Empire was presented as resting on a logic of opium. In an interview published in *The Times* on 11 June 2011, Ghosh claimed: 'It was their financial basis for Empire. In India it was the single largest sector of the economy. Everyone was connected to it'. Moreover, with the ahistoricism that is all too common in the discussion of empire, Ghosh compared the Opium Wars to the 2003 Iraq War: 'when national identity, a colonising power and a battle for control for profitable natural resource collide. People may not know it, but the Opium Wars were as important as the French Revolution'. The extent to which the nineteenth-century British empire readily served to inscribe foundation accounts and critical accounts of British power was easily apparent. In addition, the theme taken by the paper was clear, as the interview was headlined, 'Opium was the single largest sector of the Empire's economy', a claim that would have surprised the shipbuilders, financiers, and coal-miners of Britain.[51]

In 2010, the trade delegation led by David Cameron, the prime minister, visiting Beijing was asked to remove the poppies they were wearing because they were taken to refer to the Opium Wars. The British, however, refused to put aside the poppies, which are worn in memory of the war dead. As a reminder of the slippery case of drawing parallels, the British poppies, which symbolise French poppies from the World War One battlefields, are very different to those from which opium is derived.

Ending Slavery

The standard defence of the British empire makes much of Britain's role in ending first the slave trade[52] and then slavery. Each of these acts certainly challenged important interests in the empire, both in the colonies and in the metropole. Slaveholding was a major investment, and there was no sense on the part of slaveholders that Abolitionist pressure would inevitably succeed. Instead, their response to metropolitan pressures was hostile, and there was an often violent response to agitation for change by the black population. The destruction of the

51 For a far more subtle analysis of a symbiotic relationship, D. Sunderland, *Financing the Raj: The City of London and Colonial India, 1858–1940* (Woodbridge, 2013).

52 S. Farrell (ed.), *The British Slave Trade: Abolition, Parliament and People* (Edinburgh, 2007).

newly built mission chapel at Salter's Hill, Jamaica by white militiamen at the beginning of 1832 was a significant attack, intended to shock and intimidate black Christian converts and their allies. Such intimidation, however, failed, with the mission there re-established in 1834. Moreover, the white West Indian colonists did not defy the empire in order to protect slavery. Thus, Barbados did not prefigure South Carolina in 1861 in rejecting the larger state of which it was part. Contrasts in slaveholding societies between the West Indies and the USA were significant, notably the extent of absenteeism in the white society of Jamaica, the largest British colony in the Caribbean, and therefore its links with Britain.[53]

Once the slave trade and then slavery were ended, Britain was keen to spread Abolitionism. States that had either were urged to abolish them, and considerable diplomatic pressure was expended to that end. The British conception of the international order came in part to rest on Abolitionism. Thus, Texan independence from Mexico was recognised by Britain in 1840 in return for Texas agreeing to suppress the slave trade. In response in part to the role of Abolitionism in the defence of the empire's reputation, critics have attacked the British stance, emphasising self-interest. It is more accurate to argue that, although reforming ideas played the key role in metropolitan support for Abolitionism, self-interest and ideology were related in the subsequent implementation of policy. As a key instance of the fusion of materialist and idealist drives, trade and Abolitionism were linked as remaining slave economies, notably Spanish-ruled Cuba, seemed a threat to the economic viability of the British West Indies once slavery had ended in the latter in 1838. Free trade after 1846 enabled Cuba, with its comparative advantage of slave labour, to compete in British markets. The end of slavery certainly transformed the established socio-economic system in the Caribbean. Investment there fell; while the planter society crumbled. For example, the white population in Jamaica declined, many emigrating to America, while potential immigrants were attracted by opportunities elsewhere.

In public debate, the emphasis to be placed on ideology or self-interest when considering Abolitionism tends to be linked to political preferences. As a result, there is scant reason to anticipate an end to such debates. The moral character of this debate today captures its nature in the early nineteenth century. It will probably become more charged if a legal case for reparations is brought before the International Court of Justice as was considered in the West Indies in 2014.

---

53 C. Petley, *Slaveholders in Jamaica: Colonial Society and Culture during the Era of Abolition* (London, 2009).

Conclusions

In pushing Abolitionism, Britain came up against most of the powers of the world, whether other European empires, newly independent New World states, or non-Western countries, and devoted much effort to ending first the slave trade and then slavery. For example, great pressure was exerted on Brazil. Assessing Britain harshly can involve a lack of comparative rigour, or, rather, a preference for judging across time rather than in the context of the powers of the period. For example, as a ruler of Caribbean colonies, Britain was far less harsh than Spain in Cuba. As a ruler of settlement colonies, Britain, in Canada and New Zealand, was less harsh in its treatment of the indigenous population than the USA or Brazil, which called itself an empire after the end of Portuguese rule; although the situation in Australia was less favourable than that in Canada. In terms of territorial expansion, moreover, the British empire behaved like non-Western states such as Siam (Thailand), Abyssinia (Ethiopia), and Afghanistan. The criticisms visited on British imperialism are frequently ahistorical. At times, they also appear to reflect an anger that Britain was more successful than other powers. This anger then draws on a mistaken belief that there was something inherently wicked about British intentions and policies.

In its own terms, there was nothing static about the empire. Its dynamism was not just economic and military, but also political. The development of responsible government, and the establishment of Dominions, were an important aspect of the extent to which imperial expansion and governance witnessed considerable change, as well as testing assumption about how best to devise and sustain political arrangements. Although the Colonial Laws Validity Act of 1865 declared colonial legislation that clashed with that from Westminster invalid, the Act was rarely invoked. Dominion status enabled Britain to focus its military strength elsewhere, a process made particularly necessary by opposition, in both Britain and the Dominions, to conscription and concern to keep taxation low. Indeed, those factors helped frame the character of the British empire, while also reflecting the particular circumstances of its development. In part as a consequence of Dominion support, empire was relatively cheap. The Dominions were encouraged to develop their volunteer forces, a process that bore fruit with the assistance they provided to Britain in the (Second) Boer War of 1899–1902. At the same time, this assistance played a part in the definition of distinctive identities for individual Dominions. This process of national identification, which gathered pace in the 1890s and 1900s,[54] did not establish a challenge to

54 R. Palenski, *The Making of New Zealanders* (Auckland, 2012).

the empire in the short term, but had implications as a result of developments and difficulties that were to come. In the twentieth century, in contrast, empire became far more expensive for Britain (and the Dominions), and this expense helped erode political and popular support for it. However, this characterisation and explanation of the trajectory of empire is overly simplistic. In 1914 and 1939, Britain went to war not to protect the empire, but for reasons of European power politics heavily tinged with an opposition to expansionism in Europe by menacing authoritarian powers.[55] In contrast, in 1885, 1898, and 1937, war was avoided with Russia, France, and Japan respectively when imperial interests were at stake.

55 Britain itself acquired many and extensive new territories as a result of World War One.

Chapter 5

The British Empire, 1900–1945

From the perspective of the end of the British empire, the twentieth century might seem to be a case of decline, obsolescence, and inevitability. Moreover, if empire is the past, it can be understandable to focus on themes that appear more familiar today, notably the rise of the welfare state and Britain's post-imperial situation, particularly the relationship with the European Union. This, however, would be not only less than a full account and one that fails to pay due attention to the experience of the past. It would also present a misleading coherence in the discussion of British history and the fate of the empire. Indeed, it is important to note complexities in developments and ambiguities in analysis, to avoid anticipating decline and crisis, and to be aware of the problematic character of any assumptions of inevitability. Commentators in the eighteenth century focused on the moral aspects of strength and ideology, and saw the seeds of imperial decline in self-indulgence and a lack of public spirit, notably in the response to Edward Gibbon's *Decline and Fall of the Roman Empire* (1776–88).

In contrast, their twentieth-century counterparts, although also ready to look for moral aspects, were more predisposed to search out economic causes for decline. Here a crisis can, and could, be discerned for Britain from the late nineteenth century, in large part because of American and German economic growth, in both quantitative and qualitative terms. No longer the world's leading economic power, how could Britain expect to be the leading empire? This argument can then be traced forward to note the interaction between economic decline and the strains of international competition, as armaments and war placed a formidable burden on the economy and, even more, the public finances. Moreover, the difficulties of both made it harder to sustain Britain's imperial position. This situation remains pertinent today as far as Britain's international position is concerned, and will probably continue to be relevant in the future.

Before World War One, 1900–1914

Yet, prior to World War One, Britain was doing very well in the liberal international economic order, despite pressure, sometimes acute pressure, in particular sectors, and a related sense of anxiety that led to (unsuccessful) support for protectionism. Indeed, Britain continued to preside over this order, and notably in the financial and shipping sectors. The adoption of the Greenwich meridian as the zero meridian was a potent symbolic indication of this success. The powers had used different standard meridians, that for the French, for example, passing through the Observatory in Paris, while, in 1850, Congress decided that the National Observatory in Washington should be the standard meridian for the USA. Consistency was established with difficulty, and then only as a grudging acknowledgement of the need for uniformity and of Britain's maritime dominance. An international meeting of 1884, held in Britain, chose the Greenwich meridian as the zero meridian for time-keeping and for the determination of longitude. The response was sometimes grudging, but the French abandoned the Paris meridian in 1911, and the American legislation of 1850 was repealed in 1912.

The standardisation of the zero meridian was an important aspect of a more general consequence of British imperial power in terms of the implementation of British norms, for example in legal disputes. This process was pressed furthest within the empire, notably with the use of standard weights and measures, the development of currency and postal links, and the imposition of British concepts of time.[1] Many of these still have an echo today. Nevertheless, this process of implementing British norms was not only seen in the empire. The choice of whether to say that implementation involved *adopting* or *imposing* British norms provides an instance of the extent to which the language chosen, both by contemporaries and today, creates differing impressions. Responses by other scholars to draft versions of this book makes this point abundantly clear.

The ability to place a process in different lights is readily apparent. For example, in charting the inshore waters of the world, the Royal Navy played a key role not only in furthering the interests of British power, but also in spreading a Western form of knowledge. Knowledge over inshore waters was crucial to British naval power, as in the Crimean War (1854–56) with Russia, but also more generally. Knowledge was central to the process by which it became possible to anticipate

1 C. Blaise, *Time Lord: Sir Sandford Fleming and the Creation of Standard Time* (London, 2000); G. Nanni, *The Colonisation of Time: Ritual, Routine and Resistance in the British Empire* (Manchester, 2012).

and manage risk. Such management was highly significant in, and important to, the success of the informed, self-consciously rational, planning processes gaining visibility in Britain. These processes were linked to the practice of scientific investigation and discussion, both newly normative in a society increasingly impressed by the idea that authority should take scientific form. Britain was at the centre of this practice.[2] Britain's crucial role in exploration, both maritime and on land, was also a major source of global influence.[3]

Looked at differently, the use of knowledge by and on behalf of the British empire in the nineteenth century is an aspect of this empire becoming and being an imperial hegemony, which is then seen as stretching across the world. This approach has value, and anticipates some current views of America's position. However, such an approach neglects the extent to which there were other empires than that of Britain in the nineteenth and early twentieth centuries. That situation did not necessarily mean hostility towards Britain, but it did limit the nature and extent of imperial hegemony.

The meaning of empire to the British and imperial public at the start of the twentieth century has been a matter of discussion, not least on the degree of commitment to empire and on how Britons and colonists identified themselves; whether nationally, imperially, or as a compound of both. The extent of imperial support among the working class has been especially contentious, and considerable doubt has been raised, not least based on research on the situation in Coventry, Leeds, and Portsmouth, as well as in Australian cities.[4] At the level of popular culture, there has also been considerable debate over the imperial content of such varied, and apparently emblematic, works and events as the music of Sir Edward Elgar, accompanying for example 'Land of Hope and Glory' (words by A.C. Benson), and the popular celebrations of the relief of Mafeking in South Africa from Boer siege in 1900. These and other episodes can be seen as patriotic, chauvinistic, and national, rather than imperial. Alternatively, it can be argued that such a distinction is of limited value, not least because the empire was regarded as both product and part of the nation. These points are also pertinent for the 'Khaki election' held in 1900 during the Boer War (1899–1902), an election in which the pro-war Conservatives did very well at the expense of the very divided Liberals. The large-scale volunteer effort in the

2 M. Reidy, *Tides of History: Ocean Science and Her Majesty's Navy* (Chicago, Illinois, 2008).

3 E.J. Larson, *An Empire of Ice: Scott, Shackleton, and the Heroic Age of Antarctic Science* (New Haven, Connecticut, 2011).

4 B. Porter, *The Absent-Minded Imperialists: Empire, Society, and Culture in Britain* (Oxford, 2004).

war and the extensive coverage of the conflict in the rapidly expanding press ensured that it had a greater public impact in Britain than conflicts over the previous four decades. The memorials subsequently erected, and the major events staged when they were unveiled, were designed to encourage these inclusion. Memorialisation was linked to the expression of a patriotism that was both national and imperial.[5] There was also the question of what might be called 'banal imperialism', of imperial influences on people's everyday lives of which they might not be conscious or aware, but which were still very much there. The imperial source of consumer goods provides a prime instance.

'Wider still and wider', as 'Land of Hope and Glory' proclaimed, the British nation was not regarded as limited to one state or country. The values that accrued to empire offered therefore an extensive range and fluidity that encompassed Britons abroad. However, in a racist sense, these values could also serve to exclude immigrants. Indeed, the late nineteenth and early twentieth century saw anti-immigrant panics directed, in particular, at Jews and the Chinese. These panics affected imaginative literature, as in the Fu Manchu stories of the journalist Sax Rohmer about a deadly conspiracy against the empire directed by a sinister Chinaman based in London. There were similar panics in parts of the 'white' empire, notably against Chinese immigrants in Australia and South Africa. In Australia, there was also concern about Japanese power. Such panics had existed in earlier episodes in British history, but there was nothing as murderous in Britain in the early twentieth century as the anti-Jewish pogroms of the Middle Ages. However, a sense of racial tension became more pronounced in the late nineteenth century. In part, this reflected the increased rate of migration, and in part the ideas of inherent racial competition. As well as concern about immigration into the empire, there was the issue of migration within it. The volatility of societies, in which large-scale urbanisation was accompanied by the breakdown of previous patterns of social linkage and by the disruptive impact of economic cycles, contributed greatly to racism. On the one hand, there was a wish to understand and fix social patterns, and, on the other, racism served to express, focus, and formulate fears, anxieties, and hatreds.

Racism, however, was not the only form of imperial expression, and it existed alongside the view that the empire should serve to lead and incorporate all races to a common purpose. The monarchs positioned royal ceremonial to that end. In addition, there were many voluntarist bodies pledged to national *and* imperial assertion. Moreover, the pressure for tariff reform (protectionism), a key element

5 P. Donaldson, *Remembering the South African War: Britain and the Memory of the Anglo-Boer War from 1899 to the Present* (Liverpool, 2013).

in politics from the 1900s to the 1930s, was linked to support for an imperial preference in trade that was designed to contribute to imperial federation. If such bodies and political concern was dominated by the middle class, that was more generally true of the voluntarist sector, although a long-established aspect of criticism of empire is to present it in class terms. That criticism qualifies, but possibly also underplays, the degree of popular participation and support for the empire.

There was a potent image of empire as masculine or, rather, pertaining to values, such as fortitude, seen as masculine. That presentation, however, did not exclude an explicit role for women, alongside the reality of their largely unacknowledged activities as wives, mothers, and workers, all of which were activities that contributed greatly to imperial activity. Given the unfavourable sex ratio in Britain, women went overseas to look for husbands. They were encouraged to do so by groups such as the Victoria League, which was the leading voluntarist movement in this sphere. In supporting female emigration to the empire, the League served to underline the role of empire as a place of domesticity, family, and the virtues of home, as well as the masculine assertion more prominently discussed and celebrated in the memoralisation and literature of the period, and subsequently. Female emigration was regarded as the best way to ensure that the empire became a site and source of the expansion of the British nation. It therefore addressed longstanding concerns about deracination (interbreeding) through imperial activity as men formed relationships with native women. In practice, moreover, many British emigrants, both men and women, went to the USA, rather than the colonies; although their role in the USA is underrated because, unlike the Irish, they did not form a coherent group or lobby there. Single British women emigrated for a wide variety of other reasons, just as men did. Women went overseas to do Christian mission, to explore, to enhance their economic opportunities, to engage in scientific research, and to escape the rigours of British domesticity. Thus, just as some women emigrated as members of families and communities with the mission of replicating British domesticity in the colonies, so others sought to escape this life.

Attitudes to empire were closely related to domestic politics and to related visions of the future for Britain and the wider world.[6] The important link was supplied by Ireland, the future status of which contributed strongly to successive crises in politics and national identity in the late nineteenth and early twentieth centuries. The Liberal Unionists, such as Joseph Chamberlain, Colonial Secretary

6 J. MacKenzie, *Propaganda and Empire: The Manipulation of British Public Opinion, 1880–1960* (Manchester, 1984).

from 1895 to 1903, who had abandoned the Liberals to join the Conservatives in opposition to Irish Home Rule (limited self-government) in 1886, tended to press hard for measures to strengthen the empire as a whole. They and the Conservatives felt that what they saw as a Liberal threat to the empire was a matter of Liberal views on domestic politics, on Ireland (a key issue at once British and imperial), and on colonial policy; in short, that there was a connected challenge. The backing by the Liberal Unionists and Conservatives for social welfare rested largely on a desire to strengthen the British people, in both country and empire. There was less of an emphasis on individual amelioration. To these paternalists, there was a threat of national degeneration, which they blamed on the alleged consequences of the country's increasingly urban and industrial nature. A weaker and less virile people appeared unable to bear the burdens of empire, an argument that helps explain the launch of the Boy Scouts Movement. Conversely, an understanding of the call of empire would hopefully produce this virility.

There was also a pronounced concern about the precariousness of the empire. In part, this concern focused on other advanced societies, most notably naval and imperial competition by Germany, especially the Naval Race of the late 1900s. There was also anxiety about the USA, which was seen as imperial rival, and yet, at the same time, as a different and disruptive form of empire. American populism was regarded as a challenge to British society. Different concerns focused on Japan. Its rise was more troubling than that of the USA, as Japan appeared able to challenge the British position in Asia: both indirect, or informal, empire in China, and direct, or formal, empire in India. There was a racial component in this concern, one more clearly seen in Australia.

Moreover, there was also a fear that the very basis of imperial rule was vulnerable in many of the colonies. This fear was based on a prescient awareness of its reliance on opinion. There was particular concern about the situation in two, very different, parts of the empire: Ireland and India. Ireland was directly represented in the Westminster parliament (in fact over-represented), but divisions over Home Rule, notably Unionist (Protestant) opposition, led in the early 1910s to fear of disorder, civil war, and, maybe, mutiny by army units unwilling to support Home Rule. In India, the splendid show of George V's coronation Durbar (ceremony) in 1911 was matched by concerns about rising nationalism directed against white rule. India was not alone. In 1904, the Director of Military Operations in the War Office warned:

> The fact cannot be too plainly stated that throughout Egypt and the Sudan, and throughout the great protectorates of Uganda and British East Africa [Kenya], our whole position depends entirely on prestige. We are governing with a mere

> handful of white officials vast populations alien to us in race, language and religion, and for the most part but little superior in civilisation to savages. Except for the small, and from a military point of view inadequate, British force in Egypt, the authority of these officials is supported only by troops recruited from the subject races, whose obedience to their officers rests on no other basis than a belief in the invincibility of the British government and confidence in its promises. If that belief and confidence be once shaken the foundations of all British authority between Cairo and Mombassa will be undermined, and at any moment a storm of mutiny and insurrection will sweep us into the sea.[7]

This view captured a sense of precariousness and also the reliance of empire on a confidence in British power. This confidence was to be maintained during World War One (1914–18), but across much of Asia was to collapse with repeated defeats at the hands of Japan in 1941–42.

World War One, 1914–1918

In the event, the nearest attempt to sweep the empire aside during World War One failed. The Germans planned to exploit pan-Islamism to destroy much of the British empire by supporting Moslem revolution in Egypt and India. Such fears of a *jihad* (holy war) played a role in British adventure fiction, notably John Buchan's novel *Greenmantle*,[8] and in government anxieties. However, support for the German scheme was limited. In part, this was because the policy was compromised by Germany's alliance with the Ottoman (Turkish) empire, which was unpopular in the Arab world. Moreover, Islam was no more a cohesive force than Christianity was.

Instead of being a weakness, empire proved a fundamental strength for Britain during World War One. The most prominent opposition, the Easter Rising in Dublin in 1916, enjoyed little support in Ireland, let alone elsewhere, and was rapidly crushed. The firm British response was to play a major role in Irish public memory, notably in encouraging opposition to Britain. Given the fact that Britain (including Ireland) was at war in 1916, and indeed not doing well, the execution of rebel leaders was scarcely surprising, but it was also part of a wider crisis in civil–military relations. The government eventually stopped the

---

7 BL. Add. 50300 fol. 176.

8 R.S. Simon, *Spies and Holy Wars: The Middle East in Twentieth-Century Crime Fiction* (Austin, Texas, 2011).

executions, although too late. A similar point can be made about the execution of British soldiers who had failed in their military duty. Australia, which did not have the death penalty for the same offences, did not suffer adverse affects.

Without the empire, it would have been much harder for Britain to succeed in Europe, and impossible to do so further afield. Britain would have been unable to mount offensive operations against the Ottoman empire in the Middle East, would have been largely reduced to the use of the Royal Navy alone against German colonies in Africa and the Pacific, and would have been forced to introduce conscription earlier than 1916. Against the German main battle army, Canadian forces proved very important on the Western Front, particularly in 1917–18. Indian, Australian, New Zealand, and South African units were also significant on the Western Front, notably the Australians in 1918, but their importance was even greater outside Europe. The Australians and New Zealanders played a major part in the Gallipoli operation of 1915, an unsuccessful attempt to knock the Ottoman empire out of the war. The costly failure of the mismanaged operation seared itself into the collective memory of the Antipodes, where ANZAC day is still observed annually. Subsequently exacerbated by the serious dispute over the distribution of imperial forces in 1941–42 in the face of Japanese aggression, Gallipoli helped foster a sense of national betrayal in Australia and, to a lesser extent, New Zealand. For both, it was also significant to the development of national identity, and thus to a weakening of imperial identity. In Peter Weir's iconic film *Gallipoli* (1981), a deeply distorted account, the British contribution to the campaign was downgraded and misrepresented. The impression offered was of British inefficiency, cowardice, and dilatoriness leading to the sacrifice of the Anzac troops.[9]

Indian forces were also significant at Gallipoli, as well as in the eventually successful operations against the Ottomans in Iraq and Palestine in 1917–18. The morale of Indian troops was generally high.[10] The conquest of the German colonies in Africa largely depended on non-British units, for example South Africans in South-West Africa (Namibia). British imperial armies operated with considerable effectiveness, melding together forces from different backgrounds and generally maintaining high morale.[11]

---

9 M. Connelly, 'Gallipoli (1981): A Poignant Search for National Identity', in J. Chapman, M. Glancy, and S. Harper (eds), *The New Film History: Sources, Methods, Approaches* (Basingstoke, 2007), pp. 41–53.

10 G. Morton-Jack, *The Indian Army on the Western Front* (Cambridge, 2014), pp. 300–305.

11 J.E. Kitchen, *The British Imperial Army in the Middle East: Morale and Military Identity in the Sinai and Palestine Campaigns, 1916–1918* (London, 2014), pp. 216–20.

In some respects, albeit not in Ireland, and, to a degree, India, the collective effort represented by the war led to a strengthening of empire. An Imperial War Cabinet, including representatives of the Dominions, met from 1917 and provided a welcome public sign of cohesion in decision-making that countered the emphasis on distinctive interests. At more junior levels, people from various parts of the empire learned to co-operate. Male sociability in war-related activities was especially pronounced, but there were also female equivalents, notably nursing.

The war also saw a measure of the economic union that had interested Joseph Chamberlain in the 1900s. Schemes for an Imperial Customs Union were considered, while Britain's role as a market for imperial goods was much fostered by military needs and political preference. The highly damaging impact of the war on European food imports to Britain ensured that the British market increased for imperial exporters such as South Africa. However, while the war provided economic opportunities, notably for food and raw material exporters, it also greatly disturbed established economic patterns and disrupted society. For example, food exports led to inflation in Sudan. The British were hard hit by economic change. The diversion of manufacturing capacity to war production encouraged the growth of industry elsewhere, notably in India, Japan, and Latin America. For example, the Japanese merchant marine increased. Trade was greatly affected by war and the German submarine assault; and this challenge hit Britain as the leading trading power. Moreover, Britain sold much of its large portfolio of foreign investments in order to finance the war effort. The USA, which did not enter the war until 1917, benefited most of all. The British war effort had swiftly become dependent on American financial and industrial resources, as well as oil, notably for the Royal Navy,[12] while the Americans were well placed to replace British exports to Canada and Latin America.

The Inter-War Period, 1918–1939

Britain was a leading victor when Germany and its alliance system was defeated and overthrown in 1918. There was a considerable sense of achievement, not least because of the major role of British and Dominion forces, alongside French and American allies, in the Hundred Days' Offensive that defeated the Germans on the Western Front. The war was followed not by a retreat of empire, but by its advance outside Europe. In contrast, within Europe, the Allied victory led to

12 K.C. Ulrichsen, *The First World War in the Middle East* (London, 2014), p. 168.

the overthrow of the Austrian and German empires, while post-war British and allied intervention in the Russian Civil War helped ensure that the Soviet Union did not match the size of the Russian empire. During the war, the British had encouraged Arab opposition to Ottoman (Turkish) hegemony.[13] Nevertheless, colonial ambitions and the imperial ethos remained strong, and the British (like the French) saw the events of the war outside Europe as reflecting the value of empire. Indeed, the defeat of Germany and its allies carried the empire to its maximum impact (as it also did that of France) and, as a result, represented the highpoint of imperialism in world history. Britain played a leading role in the peace conferences held in Paris in 1919–20 and gained League of Nations' mandates for Tanganyika (the mainland part of Tanzania), part of Togo and a sliver of Cameroon, all conquered German territories in Africa, and also for Nauru Island in the Pacific. In addition, Australia, New Zealand, and South Africa all made gains from Germany: German New Guinea as well as the Bismarck Archipelago, Western Samoa, and South-West Africa, respectively. Moreover, the partition of the Ottoman (Turkish) empire led to British mandates over Palestine, Transjordan, and Iraq, while in 1914 Kuwait had already become independent under British protection. British power along the Suez Canal route and in the Islamic world was now far stronger, while the British empire made the greatest gains in Africa.

Ardent imperialists, such as Viscount Milner, Colonial Secretary 1919–21, and Leo Amery, Milner's Under-Secretary in 1919–21, and Colonial Secretary in 1924–29, pressed for the further strengthening of the empire, partly in the hope that it would never again be dragged into the Continental mire. There were attempts to extend British influence and control beyond the peace settlement. Hopes that Syria would be ruled by the pro-British Arab Hashemite dynasty, a key means of British influence in the Arab world, were thwarted by the French. However, British influence initially increased in both Persia (Iran) and Turkey, in the latter of which the victorious allies staked out zones of influence. Having conquered Jerusalem and Baghdad in 1917, the British occupied Constantinople (Istanbul) in 1920. Prior to the end of World War One, British forces began to take a role against the Communists in the Russian Civil War that followed their coup in 1917. This intervention continued after the end of the war, as the British moved into the Caucasus, Central Asia, and the White Sea region, and were deployed in the Baltic and the Black Sea. In 1919, George, Viscount Curzon, the bold and arrogant Foreign Secretary, advocated control over parts of the former Russian empire, a policy seen as a forward defence for the India where earlier

13 M. Darlow and B. Bray, *Ibn Saud* (London, 2010), pp. 196–252.

he had been Viceroy. Sir Halford Mackinder, a MP as well as Britain's leading geopolitician, pressed for the occupation of the Baku–Batumi railway (from the Caspian to the Black Sea) in order to give coherence to Britain's position in the Caucasus and to provide protection for Iraq and Persia (Iran). Baku was a key centre of oil production.

Such ambitions, however, could not be sustained, and the high tide of empire was to ebb very fast. The strain of World War One, the men lost, the money spent, and the exhaustion produced by constant effort, was heavy enough. The war had left a burdensome debt, notably to the USA, so that Britain had been transformed from the world's leading creditor nation to its greatest debtor, which affected Britain's international position. Debt made fiscal retrenchment and, even more, economic recovery necessary, and the British sought to recreate a liberal economic order focused on free trade and a revived gold standard. This was a self-interested internationalism, for the liberal order very much served British interests. In the face, however, of the economic nationalism of rivals, especially France and the USA, the major problems of servicing debts, and the limitations of conventional financial and monetary concepts, the British had only limited success in their plans for the world economy. Moreover, Russia under Communism became a markedly anti-liberal power, not least renouncing its debts. Economic nationalism at the level of the major powers interacted with an extensive opposition to market mechanisms. There was a widespread state-backed and tariff-enforced emphasis on domestic industrial production, for example in the newly independent states of Eastern Europe, such as Poland. Britain was also affected by the extent to which the terms of the world economy were now set by America, which became not only the world's greatest industrial power but also the largest creditor. New York replaced London as the world's leading financial centre.

Financial and economic problems affected British capability as a major power, but were not the root causes for the reversal of the post-war imperial optimum. Instead, both the expansion of imperial rule and Britain's international commitments involved intractable problems. Armed intervention in Russia against the Communists had been supported by Winston Churchill, the bellicose Secretary for War, and led to British tanks appearing at Tsaritsyn (Stalingrad) in 1919 and outside St Petersburg. However, due to the weakness and divisions of the Whites, on whose behalf the British acted, intervention proved a failure and was abandoned. The intervention had been opposed by left-wingers, sympathetic to the Communists, and by conscripts eager for demobilisation, notably in the Baltic fleet, but failed due to the difficulty of the task.

Revolts in Egypt (1919) and Iraq (1920) were crushed, but helped lead Britain eventually to grant their independence. Nevertheless, thanks in part to the Anglo-Iraqi treaty of 1930 and the Anglo-Egyptian treaty of 1936, Britain maintained considerable influence in both, in what was to be, until 1954 and 1958 respectively, despite serious clashes, a generally successful exercise in informal empire.

The revolts of 1919–20 were but part of a wider post-war crisis for the empire. The Third Anglo-Afghan War, in 1919–20, underlined the difficult situation on the North-West Frontier of British India (now Pakistan), where there was a revolt in Waziristan; while there were also serious disturbances in the Punjab in 1919. British influence collapsed in Persia (Iran) in 1921, when the pro-British Shah was overthrown by Reza Khan, who exploited nationalist sentiment and rejected British pretensions, the pattern that was also to be followed by nationalists in China. More prominently, in the Chanak crisis of 1922, the government backed down in its armed confrontation with the nationalists in Turkey led by Kemal Atatürk, who rejected the peace settlement in so far as it affected Turkey. There was little support, in Britain or, even more, the Dominions, for war with Turkey. Indeed, the attitude of the Dominions indicated the limits of imperial cohesion. This crisis precipitated the fall of David Lloyd George, the prime minister, when many Conservative backbenchers opposed him in a decisive blow to the coalition.

More seriously, the loss of Ireland was a major change, as the empire began at home. This was not a failure at the periphery and at the hands of a totally alien population, as in Persia, a failure that can be seen in terms of imperial overreach. Instead, this was a failure at the centre in what had been a part of Britain for centuries and had been represented in the Westminster parliament since the Act of Union of 1800. In the event, the weakness of British imperialism when confronted by a powerful nationalist movement was exposed. World War One had destroyed the basis for the Irish Home Rulers, those who sought self-government as part of a commitment to empire. In the 1918 general election, 47 per cent of the vote and 73 out of the 105 parliamentary seats, including most of those outside Ulster (the historic northern province), were won by Sinn Féin, a party of nationalists who refused to attend Westminster and who demanded independence. In 1919, a unilateral declaration of independence was issued, and fighting broke out. A terrorist struggle denied Britain the reality and semblance of control, and ended with the Anglo-Irish Treaty of December 1921. This treaty accepted both partition of the island, essentially on sectarian (religious) grounds, and effective independence (rather than Home Rule) for the new Irish Free State (Eire). It became a self-governing Dominion within the empire, with a Governor-General appointed by the Crown.

This was the same status in the 'Community of Nations known as the British Empire', as Australia (1900), Canada (1867), Newfoundland (1907),

New Zealand (1907), and South Africa (1910), although, in the constitution of the Irish Free State, it was described as being a 'co-equal member of the community called the British Commonwealth of Nations'. The Commonwealth became a term used in this context from the start of the twentieth century, and became a more central concept from the 1920s as a result in large part of the major contribution of the Dominions to the war effort. Irrespective of the constitutional relationship, however, the new Irish Dominion was far more alienated from Britain and the empire than the others. Indeed, that situation suggests what might have happened had India become a Dominion, or, at least, done so after a violent independence struggle. In the new Irish Free State, there was a civil war as nationalists opposed to partition were defeated by the government. In Northern Ireland, there was continued terrorist violence, as well as the establishment of a sectarian Protestant state that, fearful of betrayal by the large Catholic minority, was inherently and overtly discriminatory.[14] Britain and the Irish Free State were involved in an economic war in the 1930s.

At the same time, the Irish settlement indicated the range of options offered by imperial links. The same was true of India, where there were moves towards a less authoritarian system and practice of control. In 1919, under the Montagu–Chelmsford Reforms, a Government of India Act established the principle of dyarchy in the provinces. This Act, which reflected Liberal aspirations that were not shared by all Conservatives, allowed responsible self-government in areas of competence by Indian ministers under the supervision of provincial legislatures, while the British government retained finance and foreign policy in its control.

Across the range of imperial interests and commitments, there was, in the context of post-war exhaustion and pressing domestic economic problems, a lack of resources and will to sustain many international ambitions, especially schemes for imperial expansion. Such schemes were expensive. It had cost £40 million to suppress the 1920 Iraq rising and the garrison there cost £25 million per year. Retrenchment and judging between commitments were increasingly the order of the day. The cuts in public expenditure recommended by the Geddes Committee in 1922 – the Geddes Axe – hit military expenditure most heavily. Indeed, costs and cuts encouraged a turn to new technology in order to protect imperial commitments. This was an example of a more general process whereby empire, far from necessarily being an anachronistic force and sphere representing all that was most backward-looking, instead presented an opportunity and need for new solutions. Constructive imperialists such as Amery saw themselves as

14 A.F. Parkinson, *Belfast's Unholy War: The Troubles of the 1920s* (Dublin, 2004).

modernisers. Modernisation was not always attractive. Thus, the problems of Iraq and elsewhere saw the use of the Royal Air Force to provide 'air policing'. The punitive character of the resulting bombing and strafing, which led to numerous Iraqi casualties, attracts present-day criticism. The discussion of the possibility of using gas is repellent. British expenditure on maintaining control fell, although at a high cost in the lives of those thus 'policed'. It is also possible to point to the self-interested arguments of RAF leaders, notably Sir Hugh Trenchard, the Chief of the Air Staff from 1919 to 1929; as well as to note the extent to which opponents learned to counter aerial surveillance and attack. The latter problem also faced the Americans in Nicaragua in the 1920s.[15] Nevertheless, the central point is that empire required and produced new solutions. This was a situation repeatedly seen, for example in the debates over the administration and government of India, notably in the 1780s, 1850s, 1910s, and 1930s. There was also an emphasis on the scientific administration of empire.

As so often when discussing the problems of a particular empire, it is important to place them in perspective, both chronologically and geographically. There had always been issues of prioritisation for the British empire, while apparent opportunities had frequently proved unobtainable as with Cartagena in 1741 and Buenos Aires in 1807. In addition, at one level, the picture for Britain was one of continued strength, certainly in comparison with other European powers: France, and, especially, Germany and Russia, let alone Austria, suffered even more from the war. The German, Russian, Austrian, and Turkish empires were overthrown. The territorial growth of the British empire as a result of the war was more than that of any other state or empire. Moreover, American isolationism helped to mask the political consequences of the shift of financial and economic predominance to the USA. The British position in Latin America markedly declined, but the region already had been increasingly under American influence from the mid-nineteenth century. British influence in Central America had fallen in the 1850s.

Returning to the 1920s, the loss of the bulk of Ireland did not herald the collapse of other links within the British Isles nor any serious pressures in them. There was scant sign of separatism in Scotland or Wales. Moreover, in India, the non-cooperation movement led by Mahatma Gandhi ebbed in effectiveness from 1922. In addition, the Indian Army enabled Britain to discharge its military commitments, especially in Iraq, without conscription, although the modernisation of that army was not pressed forward. Furthermore, in

15 D. Omissi, *Air Power and Colonial Control: The Royal Air Force 1919–1939* (Manchester, 1990).

Egypt, Britain retained control of the Suez Canal zone, as well as of defence and foreign affairs. Financial strength was suggested by Britain's return to the Gold Standard (convertibility of sterling with gold) in 1925. This measure was actively pressed as a sign of imperial power by Churchill, then Chancellor of the Exchequer. However, the over-valuing of sterling was to be a major burden on the economy, and Britain left the Gold Standard in 1931. Meanwhile, helped by the destruction and confiscation of the German mercantile marine in, and as a result of, World War One, Britain remained the world's leading shipper and shipbuilder. The British also had the leading stake in international aviation and telegraph routes.

The empire was fostered in British consciousness in a fashion that would seem surprising to most readers today. On Empire Day, every year, schools staged pageants and displays, souvenirs were issued, and large parades were held in Hyde Park. As an instance of adaptability, the character of Empire Day celebrations changed in the inter-war years, with a concerted effort to link them to remembrance of the war dead. The British Empire Exhibition in 1924–25, for which Wembley Stadium was built in 1923, was a major public occasion, celebrated in the press and the newsreels, and commemorated by a set of stamps, an unusual development. The disappointing performance of the nervous George, Duke of York, later George VI, at the opening of the Exhibition was fictionally presented in the film *The King's Speech* (2010). Another major empire exhibition followed in Glasgow in 1938, an important indicator of Scotland's major role within the empire.

Far from slackening, integration within the empire was pressed forward by the extension of new communication systems. Railways attract less attention than air routes, but their development helped move goods, notably minerals and cash crops for export, to the ports where harbour facilities were constructed and improved. These railways made colonies economically coherent, as well as a more active part of a developing imperial economy. Railways were significant for the production of cash crops, such as cocoa, providing both economies of scale and export outlets. The railways, conspicuously, did not link British colonies to those of other powers. Thus, Gambia, Sierra Leone, Ghana, and Nigeria were cut off from French West Africa. More prominently, new air routes were pioneered both by the Royal Air Force, which was keen to develop routes along which aircraft could be sent to reinforce vulnerable points, and by Imperial Airways, a company founded with government support in 1924. In 1932, the Britain to Australia airmail service began, as did weekly flights to Cape Town. Weekly flights to Hong Kong followed in 1936. Flying boat traffic across the empire rose from three million letters in 1928 to 17.5 million by 1934. In contrast, thanks to the problems of flying the Atlantic, such flights only began to New York in 1946. However, imperial links also provided an opportunity for competing commercial strategies and political aspirations within the empire, notably in Australia, New Zealand, and India.

Regular air and sea services, as well as the radio links provided by the BBC Empire Service,[16] helped develop the integration of British and colonial élites. For example, international shortwave radio services from Britain to Canada began in 1926. In part by supporting the establishment and consolidation of public broadcasting authorities around the empire, and by co-operating with them, the BBC served as a way to integrate the empire, notably the settler diaspora.[17] This integration sustained mutual interest and interests, and ensured the neo-Britishness that was characteristic of settler life, and that contributed greatly to a sense of empire. This process did not only occur at the level of the comfortably off. These services were used by sports teams and touring theatrical companies, as well as officials and businessmen. To take the case of higher education, the scholarly networks that had been much strengthened by World War One extended, into the inter-war period, the intimate scholarly connections that had tied the British and settler universities to each other. There was a reshaping of earlier imperial networks by centralised and professional systems of university governance and administration. Committees of vice-chancellors and principals met with increasing frequency in Britain, and national conferences in the Dominions assumed a more active role. This was an aspect of Dominion independence, and also a repurposing of the mechanisms that had linked settler universities to Britain. At the same time, universities, and those who worked in them, asserted the ongoing independence and interdependence of the extensive and expansive British academic community.[18] This was a particular instance of the wider process of imperial webs: individual and collective links with varying institutional consequences that helped to provide a coherence to the world of variety that represented the empire. Britons overseas were but part of a wider system of adaptation to particular and changing circumstances, ensuring that the empire as a practice was locally contingent at the same time that there were ideas, beliefs, and policies of unity. Both adaptation and unity captured the impact of the social, gender, religious, and racial views of British society, and sought to

16 A. Anduaga, *Wireless and Empire: Geopolitics, Radio Industry and Ionosphere in the British Empire, 1918–1939* (Oxford, 2009).

17 S.J. Potter, *Broadcasting Empire: The BBC and the British World, 1922–1970* (Oxford, 2012), pp. 78–9.

18 T. Pietsch, *Empire of Scholars: Universities, Networks and the British Academic World 1850–1939* (Manchester, 2013).

maintain them at the same time that the friction of particular circumstances sustained a significant measure of diversity.[19]

Family and friendship links across the empire could be readily maintained, as could associational movements, such as the Freemasons or the Boy Scout Movement, the latter very much a legacy of the idea of imperial manliness. Founded in 1908 by Robert Baden-Powell, a hero of the Boer War, the Movement was intended to prepare young men for the active life required if the empire was to remain a vital force. As such, empire was seen as a counter to the supposedly weakening consequences of urban life, which was associated, variously, with degeneration, effeminacy, and socialism. Such views serve as a reminder of the extent to which the empire played a central part in debates about the character and future of the British people, with accounts of the future bound up in notions of identity. The supposed relevance of the empire to the people gave it a resonance very different to that of state interest. These debates occurred in Britain, but also in the Dominions.

Discussion of the relevance of empire was more difficult for the Left, as part of it moved leftwards away from predominantly liberal or evangelical concepts of progress and, instead, towards more socialist views that were often inherently opposed to empire, or at least indifferent to it. At the same time, empire provided an opportunity on the Left to spread institutions and beliefs, for example to encourage the development of trade unions. Moreover, the Left displayed some interest in moves to enhance autonomy in India.

Critical accounts of empire can be framed from modern perspectives, although some, such as the environmental one, may seem ahistorical. Indeed, far from attracting criticism, attempts to control the environment, for example by introducing irrigation schemes and constructing dams, were the norm in this period. If such schemes dislocated traditional economic relationships, and brought opportunity and profit very differently to particular groups, that was true of change as a whole. Thus, in Sudan, the Gezira plain was used to grow grain for the nearby city of Khartoum. However, the attempt to develop cotton cultivation there was pressed with the construction of an expensive irrigation scheme that was officially opened in 1926. This scheme served to produce a cash crop designed to further the imperial economy, by increasing supplies from within the empire, and was therefore an example of the process by which distant regions were more intensely integrated into the imperial economy. Production in Sudan lessened dependence on India and was also part of a strategy focused on imperial self-sufficiency and, therefore, not needing cotton imports from the

19 R. Bickers (ed.), *Settlers and Expatriates: Britons Over the Seas* (Oxford, 2010).

USA. Similarly, imperial economic links that did not centre on Britain were developed. Myanmar became the largest rice exporter in the world, in large part in order to help feed India, especially Bengal. This helps explain the problems caused in World War Two when Japan conquered Myanmar in 1942, problems accentuated by the need to support the large army confronting the Japanese and by difficulties in supply from within India. The terrible Bengal famine of 1943, now used as a major basis for criticism of imperial rule, notably in India, should, at least in part, be understood in its wartime context.

At the same time as they were used in the British empire, dams and irrigation were to be central during the century to the development strategy of independent countries, for example the USA and in Latin America, as well as of left-wing states, notably the Soviet Union in Central Asia and also Communist China. Alongside criticism of Western empires on environmental grounds, it is appropriate to note that the determination to control the environment and to profit from this control, was seen as a central aspect of modernity around the world.

There was a racial dimension to inter-war economic development. Thus, in Africa, much British investment was linked to the imposition of a white settler and company control. In Kenya, both the African and the Indian population suffered discrimination, while white settlers extended their control over the land and notably over the highlands that offered economic productivity as well as a degree of freedom from disease. The continuation in peacetime of the pass system introduced for Africans during the war was both indicative of attitudes and a cause of hostility. It would be mistaken to view the entire empire in this light. In Malaya, the development of a strong British role in rubber and tin production was not affected by a white settler presence comparable with that in Kenya. Instead, Britain offered an important degree of economic modernisation. British companies in Malaya, and elsewhere, benefited, as a result of participation in the empire, from the ready availability of investment capital, and also from their easy access to international commercial networks. The British role in industrial technology was seen with the machinery used in tin production, especially for dredging. In Sri Lanka, Kerala, and Assam, tea production focused on the distant metropolitan market developed. Tea production, moreover, benefited from the demand for tea elsewhere in the empire, especially in the Dominions. However, economic benefits were not shared equally. Thus, in tea production, the peasants, especially in Assam in the late nineteenth century, were treated like serfs, with the indentured system keeping them heavily dependent on their employers. Managerial roles in Assam, Kerala, and Sri Lanka were taken not by the local population but by British expatriates, notably Scots, a situation that lasted until independence in 1947.

Aside from such ethnic issues, which is one way of referring to the very harsh consequences of the differential pricing of labour and of related labour controls, there were also governmental tensions within the empire over the terms of trade. These were a source of disagreement in the 1920s as post-war economic pressures created and accentuated differences. As part of a more general loosening of imperial ties,[20] the Dominions sought to protect their industries from British competition and were concerned that free trade within the empire would harm them. In turn, Imperial Preference was, foremost, the attempt to overcome these tensions and strengthen the empire, not least by presenting it as a collegial affair rather than one focused on British military power. Such economic strength was a cause championed from 1930 by the press baron William, Lord Beaverbrook, the owner of the *Daily Express*, in his 'Crusade' for Empire Free Trade, as well as by Harold, 1st Viscount Rothermere, another press baron, owner of the *Daily Mail*. This was a period when such owners of newspapers were particularly influential. Imperial Preference (which was not the same as free trade) already existed to a degree and was eventually extended in agreements reached at the Imperial Economic Conference held at Ottawa in 1932. Yet, British exporters benefited less than Dominion producers because, while the Dominions raised tariffs on non-British imports, they were unwilling to cut tariffs on British imports as they feared the impact on Dominion producers. Indeed, the Ottawa agreement was a cautious agreement that contrasted with the bold views of the Conservative politician Leo Amery, who pressed for a common economic policy and currency, and thus an empire bloc.

Nevertheless, in light of rising protectionism elsewhere during the Depression, the agreements were promising. Furthermore, the tension and lack of warmth shown at Ottawa suggested that it would be difficult to achieve more. The protectionism introduced in Britain, with the general 10 per cent tariff under the Import Duties Act of 1932 that brought an end to free trade, was made more politically acceptable by Imperial Preference; but its essential thrust was concern about the economic position in Britain. Thanks in part to Imperial Preference, the empire took 49 per cent of British exports in 1935–39, compared with 42 per cent a decade earlier. Indeed, in the late 1930s, the British exported more to South Africa than to the self-sufficient and protectionist USA. Yet, this increase reflected the more pronounced fall in world trade as British exports to the empire actually declined in value. Import substitution in some colonies, such as India, was significant, and in Canada was related to the

20 Memorandum by the Chief of the Imperial General Staff, Oct. 1932, NA. CAB. 24/234 fol. 165.

spread of American-owned branch-plant operations. Moreover, the important growth of motor-car and white-goods manufacture in Britain did not depend on colonial products nor markets, although the supply of petrol reflected Britain's position in the Gulf.

In a reminder of the flexibility and porosity of imperial ideas, British policymakers, instead of thinking, as in the Victorian era, primarily in terms of the global economy theoretically made possible by free trade, were increasingly discussing the future in terms of an economic bloc that played a central role in strategic planning. This bloc was to be led by Britain, but with major contributions from the Dominions. Both Stanley Baldwin, prime minister in 1923, from 1924 to 1929 and from 1935 to 1937, and Neville Chamberlain, Chancellor of the Exchequer from 1931 to 1937 and prime minister from 1937 to 1940, thought in these terms. The pre-1914 liberal internationalism, that had been partly revived in the 1920s, was superseded thanks to the Depression by a corporatist patriotism at once nationalistic and imperial. Although the sterling bloc and the empire were not coterminous, the empire certainly lent strength to sterling and thus contributed greatly to the strength of the bloc. Until the 1967 devaluation of sterling, the currencies of most Commonwealth countries, bar Canada, were fixed in value relative to sterling. Moreover, these states conducted their international trade in sterling. Many of these states held large sterling balances that helped support the currency and thus the financial stability of Britain and its government. However, the abandonment of the gold standard in 1931, and of free trade in 1932, meant that Britain's hitherto-pivotal role in the global economy declined.

This emphasis on the empire was linked to a political assertiveness that presented the empire as a leading world power that possessed coherence and had distinct political interests. The British press went into overdrive on this topic at the time of the coronation of George VI in 1937. In part, however, this assertiveness arose from a sense of vulnerability. The economic benefits stemming from empire helped justify imperial strategic commitments. The latter included interests in the Middle East, the British presence in South and South-East Asia, and the route to Australasia. The ministerial report on defence requirements, amended and approved by the Cabinet on 31 July 1934, noted that the 'dependence for security of that vast portion of the Empire whose shores are washed by the southern Pacific and Indian Oceans on the maintenance of our naval position in the Far East has long been recognised'.[21] The construction of a naval base at Singapore was regarded as crucial to this position.

21 NA. CAB. 24/250 fol. 111.

The stress on imperial links was enhanced by the degree to which for Britain there was no international strategic or political substitute for these links, both with respect to the defence of the Dominions and as far as the views of the British government were concerned. The combination of Britain's worldwide commitments, however, posed a problem in responding to particular crises, and in considering how best to react to crises that might occur. Reporting on 9 February 1937, about the possibility of confronting Japan, Germany, and Italy, the Chiefs of Staff noted: 'We could send a fleet to the Far East adequate in heavy ship strength for a defensive strategy [against Japan], while retaining sufficient strength at home to counter the German forces ... would leave nothing available for the Mediterranean, where we should have to rely upon the French fleet to deal with Italian naval forces'.[22] In a parallel with the contemporary situation facing the USA, others acted as free-riders. The desired benefit from the cover provided by British military strength enabled the Dominions to feel safe with only a modest expenditure on defence. For example, the Canadian navy was largely run down after World War One. At the imperial conferences of 1923 and 1926, the Canadian Prime Minister William Mackenzie King, in response to the Chanak crisis of 1922, made it clear that his country would not fight in a war simply at Britain's behest, but, instead, that its interests had to be at stake and that the Canadian parliament would play a crucial role in validating this. The limited provision by the Dominions for defence contributed greatly to the more general military vulnerability of the empire that became apparent in the 1930s. The Commonwealth also failed to develop workable processes for effective co-operation on defence and international relations. Although the threat posed by rising Japanese power was appreciated, indeed pressed by Australia and New Zealand, there was no effective response by the Dominions to supplement the British government's financing of a major naval base in Singapore and the plans for British naval deployment there in the event of a crisis with Japan.

Meanwhile, economic and political ties in the 'informal empire' faced serious difficulties. In Latin America, American businesses made major inroads in most markets, with the British doing best at retaining their position in Argentina. The British presence in China was affected by different pressures. China became more assertive as a republic, with the rise of nationalism making foreign interests a conspicuous target; and was becoming harder to manage because of its acute divisions. Chinese nationalists attacked British commercial interests in 1926, leading to the dispatch of a major British force, including planes and an aircraft carrier, to Shanghai. However, whereas old China hands wanted this force to

22 NA. CAB. 24/268 fol. 104.

move up the Yangzi valley, in order to protect British interests, notably at Hankou, a major inland entrepot, the government responded far more cautiously, and the Hankou presence was abandoned. When the Kuomintang (nationalist) leader, Jiang Jieshi, broke with the Communists in 1927, that helped satisfy British concerns. In another light, this was British appeasement of the Kuomintang. Moreover, there were economic problems: the export of British cotton goods to China was hit by Japanese competition and by the development of Chinese production. From 1931, when the Japanese occupied Manchuria, British interests in China were affected by Japanese expansionism and this became more significant when a full-scale invasion was launched in 1937.[23]

There were also significant political problems in some parts of the colonial empire. The growth of anti-imperial feeling was related to indigenous notions of identity and practices of resistance, many of them central to a peasant culture of non-compliance with ruling groups. New organisations, such as the All-India Muslim League, founded in 1906, the National Congress of British West Africa (1920), the Young Kikuyu Association in Kenya (1921), and the African National Congress in South Africa (1923), fostered demands for change. They drew heavily on the activism of individuals educated in new institutions established by colonial governments, in part in order to provide officials.

An awareness of challenge was captured in a memorandum of 15 March 1920 by the General Staff urging a more accommodating attitude to the Turkish nationalists. Aside from the need to keep Turkey out of the Russian/Communist camp, there was a concern with the opinion of the Islamic world,

> the effect which the severity of the proposed peace conditions may produce amongst the Mahomedan population of other portions of the British Empire; it will suffice here to say that the Arab inhabitants of Palestine and Mesopotamia and the Mahomedan portion of the Indian population will certainly not receive the news with indifference.[24]

Similar concerns had been expressed in 1882 at the time of the invasion of Egypt. They were more pressing in 1920 due to the Russian Revolution, the problems Britain was facing in the Islamic world, and the impact of President Woodrow Wilson's emphasis on national self-determination. There was a sense of a transformation in the context of empire due to the rise of nationalism.

---

23 S.K. Fung, *The Diplomacy of Imperial Retreat: Britain's South China Policy, 1924–1931* (Oxford, 1991).

24 NA. CAB. 24/101 fol. 315.

The issue of the relationship between this and religious hostility is pertinent for modern discussion about a 'clash of civilisations'. The memorandum referred to

> the great change which has been influencing the nature of popular movements in Asia during the last 15 years, owing to the success of Japan. In the past it has always been religion that has moved the East. Now, with the improvement of communications and greater frequency of intercourse, familiarity with Europeans and their methods has inevitably bred contempt, or, at least, a practical perspective. Whether the Easterner believes more in himself or less in the European, it would appear that the dominating factor of the future is nationality. The international agitator is quick to manipulate this factor, as is seen in Egypt, where Copt and Muslims vie in vehemence; in India, where Hindu shows an inclination to common cause with Mohammedan; in Palestine, where anti-Zionists work to combine Christian and Arab against the Jew.
>
> The Arab rising [in Arabia against Turkish rule] was nationalist, not religious ... The Young Turk revolution of 1908 and the Persian movement of 1906 were nationalist. The present movement in Turkey is definitely nationalist and not religious. Though the weight of religions and quasi-religious factors will decrease and the weight of territorial considerations will increase in proportion to the strength of nationalism, yet religion will always be the instrument of nationalism.[25]

Concern with subversive ideas encouraged British intelligence organisations and operations that relied heavily on the co-operation of supportive imperial subjects, without whom these operations were in a very weak position. These organisations and operations reflected the fear that colonial populations were readily manipulated, as well as the range, and ambiguities and nuances involved in the term co-operation, and the related concerns these gave rise to.[26] In colonies such as India and Jamaica, administrators and officers had for a long time been concerned as to how best to control populous territories with very small forces. The military strength available was regarded as the crucial support of a moral authority on which rule and control rested. This was an attitude that helped lead some in Britain and among the British in India to support General Dyer's harsh and bloody resort to disturbances at Amritsar in 1919. The extent to which this authority was accepted, indeed even accepted, by the colonised

25 NA. CAB. 24/101 fols 311–12.

26 M. Thomas, *Empires of Intelligence: Security Services and Colonial Disorder after 1914* (Berkeley, California, 2008).

in the nineteenth century should not be exaggerated, but there is little doubt that it was under far more challenge by the inter-war years. In part, this was because World War One had encouraged not only imperial consciousness but also a separate awareness in individual colonies.

The use of this military strength has proved an important issue in the modern recollection of the empire. This is particularly so in the case of Ireland and the British opposition to independence, notably the use of auxiliary police, especially the Black and Tans, recruited from ex-soldiers. They became associated with reprisals against terrorism by the IRA (Irish Republican Army), and the use of civilian clothes by the IRA helped encourage lack of care in the targeting of reprisals.[27] Amritsar remains an important issue in Indian public history, supporting the argument that British authority had an inherently repressive character.[28]

The British government has found it appropriate to be contrite. In 2013, Prime Minister David Cameron laid a wreath at the memorial, as well as bowing his head, and standing in silence to pay respect to those who died. He was shown around the site of the massacre by descendants of some of those who came under fire in 1919, and they pointed out walls where bullet holes can still be seen, as well as the Martyrs' Well where many people died after seeking shelter from the volley. The memorial plaque declares: 'This place is saturated with the blood of those Indian patriots who were martyred in a non-violent struggle to free India from British domination'. As such, the massacre is implicitly contrasted with the violence used, notably in the 1980s by Sikhs seeking independence from India for the Punjab, the very region in which Amritsar is located. Thus, the highly militarised nature of the Indian response in storming sacred sites occupied by Sikh militants, especially the Golden Temple in Amritsar in 1984, is implicitly excused by the plaque. In the hyper-critical Indian press, Cameron's remarks were condemned as too late by some Indian commentators and, separately, as designed to appeal to Sikh voters in Britain. However, his remarks associated Cameron both with Churchill – a positive, indeed iconic, figure in British, specifically Conservative, history – and with a goal that presented the modern British government in a benign light. Whereas Queen Elizabeth II, when she laid a wreath at the Amritsar memorial in 1997, described the massacre as a 'distressing' example of the 'moments of sadness' in Anglo-Indian history,

---

27 D.M. Leeson, *The Black and Tans: British Police and Auxiliaries in the Irish War of Independence, 1920–1921* (Oxford, 2011).

28 N. Collett, *The Butcher of Amritsar: General Reginald Dyer* (London, 2005), pp. 251–67.

Cameron wrote in the book of condolence: 'This was a deeply shameful event in British history, one that Winston Churchill rightly described at the time as "monstrous". We must never forget what happened here, and in remembering must ensure that the United Kingdom stands up for the right of peaceful protest around the world'. The last was a remark that spoke more to the 2010s, when Britain supports such protests, than to the 1910s. On both sides, there was a strong ahistoricism that failed to place the massacre, a terrible event in which there was a disproportionate use of force, in the context of the difficult situation in the Punjab in 1919.

British rule in the 1920s and 1930s confronted serious problems in a number of colonies. In part, this was an aspect of the way in which (throughout) empire was not a pacified or finished product, so that the imperial project and decolonisation were concurrent, or at least greatly overlapped. This was notably so if the focus is on effective, rather than formal, control. The strengthening of empire could also cause a reaction. Thus, the deployment of a large British garrison in Waziristan in the 1920s helped provoke a major rising there in 1936. In addition, the combination of opposition in the colonies and financial problems in Britain ensured that, despite improved communications and the availability of air power, colonies became harder to administer and difficult to provide sufficient resources for. For example, drawing on religious and political antipathy, the Saya San rebellion challenged the British position in Myanmar in 1930–32. Opposition to British rule was exacerbated by the effects of the economic depression, helping to create a rebellion in the Irrawaddy delta region. Religious identity and anger played a role. There was also considerable trouble along, and near, the Mediterranean axis of the empire. Greek Cypriot nationalists rioted in 1931, with British troops flown in from Egypt in response. In Malta, the British were opposed by the Nationalist Party, which looked for support to Fascist Italy under Mussolini as did other opponents of Britain, including in the Muslim world, for example Egypt and Iran, as well as some Indian nationalists.

Arab action in Palestine – a pogrom in 1929, a general strike in 1936, and a rebellion in 1937–39 – was largely directed against Jewish immigration. The rebellion was suppressed and did not have political consequences in Britain comparable with the question of the future of India. However, there was concern about the impact of growing Arab nationalism in Palestine and elsewhere. In 1938, the Chiefs of Staff warned of 'a danger that the infection of lawlessness may spread to neighbouring Mohammedan countries'.[29] In 1939, anxiety about

29 Chiefs of Staff, 'Appreciation of the Situation in the Event of War against Germany', 14 Sept. 1938, NA. CAB. 24/278, p. 346.

the developing international crisis led to the issue of a White Paper designed to defuse this Arab nationalism by rejecting the idea of partition for Palestine between Jews and Arabs. The use of force and of surveillance in Palestine indicated the extent to which policies of divide and rule, and of the co-option of élites, were not sufficient to ensure political control unless force was also available. To a varying extent, the same was true in other colonies.

The state of the empire in the inter-war years is an important subject, for it helps address the question of what might have happened to the empire bar for World War Two. The differing ability of local societies to cope with the pressures of change created difficulties for colonial governments and exacerbated contrasts between colonies. In addition, economic developments and tensions within the empire helped cause political problems. In India, as elsewhere, rent disputes provided a link between economic troubles and political division, while in Myanmar tension owed much to the consequences of the spread of rice production geared for the Indian market, as well as to the fiscal demands of the British state. The response in Myanmar in the 1920s included a tax boycott. The world Depression of the 1930s reduced investment for colonial development, limiting the resources available to provide jobs at all levels, while the decline in markets for colonial goods hit local financial systems, cutting off credit and investment. As a result, social tensions became more potent. Economic strains linked to the global Depression weakened political bonds, and the practices of consensus, by encouraging resistance to the tax demands and other fiscal measures of government. This resistance often took a violent form and, in turn, was countered by the use of force by government, including raids on villages. In Nigeria, there were rebellions against taxation as well as strikes and a marked rise in crime. In response, the government launched numerous tax raids.[30] In the Gold Coast (modern Ghana), there were agrarian disputes linked to cocoa production in 1930–31 and 1937–38. In Jamaica, where unemployment was high, labour tensions were in part related to activism by the League of Coloured Peoples.

In South Asia, the gravest difficulties did not arise from Waziristan on the North-West Frontier, where a major revolt, under the Faqir of Ipi, that broke out in 1936, met with a formidable and ultimately successful British military response. Instead, they were due to the growing strength of the non-violent Indian National Congress Party. Mahatma Gandhi's mobilisation of popular action in non-violent criticism of, and opposition to, British rule helped to turn

30 M.E. Ochonu, *Colonial Meltdown: Northern Nigeria in the Great Depression* (Athens, Ohio, 2009).

Congress into a mass movement. This was particularly so of his flouting of the tax on salt in 1930, with a 'salt march' to the sea to make untaxed salt. The habit of deference to British authority was seriously challenged.[31] Such activity led in Britain to uneasiness about the imperial position. However, visual confidence was expressed in the majestic buildings designed by Sir Edwin Lutyens and Sir Herbert Baker for the official quarter in New Delhi finished in the 1930s, notably the immense Viceroy's palace.

The British government sought a legislative response to pressure for change. The Government of India Act of 1935, although designed to ensure British retention of the substance of power, moved India towards self-government and eventual Dominion status. The principle of dyarchy established under the Montagu–Chelmsford Reforms of 1919 was extended to central government. Moreover, as an aspect of modernisation, the Act proposed the creation of an All-India Federation, entailing an incorporation of the hitherto-autonomous princely states, such as Hyderabad and Kashmir. However, opposition by most of the princes ensured that this measure was not implemented. A section of the Conservative Party, led by Churchill, out of office from 1929, bitterly opposed the 1935 Act, seeing the moves towards self-government as a crucial step towards the abandonment of empire. For Churchill, the new policy on India was more than a tactical step, and he offered an apocalyptic vision of its consequences, as well as a call for the maintenance of the existing system that appeared impractical and out of place to many. Churchill was not alone. The Indian Empire Society, under the presidency of John, Viscount Sumner (1859–1934), a key spokesman of the Conservative diehards, who had voiced unpopular views on Amritsar and the Irish settlement, campaigned vigorously against self-government.

However, Stanley Baldwin, the Conservative leader, was no friend of the diehards. Edward, Viscount Irwin (later Earl of Halifax), Viceroy of India from 1926 to 1931, described Churchill as an 'Imperialist in the 1890–1900 sense of the word', and that sense now appeared less relevant. Churchill was portrayed as a 'Victorian', this now being a term of abuse, even from people of a similar vintage to him.[32] The success of Baldwin's brand of 'moderate Conservatism' in Britain, notably in the 1935 general election, helped to explain the limited purchase and effect of the diehard defence of empire. The bitterness of the parliamentary rebellion against the 1935 Act was a testimony to the continued

31 J. Darwin, *Unfinished Empire: The Global Expansion of Britain* (London, 2012), p. 344.

32 K. Robbins, *Churchill* (Harlow, 1992), p. 108; R. Toye, *Churchill's Empire: The World That Made Him and the World He Made* (London, 2010).

pull of traditional notions of empire and the rebels' sense of danger, but also to their failure.[33] This episode underlines the centrality of domestic British politics for the peacetime course of empire.

In the event, the provincial elections of 1937 were a success for the Indian National Congress. This was contrary to the predictions of the Act's supporters, who had hoped to use provincial self-government in order to divide and rule India. Another sign of changing attitudes was provided by sensitivity to Indian opinion in the films shown there. In 1938, *The Relief of Lucknow*, a proposed film dealing with a iconic episode in the Indian Mutiny, one judged heroic by Victorians, was banned by the India Office, as were later moves to film stories from the Mutiny. Moreover, in 1939, the American film *Gunga Din* was prohibited following opposition to its showing by Indian newspapers. This episode led to the issue of guidelines by the India Office that banned films based on episodes in the history of British India, adaptations of the stories of Rudyard Kipling, such as *Gunga Din*, and films that presented Indians as villains.[34] Films continued to be sensitive. Students at Calcutta University gathered to set fire to the set, while chanting, 'Foreigners out!', when *The River*, based on Margaret Rumer Godden's bestselling novel, was being filmed in 1945–46.

However, the market for empire among the British public was seen with films such as *The Drum* (1938) and *The Four Feathers* (1939), the latter, based on A.E.W. Mason's novel of 1902, a presentation of imperial endeavour, in Sudan in the late nineteenth century, as a definition of manliness and heroism. The audience for imperial adventure films stood up well in the 1930s and 1940s. Examples included the American film *The Charge of the Light Brigade* (1936), much of which was set in India with a hostile portrayal of resistance to the British. Thereafter, interest in such films began to wane. Despite the popularity of *Zulu* (1964), which was based on the successful defence of Rorke's Drift against a large force of attacking Zulus in 1879, Hollywood had much less appetite for producing them by the 1960s. More recently, instead of these heroic attitudes, there is a pervasive anti-imperial liberalism that excludes earlier narratives of national glory, presenting them as anachronistic. The recent remake of *The Four Feathers* (2002) was critical. In contrast, *Elizabeth: The Golden Age* (2007) was unusual in endorsing a key element of the English national account, with opposition to the Spanish Armada of 1588 presented as affirming national

33 G. Peele, 'Revolt over India', in G. Peele and C.P. Cook (eds), *The Politics of Reappraisal, 1918–1939* (London, 1975), pp. 114–45; C. Bridge, *Holding India to the Empire: The British Conservative Party and the 1935 Constitution* (London, 1986).

34 P. Chowdhry, *Colonial India and the Making of Empire Cinema: Image, Ideology and Identity* (Manchester, 2000).

liberty and offered in an anti-Catholic fashion. This film was praised by Michael Gove, later Conservative Secretary of State for Education.

As part of a conviction of the importance of empire, there was a general sense among policymakers in the 1930s that it had to change. Reform of the government of India was, alongside Imperial Trade Preference and more equal relations with the Dominions, presented as the best means to strengthen the empire. It was to that end that Amery, an ardent imperialist, supported the Government of India Act in 1935, while Irwin backed eventual Dominion status for India. As with prayer book reform in the 1920s, the parliamentary time devoted to the government of India underlines what seemed important and controversial to contemporaries. Ignoring their values can ensure a failure to appreciate what was at stake. Moreover, the 1935 Act was to prove highly significant for the structure of post-independence India. This was not the sole type of interest in imperial development. Such development drew on a range of idealistic notions as well as on prudential considerations. At Blickling Hall, Philip Kerr, 11th Marquess of Lothian, held regular meetings of the Round Table Movement, an influential body of idealists established in 1909, that sought what they saw as a modern future for the empire based on greater unity and informed public support. There were also significant shifts in missionary rhetoric away from the ethnocentrism of the later nineteenth century and early twentieth century, as other strains of liberal theology and Christian universalism, based more upon feelings of racial equality and brotherhood, came to the fore. The International Missionary Council took up anti-racism as a cause. In addition, the creation after World War One, of mandates by the League of Nations, for the colonies allocated to the victors, had introduced the idea of an oversight of imperial rule from the outside. Although this oversight did not amount to much, it contributed to a stress on such rule as a trust, which indeed had Victorian antecedents.

Empire was certainly changing in the 1930s at its closest point. In Ireland, relations between the Free State, under Thomas Cosgrave, and Britain remained good until the Fianna Fáil Party under Eamonn de Valera, like Cosgrave a veteran of the Easter Rising of 1916, gained power after the 1932 election. He successfully pressed the British to recall the Governor-General, and the new one, nominated by de Valera, undertook no public duties. Moreover, the Executive Authority (External Relations) Act of 1936 limited the role of the Crown in the Free State to diplomatic formalities, and then only as advised by the Executive Council. In 1937, a new constitution, passed after a referendum, asserted the Irish State's territorial claim to Northern Ireland, while the oath of allegiance to the Crown that MPs had been obliged to take under the Anglo-Irish Treaty of 1921 was abolished. The constitution described the Irish State, now rechristened Eire (Ireland), as a 'sovereign, independent, democratic state', and stipulated that the head of state was to be a directly elected President. Moreover, Irish was to be the first language, an important symbolic declaration of cultural independence. However, Ireland remained in the Commonwealth and did not become a republic (under the Republic of Ireland Act passed in December 1948) until 1949. After coming to power, de Valera, in addition, set off an 'Economic War' with Britain by suspending the payment of land annuities from Irish farmers to the British government. A cycle of retaliation led to protectionism by both sides, hitting Irish agricultural exports to Britain, and the 'war' was ended by agreement in 1938. Also in 1938, Britain gave up its rights to use particular harbours in southern Ireland for naval purposes. This step was to hit Britain hard during the battle of the Atlantic with German submarines in World War Two.

Although far less serious, there were also indications of tension in colonies ruled by the Dominions. In 1929, protest in the Pacific island of Samoa arose due to the suppression of the Fono of Faipule, Samoa's democratic assembly. Organised by the Mau movement, this protest led to an armed police response in which the High Chief was killed, and to the deployment of New Zealand troops.

It is unclear what would have happened to the empire but for World War Two, which broke out in 1939. There were already serious problems, but it is worth remembering that the 1930s, as a frame of reference, was greatly affected by the global Depression. Similarly, it is unhelpful, when considering the development of the welfare state in the late 1940s, to judge the nature of health care and social welfare in the 1930s without making allowance for the important constraints stemming from the Depression. Towards empire in the 1930s, British policy was in a state of flux. Policy towards India was at a stage between the traditional co-option of local support and democratisation. The attitudes of the constituent parts of the empire were also in a state of flux. Moreover, Britain itself was changing, with both political culture and ideological drive altering before the inroads of World War Two were to cause a crisis of imperial survival.

As an instructive indication of new assumptions in both Britain and its empire, American influence in British life and culture, for example popular music, fiction, and film, was growing. Moreover, the sway of America was also increasing in parts of the empire, notably Canada, and in areas of British influence, especially South America. In July 1939, Lothian, en route to take up the embassy in Washington, spoke of 'the extent to which we in Britain have become Americanised, in the best sense of that word, in the last twenty-five years – not merely in the mechanisation of our private lives but in our social and democratic life'. Yet, America could also serve to support ideas associated with the empire, notably that of the Anglosphere. In the long run, the ideas and practices summed up by this concept weakened the empire by providing a means for America to replace Britain, notably by taking over its role in Australia, Canada, and New Zealand. However, the Anglosphere also helped recruit American sympathies to the cause of Britain. It developed institutionally in the early twentieth century. In 1903, the Rhodes scholarships had been established in accordance with Cecil Rhodes's will, which sought to foster 'the union of the English-Speaking peoples throughout the world'. From 1925 to 1939, Lothian was the Organising Secretary of the Rhodes Trust. In 1918, the English-Speaking Union was established, Churchill becoming President in 1921.[35] The idea enjoyed particular currency in the 1920s when there was a peak in the newspaper use of the term 'English-Speaking Peoples'.[36]

World War Two, 1939–1945

The record of the empire during World War Two throws some light on its state and potential in the late 1930s. In the event, despite the serious weaknesses that the war revealed, and the vulnerability of Britain in 1940 and of India in 1942, the empire successfully rallied to fight Germany, Italy, and Japan. In contrast, Irish neutrality was a powerful affirmation of independence from Britain and one that was much resented, not least because Britain was deprived of the use of ports that would have helped greatly in the struggle against German submarines. Some Burmese (Myanmar) and Indian nationalists fought for the Japanese. However, the absence of large-scale sustained opposition to British rule within the colonies ensured that military resources could be concentrated on war with the Axis powers. Moreover, the empire provided strategic depth. When, in the House of Commons on 4 June 1940, Churchill pledged to fight on, he added that, even if Britain was conquered, 'our Empire beyond the seas, armed and guarded by the British Fleet, would carry on the struggle'.[37] Plans were made to move George VI and the gold reserves to Canada. There was an echo of Gibbon's aside in his *Decline and Fall of the Roman Empire* when he considered the possibility of renewed 'barbarian' invasions bringing down European civilisation. Gibbon

35 P. Ziegler, *Legacy: Cecil Rhodes, the Rhodes Trust and Rhodes Scholarships* (New Haven, Connecticut, 2007).

36 P. Clarke, 'The English-Speaking Peoples before Churchill', *Britain and the World*, 4 (2011), p. 203.

37 R. Toye, *The Roar of the Lion: The Untold Story of Churchill's World War II Speeches* (Oxford, 2013).

thought this unlikely, but added that this civilisation had already been reborn on the other side of the Atlantic, by which he meant British North America.[38]

Over five million fighting troops were raised by the empire during the war, the largest number in India, while Britain's pre-war position at the centre of a vast global production system ensured that the empire provided an effective war production machine.[39] The empire's role was crucial before December 1941, when America entered the war and the Red (Soviet) Army stopped the German advance outside Moscow; and was also very important thereafter. The outbreak of war in 1939 was followed by the convoying of Australasian troops to Egypt, providing a vital fill-up to the British strategic reserve in the Middle East, one that was to be crucial to the defeat of Italy. In 1940, at a time of threatened German invasion of Britain, the presence of Canadian forces greatly strengthened the ability to repel attack, not least because the British Expeditionary Force had been badly battered in France and in the retreat from Dunkirk. By 1942, 500 Canadian warships were in commission. Canadian troops played a major part in European operations in 1944–45, and Canada, at the close of the conflict in 1945, had the world's third largest navy and the fourth largest air force. It also provided Britain with crucial financial support and on more generous terms than the USA. The entry of Italy (1940) and Japan (1941) into the war gave a far greater role to imperial forces. Indian and African forces proved crucial in the defeat of the Italians in East and North Africa, as well as in the conquest in 1941 of Iraq and Vichy-ruled Syria, which were seen as potential German supporters. Australian and New Zealand forces were also vital in the Middle Eastern conflicts. Indian and Australian forces were crucial in halting Japanese expansion and, subsequently, in driving the Japanese back.

To move into the area of moral judgements is tricky and frequently anachronistic. However, this is an area that public discussion engages with, and that academics therefore should consider. By modern standards, nineteenth-century imperialism lacked a clear moral base. In contrast, the empire demonstrated one in 1940–41 by giving Britain the ability and, in part, the will to fight on against Nazi Germany. This imperial role, however, has been underplayed in many subsequent attempts to provide a sense of common British history that could include immigrants from the Commonwealth. In part, this underplaying may be because much liberal opinion is unhappy about military values and references.

38 E. Gibbon, *The History of the Decline and Fall of the Roman Empire*, ed. J.B. Bury (7 vols, London, 1897–1901), IV, 166.

39 D. Edgerton, *Britain's War Machine* (London, 2012).

At the same time, the defence of empire created serious tensions between Britain and the Dominions. In particular, Britain and Australia differed considerably in 1941 and 1942 over competing military priorities, with the Australians seeking a greater emphasis on the challenge from Japan, whereas Churchill wanted Australian forces committed to the Middle East. Mackenzie King, the Canadian prime minister, was initially unenthusiastic about deploying forces in the Mediterranean, but the Canadians played a major role in the conquest/liberation of Italy from 1943.

The USA played a larger role than Britain in the war with Japan, not least because, after conquering Myanmar and sending a fleet into the Bay of Bengal in early April 1942, the Japanese did not press on against India. Instead, the Japanese focused on the South-West Pacific and then the Central Pacific, leading, in 1942, to the battles of the Coral Sea and Midway respectively. Had, instead, the Japanese invaded Sri Lanka in April 1942, as Field Marshal Alan Brooke, the Chief of the Imperial General Staff, feared, then the pressure on the British empire would have been much stronger. Instead, by occupying Iran (with the Soviet Union) and conquering Vichy-ruled Madagascar, both in 1942, the British greatly strengthened their position in the Indian Ocean, taking the empire there to its greatest extent. By late 1944, however, Britain was clearly a subordinate partner to the USA in the conflict as a whole, although the importance of British and empire forces to the land, sea, and air assault on Germany and German-occupied Europe that year, should not be underrated. The American role had significant implications for parts of the empire, notably for Australasia and the British colonies in the Pacific, as, throughout the war, there was a marked increase in the American military presence in both. This increase was a matter not only of bases and the presence of troops, warships, and plans, but also of defence-planning. Although there was tension, not least over the role of the USA in the South-West Pacific, the war ended with closer strategic relations between the USA and both Australia and Canada.

Moreover, economic as well as strategic links between the Dominions and Britain became less important. The development of industries in Canada and Australasia was linked to a longer-term decline in dependence on imports of British manufactures, while, more generally, their economies and societies changed. War also brought a fluidity in assumptions and relations, and a decline in deference, that affected attitudes towards imperial links, in the Dominions, the colonies, and in Britain itself. More seriously for Britain, the Roosevelt administration in America was opposed to colonial rule, and, instead, in favour of a system of 'trusteeship' as a prelude to independence. Roosevelt pressed Churchill on the status of both Hong Kong (which he wanted returned to China, then ruled by the Nationalists) and India. British officials were made well aware of a fundamental contradiction in attitudes. In 1943, at the Tehran Conference of Allied leaders, Roosevelt told Churchill that Britain had to adjust to a 'new period' in global history and to turn its back on '400 years of acquisitive blood in your veins'. Roosevelt did not propose that America provide independence to Puerto Rico, Alaska, or Hawaii; although the Philippines, in America's eyes an equivalent to India, had already become a self-governing Commonwealth and full independence from the USA was to follow after the war. In the longer term, ironically, some American commentators have regretted the destabilising consequences of helping undermine the British empire.

In India, there were major changes during the war. An upsurge in volunteering for the army was matched by a change in military policies to encourage both the recruitment of traditional 'non-martial' races and a degree of Indianisation of the officer corps. At the same time, the war witnessed an increase in pressure for independence. The British government offered the Hindu-dominated Congress Party a constituent assembly after the war with powers to draft a new constitution, with Congress being invited to join the central government in the meanwhile. Congress, however, sought a bigger role at once, including in the direction of India's war efforts, which Churchill was unwilling to grant.[40] From April 1942, at a time when Britain's position in Asia was under great challenge from the Japanese advance, Gandhi started to employ the slogan 'Quit India', and he swiftly pressed for a civil disobedience campaign to thwart the government. The crisis built up in August 1942. As Congress increased the pressure for the end of British rule, Gandhi and other leaders were arrested. In response, rioting, strikes, and sabotage spread, with many attacks on the railways. These affected the British ability to respond to the Japanese advance in Myanmar. Under the pressure of war, the government relied on force. Most of the police and civil administration remained passive. Instead, large numbers of troops were deployed in an attempt to restore order, and tens of thousands of Congress supporters were arrested, many for the remainder of the war, while the party was banned. The crisis ended swiftly, in part because much of the population was not involved, but Congress became more hostile to the continuation of British rule. The British realised that in case of a further dispute they could not rely wholesale on the police or administrators. Although the army was loyal, there were murmurings about a desire for independence once the war was won. Post-1947 Indian historiography underplays the genesis

40 R.J. Moore, *Churchill, Cripps and India* (Oxford, 1979).

of Indian nationalism in the Indian Army and overplays the non-violent culture of Congress.

India in 1942–45 was no repeat of the Thirteen Colonies in 1775–83: there was less dissidence and, after their loss of four aircraft carriers to American planes in the battle of Midway in June 1942, the Japanese could not play the role of the French. Congress did not collude with the Japanese, while those nationalists who did ally with them were a much smaller group. The Japanese-backed Provisional Government of Free India and Indian National Army formed by the Indian nationalist Subhas Chandra Bose had little impact. The subsequent attempt to praise Bose by a strand in Indian liberal nationalism[41] fails to engage adequately with the implications of his alignment with Japan and Germany, both of which were very different as empires to Britain. Bose's visit to Port Blair in the Andaman Islands in the Bay of Bengal, where nationalists had been imprisoned pre-war, was intended to make a point about the cruelty of British rule, but was made redundant by his failure to engage with the brutal, indeed murderous, character of the Japanese occupation of the Andamans. Bose was used by the Axis powers. Several of the anti-imperialist movements during the war were pro-Axis.

A terrible famine in Bengal in 1943 that owed much to grave shortages of shipping, to wartime inflation, and to the end of rice imports from Japanese-ruled Myanmar, was responsible, by 1946, for maybe three million deaths above expected levels. This appalling calamity led to criticism of the government, but not to political breakdown. However, since the war, the crisis has served as the basis for criticism of British rule, comparable to arguments about the Irish Famine of 1846–48. A context of racialist attitudes is emphasised rather than that of the practicalities of the period.[42] At the time, there was a degree of general foreboding about the future for British India, as the suppression of the 'Quit India' campaign had increased nationalist feeling. The Viceroy, Field Marshal Wavell, wrote in July 1944: 'On the whole, India is getting along reasonably well ... Once the Japanese war is over, our troubles out here really will begin'.[43]

Aside from active dissidence, war encouraged native politicisation in colonies, for example Sudan. Furthermore, the experience of military service

---

41 S. Bose, *His Majesty's Opponent: Subhas Chandra Bose and India's Struggle against Empire* (Cambridge, Massachusetts, 2011).

42 M. Mukerjee, *Churchill's Secret War: The British Empire and the Ravaging of India During World War II* (New York, 2010).

43 Wavell to Field Marshal Brooke, 4 July 1944, Kings College, London, Liddell Hart Library, Alanbrooke papers 6/4/12.

expanded horizons. More generally, participation in the war altered political, economic, and social relations within the empire including in Northern Ireland.[44] The likely long-term consequences were unclear. Meanwhile, empire provided politicians, in Britain, but also in the colonies, with an opportunity to hope and plan in accordance with their different assumptions. Thus, although they held views about the value of empire, Labour politicians assumed a progressive and democratic outcome for India, while Conservative counterparts, notably Churchill, were less willing to think through the implications of major change. These politicians were to compete for power anew in 1945 as the first general election since 1935 was held.

44 P. Ollerenshaw, *Northern Ireland in the Second World War: Politics, Economic Mobilisation and Society, 1939–45* (Manchester, 2013).

Chapter 6

From World War Two to the Present

> It is difficult to tie ourselves up with Europe and consolidate the Empire at the same time.
>
> Memorandum for the Prime Minister, Ramsay MacDonald, by the Chief of the Imperial General Staff, October 1932[1]

The Late 1940s

The British empire was largely to disappear within two decades of the end of the war in 1945, one of the most significant shifts of authority in global history, as well as an important aspect of the more general decline of Europe's place in the world. The other Western European empires were also to disappear within three decades of the end of the war. The extent to which this outcome was likely was unclear to those who lived through the process, as, separately, is agreement over the cause of it. For example, alongside the familiar argument that Japanese success fatally undermined the British empire in Asia (as well as the Dutch and French empires there), and crucially destroyed the prestige on which imperial rule rested, it is necessary to focus on the overall political and resource consequences and costs of the two world wars.

If the latter approach is adopted, then Britain's post-war decision to abandon its colonial presence in South Asia can be seen as stemming in part from conflict within the European system, rather than as simply a response to the war with Japan or to growing indigenous pressure on Britain to 'quit India'. Shrewd observers at the end of World War Two saw the weaknesses of empire, especially as Britain was financially exhausted. The dependence upon wartime loans, mostly from the USA, made Britain the world's greatest debtor nation in 1945; while a quarter of the national wealth had been lost during the war. 'The Present Overseas Financial Position of the United Kingdom', a Treasury memorandum by John Maynard Keynes, discussed by the new Labour government on 23 August 1945, warned:

> We have not a hope of escaping what might be described, without exaggeration and without implying that we should not eventually recover from it, as a financial

1 NA. CAB. 24/234 fol. 165.

> Dunkirk. Abroad it would require a sudden and humiliating withdrawal from our onerous responsibilities with great loss of prestige and an acceptance for the time being of the position of a second-class power ... At home a greater degree of austerity would be necessary than we have experienced at any time during the war.

Yet, such a result seemed far from obvious, for, just as World War One had ended with the expansion of the British empire, so it appeared likely that World War Two would be followed by the same. At the very least, it seemed likely that most of the British empire would be retained. During the war, moreover, the French feared British designs on their empire, the USA was concerned that British military planning was overly directed to imperial goals, and the British occupied Italian Somaliland and Libya, also an Italian colony, both of which were regarded as important for protecting the route to India. Churchill, indeed, considered the annexation of both territories, and there were hopes that it would be able to maintain wartime gains under the equivalent of League of Nations mandates. Italian Somaliland remained under British administration until 1950, enjoying a stability that contrasts markedly with the situation in Somalia today, while Britain gained control over most of Libya, which, again, was more stable and better governed than in recent years. Had the Germans had overseas colonies, they would doubtless have met with a similar fate. As it was, alongside the USA, the Soviet Union, and France, Britain was one of the four occupying powers in Germany and Austria. There were also hopes of a recovery of imperial military greatness, as the surrender of Japan was followed by the reimposition of control in Japanese-occupied areas, including Malaya, Singapore, and Hong Kong. British power ensured that the British played a major role in the reintroduction of Dutch and French colonial power into the Dutch East Indies and Vietnam respectively.[2] However, the former commitment, which lasted until November 1946, led to British conflict with Indonesian nationalists, a conflict that resulted in casualties among civilians. There were plans for the extension of British power in South Asia, with a protectorate from Nepal to Bhutan and an extension of influence in Tibet and even into Xinjiang.[3]

In April 1944, the Admiralty had discussed plans for a big heavy cruiser; plans for new battleships and carriers following in May. In 1946, Admiral Willis,

---

2 M.A. Lawrence, *Assuming the Burden: Europe and the American Commitment to War in Vietnam* (Berkeley, California, 2005), pp. 104–5.

3 P.J. Brobst, *The Future of the Great Game: Sir Olaf Caroe, India's Independence, and the Defense of Asia* (Akron, Ohio, 2005).

Commander-in-Chief Mediterranean, could write about his optimism for a long-term, albeit smaller-scale, presence in Egypt.

Britain was also active elsewhere. In late 1944, troops were sent to Greece to prevent a Communist takeover after the German withdrawal. Moreover, British support of the royalist government continued after the war in the Greek Civil War, which was really the first episode of the post-war Cold War. Less centrally, British policy in Antarctica and the South Atlantic also indicated a continued desire to act as an imperial power. The creation of the Falkland Islands Dependencies Survey in 1945 signalled a determination to use scientists to consolidate British influence. Moreover, the mapping of the Antarctic peninsula and nearby areas carried out by the Survey was designed to underline Britain's title to the area, not least because British maps omitted names found on Argentine and Chilean maps of the Antarctic peninsula. In 1948, the cruiser HMS *Nigeria* was dispatched to Antarctic waters in order to support British claims, which were also validated in the public mind by the release of the film *Scott of the Antarctic*.[4] In 1946, the Colonial Office established the Directorate of Colonial (later Overseas) Survey, and instructed it to map 900,000 square miles of Africa within ten years, using aerial photography as well as ground surveys.

However, the dominant role in the victorious coalition had been taken by the USA and Soviet Union, both of which, albeit from different perspectives, had anti-colonial ideologies, were hostile to the British empire, and saw no reason to view its expansion with any favour.[5] Furthermore, in complete contrast to 1919–21, the Americans were not to withdraw from helping direct the new world order, while the Soviet advance was not to be restrained by Poland and, with British assistance, in the Baltic States. Under American pressure, the Atlantic Charter, issued by Churchill and Roosevelt in the Placentia Bay Conference in August 1941, had declared 'the right of all people to choose the form of government under which they will live', and the United Nations (UN), which was founded in 1945, was to show favour for the notion of national self-determination. For example, in 1946, the UN renewed the authority New Zealand had wielded in Western Samoa under a League of Nations mandate, after New Zealand agreed on eventual independence for the territory. Indeed, Western Samoa became independent in 1962 after a plebiscite sponsored by

4 K. Dodds, *Pink Ice: Britain and the South Atlantic Empire* (London, 2002).

5 R.B. Woods, *A Changing of the Guard: Anglo-American Relations, 1941–1946* (Chapel Hill, North Carolina, 1990); A. Husein, *Mapping the End of Empire: American and British Strategic Visions in the Postwar World* (Cambridge, Mass., 2014).

the UN. Not only imperial expansion, but even empire, itself, now seemed anachronistic; at least when practised overseas in a conventional territorial fashion by Western European powers, as opposed to more indirectly by the USA in the New World and by the Soviet Union in Eastern Europe.

The British empire was also challenged by internationalism from a different direction. The new international economic order was American-directed and a challenge to the protectionism of the sterling bloc, and deliberately so. The Bretton Woods Conference, held in the USA in 1944, produced plans for post-war co-operation that led to the foundation of the International Monetary Fund and the International Bank for Reconstruction and Development (World Bank), both of which had American headquarters. Free trade was also actively supported as part of an American-directed liberal economic order. The General Agreement on Tariffs and Trade (GATT), signed in 1947, began a major cut in tariffs that slowly established or established anew a measure of free trade. More specifically, under the loan agreement of December 1945, the British government received from the Americans a credit of $3.75 billion for five years at 2 per cent interest, but, within a year of ratification, the pound had to be made convertible into the dollar, all exchange restrictions removed, and the system of imperial preference ended. The Americans also hit at the protectionism of the British imperial aviation system. British hegemony therefore had to adjust to American power,[6] although the mutual dependence of the two powers included the degree to which the British world system required American acceptance.[7]

Despite these challenges, there was an attempt to protect, if not revive, the British empire. This attempt is significant, not least because, while the age of imperial greatness in the nineteenth century has, even indirectly, faded from memory, impressions of empire in this post-war period continue to play a role for people who are alive today. Furthermore, the post-1945 period provides an instructive context within which to consider recent American activity. Empire was regarded in the late 1940s as a vital economic sphere and resource. Oil was increasingly valuable to the British economy, the discriminatory tariffs of imperial preference were crucial to trade, colonial exports earned the dollars Britain required to fund imports, and imperial financial links helped maintain sterling. Ernest Bevin, the influential Foreign Secretary in the Labour government from 1945 until 1951, and a figure from a time when Labour displayed a robust

---

6 P. Hugill, 'The American Challenge to British Hegemony, 1861–1946', *Geographical Review*, 99 (2009), pp. 403–25.

7 J. Darwin, *The Empire Project: The Rise and Fall of the British World-System, 1830–1970* (Cambridge, 2009).

nationalist patriotism and commitment to empire, was determined to preserve military strength in the Middle East, and hoped to use imperial resources to make Britain a less unequal partner in the alliance with America. Continued imperial strength was regarded as necessary to Britain's world status, indeed strategic and economic security. Imperial assumptions were strongly held among the ministers of the Labour government when it took power in 1945. These assumptions and hopes led to a determination to increase imperial productivity and, accordingly, to a variety of projects and plans. Modernisation was a key theme, with development used to strengthen the credibility of colonial policy.[8] There was an attempt to develop the economy of Tanganyika (now mainland Tanzania) with an ambitious, and ultimately unsuccessful, Groundnuts Scheme. This attempt was designed to increase the supply of vegetable oils and fats within the sterling area, in order to cut imports from non-sterling countries, and thus to help maintain the level of the currency. Similar hopes were built on African mineral resources, for example the copper of Northern Rhodesia (Zambia). These were prime examples of the second colonial 'occupation' of Africa, that moment in the post-war British imperial revival when Africa was perceived as a possible surrogate for India.[9] These hopes and a sense of imperial separateness encouraged the belief that Britain did not need to join schemes for economic co-operation in Western Europe.

There was also an ethical dimension to the furtherance of empire. Support for Indian independence played an important role in Labour Party circles.[10] More generally, there was a conviction, which drew on aspects of the liberal tradition, not least the nonconformist belief that there was a duty of care to protect the less fortunate, that imperial rule could serve the interests of the colonial peoples. Most were not regarded as equally developed and ready for independence as the Indians. There was an assumption that imperial rule was a trusteeship, a preparation for independence, but also that the Africans would not be ready for independence for a long time. Reliance on 'native authorities' in Africa meant encouraging a tribalism that did not seem to place a demand for new political outcomes. Britain's mission was presented as fulfilling its imperial potential, but in a mutually beneficial fashion, not one based on conquest and

8 S. Clarke, 'A Technocratic Imperial State? The Colonial Office and Scientific Research, 1940–1960', *Twentieth-Century British History*, 18 (2007), pp. 453–80.

9 D.A. Low and J. Lonsdale, 'Towards the New Order', in Low and A. Smith (eds), *History of East Africa* III (Oxford, 1976), pp. 1–63.

10 N. Owen, *The British Left and India: Metropolitan Anti-Imperialism 1885–1947* (Oxford, 2007).

exploitation. Eventual independence was defined in terms of the establishment of a Westminster parliamentary democracy.

In part, decolonisation involved the pursuit of empire by other means. National self-determination was certainly not regarded by the British as the antithesis of empire. By first enjoying 'self-government', locals might run the show on behalf of the British, and run it more cheaply than the British could. Eventually, 'national self-determination' would 'save' former dependencies for the 'new Commonwealth'. This, in turn, might provide Britain with a platform to act as a 'third force' internationally; in short as a major power beside the USA and Soviet Union. Thus, the local collaborators who might operate 'self-government' were to be important for transforming empire, as well as for running it.

In India, the most populous and important part of the empire, World War Two had challenged and, to a degree, undermined British rule. Post-war political volatility in India made it impossible to provide a level of stability sufficient to serve as the basis for a restoration of the processes of accommodation that ensured widespread consent. The rise of the Congress Party challenged the British position, not least by hitting the effectiveness, business, and morale of government, while the increased sectarianism of Indian politics, especially with the rise of the Muslim League, made imperial crisis management, let alone control, impossible. To the Muslims, in turn, the cause of Indian independence was compromised by Hindu sectarianism, and they called for partition. As communal rivalries, principally, but not only, between Muslims and Hindus, became worse, British control ebbed, not least with disaffection among sections of the military, although the highly professional Indian Army held up well, which prevented an even more serious collapse.[11] There was concern that any rebellion by Congress could not be defeated. In response to the Muslim League's Direct Action Day of 16 August 1946, Field Marshal Wavell, the Viceroy, pressed for a show of consistency in the shape of a commitment to 10 more years of rule, or the fixing of a date for withdrawal. His replacement, Lord Louis Mountbatten, concurred. Civil war appeared a prospect.

The timing of independence owed much not to events in India but to the situation in Britain, namely that Labour, under Clement Attlee, was in power from 1945 to 1951, not the Conservatives under Churchill, who had so bitterly opposed moves towards independence. Churchill, however, might not have been so obstructive had he won the election in 1945. He was emotional about

11 D. Marston, *The Indian Army and the End of the Raj* (Cambridge, 2014), pp. 350–51.

India; but, apart from huffing and puffing in 1947, he did not oppose Attlee, while many pragmatists, and even some of the 'old guard', in the Conservative party accepted the inevitability of Indian independence. Attlee was convinced that public opinion in Britain would oppose large-scale military action to maintain control in India. Attlee agreed, in early 1947, that the British would transfer power in June 1948. The British hope for a quasi-federation of Muslim and Hindu India fell victim to an inability to reach compromise. Congress was opposed to partition, but the Muslim League was insistent. This led Mountbatten to an agreement to partition, prefiguring the policy that was to be pursued in Palestine. In turn, the decision to bring forward withdrawal from India to August 1947 made it harder to contain communal violence.

The end of empire in South Asia was marked by large-scale violence, with the flight of over 12 million people to avoid fear of massacre. Over one million were killed.[12] The fate of the princely states left a lasting dispute between India and Pakistan over Kashmir. It is too easy to blame deep sectarian divides and their consequences on British rule, as Jack Straw, the Foreign Secretary in 2003, and others were to do, explicitly or implicitly. The history of sectarian division in South Asia was much longer and, in some respects, British rule represented an interlude of lesser conflict and tension, an interlude that lasted until the end of empire appeared imminent.

There had been much speculation about independence for India strengthening Britain's position, including talk of India being given independence only if it agreed to help in the defence of other imperial possessions, specifically Aden, Burma (Myanmar), and Malaya (continental Malaysia). There was also an expectation that an independent India would accept a continued presence by British forces, or at least co-operate closely in military matters. However, such hopes proved misplaced. Congress was resentful of the way in which partition had occurred. Unlike Britain, India was to be neutral in the Korean War (1950–53). Indeed, Indian independence greatly affected British military options. India was important to the security of British trade routes, especially to the Gulf and the Strait of Malacca en route to the Far East, but, more significantly, Indian troops were central to Britain's expeditionary capacity around the Indian Ocean and in the Middle East. The loss of those troops removed an important mainstay of the military dimension of the empire. Whereas, in 1941, Indian forces had played a major role in the successful invasion of Iraq, a decade later, when Britain was in dispute with the nationalist government in Iran over its nationalisation of British oil interests, Plan Y, the plan for a military intervention by the seizure of

12 Y. Khan, *The Great Partition: The Making of India and Pakistan* (London, 2007).

Abadan, was not pursued, in large part because the troops were not available. In 1952, the British Army had 450,000 men, but, the previous year, with British forces committed in Germany and Korea, Plan Y no longer seemed militarily viable. As a reminder, however, of the range of factors that has to be borne in mind, political pressures also played a role, as both the USA and Arab states warned Britain against invasion. In 1956, India did not support Britain during the Suez Crisis. Jawaharlal Nehru, the prime minister, strongly opposed British policy, as did much of the Commonwealth with the exception of Australia and New Zealand. Nor did India back Britain in the conflicts of the last stage of empire, such as the Malayan Emergency. The lack of such support helped oblige Britain to continue conscription, whereas it had not been retained after World War One. In addition, it became less practical for Britain to think of defending colonies when faced by sustained large-scale opposition, although considerable success was achieved in doing so in the 1950s.

Independence was also granted to Burma (Myanmar) and Ceylon (Sri Lanka) in 1948, as, with India gone, it seemed pointless to hold on to either. In Burma, the result was a rapid descent into political instability, regional separatism, military rule, and poor relations with Britain. In Ceylon, over the longer term, it proved difficult to prevent the deterioration of Tamil–Sinhalese relations into large-scale sectarian violence that continued until 2009. Palestine proved a more serious problem for Britain than Burma and Ceylon. The British managed neither to contain, let alone suppress, sectarian violence between Arabs and Jews, nor to negotiate a peaceful end to the mandate. Instead, the British presence was brought to an end in 1948, with the government keen to get an embarrassing problem off their hands. Pressure from the pro-Zionist American government was a complicating factor. Britain was to receive much criticism, from all sides, for its failure in Palestine, and was to be accused of both anti-Semitism and hostility to the Arabs. However, the subsequent problems of maintaining the peace there again suggest that more attention needs to be devoted to the serious difficulties that Britain had faced. Neighbouring Jordan became formally independent in 1946.

At a more modest level, there was also a withdrawal from areas where imperial expansion had been considered. This was the case in the Horn of Africa where Italian control was not continued. In 1948, the Ogaden was transferred from British to Ethiopian control (the Haud followed in 1954), and in 1949 it was agreed that Italian Somaliland should be restored to Italian trusteeship. Also in 1948, vestigial British authority in Eire was ended by the Republic of Ireland Act, which took Eire out of the Commonwealth. Proposing the legislation in the *Dáil* (Irish parliament), John Costello, the prime minister, claimed it would 'end forever, in a simple, clear and unequivocal way, this country's long and tragic association with the institutions of the British Crown'. In 1949, Eire became a republic, although one whose citizens had residence, and even voting rights, in the United Kingdom.

The empire, therefore, was much less extensive by the end of 1949, than it had been in 1945, in territorial terms, population, and with regard to the number of troops under arms. There had also been a major collapse of the 'informal empire' in the 1940s. In Latin America, Britain's economic and political influence had lessened as the USA became more powerful, while the war led to the slackening of economic links with Britain, which encouraged a measure of industrialisation and import-substitution in Latin America. In China, the British position had been wrecked by the Sino-Japanese war that had begun in 1937 and by the Japanese destruction of the treaty port system. Thereafter, Communist triumph in the Chinese Civil War (1946–49) cemented the rejection of Western influence. In Egypt, the assertive wartime British role increased hostility to Britain.

Unlike after the loss of America in 1783, there was no process of imperial recovery. Instead, the weakness of Britain as an imperial power was readily apparent. Whereas, under William Pitt the Younger, the finances and economy of the country had rapidly improved from 1784, helping Britain sustain her military and international position, Labour, under Attlee, in far more difficult circumstances, was unable, despite bold hopes, to match this. The war had exhausted British public finances and had seriously damaged the British economy, and, despite a major growth in exports in the late 1940s, this situation left Britain in a weaker position to sustain imperial commitments. Moreover, the wartime sale of overseas investments ensured that it would not be possible to use 'invisible exports', notably interest payments, in order to finance the serious trade deficit. In addition to these sales, much of the heavy cost of the war had been financed on credit, which left a heavy debt bill. Unlike after 1815, there was to be no period of maritime dominance, imperial hegemony, and an absence of expensive foreign challenge, that, together, would help ensure renewed fiscal stability. Instead, after 1945, there were a series of imperial crises and a confrontation with the Soviet Union, both of which posed serious financial burdens.

The extent to which Labour's expensive commitments to social welfare seriously, if not fatally, exacerbated the situation is controversial, but it was at least a serious complicating factor. Looked at differently, the alliance between labour and capital seen across Western Europe was an important aspect of resisting Communism in the Cold War, but it weakened the European empires in other respects. The fiscal situation was made worse by the conditions attached to the American loan given to assist Britain when wartime Lend-Lease help ended in 1945: the convertibility of the pound into the dollar caused pressure on the reserves of the Bank of England. The sterling crises of 1947, when the currency's convertibility was hit hard, and 1949, when there was a devaluation of 30 per cent, underlined British weakness, and also the need for the economic and financial support of the empire.

Owing to these problems, the British had little to offer those whose co-operation they sought, for example in the Middle East. Instead, it was felt necessary to seek American assistance in resisting Communist pressure in Greece and Turkey (1947), and in South-East Asia (1949). Pushed onto the defensive, the British were not in a good position to reassert themselves in areas of earlier imperial influence. The foundation of NATO in 1949 was similarly a response to the need to rely on the USA in the face of Britain's concern to resist Soviet expansionism in the absence of effective Western European assistance. The American willingness to act was also important to Britain's new role in Europe. This role was part of a larger American and British commitment to opposing Communist expansionism. Empire appeared less relevant when the Cold War was focused on Europe in the late 1940s. The Cold War, however, led to a change in American attitudes, away from hostility to the continuation of the empire and towards support for its maintenance, at least in the short term, as a way to prevent Communist expansionism outside Europe.

Still Great: 1950–1956

When Churchill regained power at the head of a Conservative government in 1951, he had no intention of further dismantling the empire. Indeed, the Conservatives had fought the 1950 election to 'make Britain great again'. In October 1952, Britain became a nuclear power, the third after the USA and the Soviet Union, a policy initiated by Labour in January 1947 and pursued at great cost. The decision to develop and manufacture the hydrogen bomb followed in June 1954. More generally, there was a sense of power and opportunity. The accession, in 1952, and coronation, in 1953, of Queen Elizabeth II led to much talk of a 'New Elizabethan Age', a reference back to Elizabeth I. This was celebrated with a Coronation Review of the fleet, while the ascent of hitherto-unclimbed Mount Everest in 1953 by an imperial team contributed to their excitement.

Although global commitments were reduced in some areas in the early 1950s, elsewhere they were maintained, and even expanded, in order to demonstrate that Britain was not weak, to protect British interests, and to enhance military capability in the event of war with the Soviet Union. These commitments, however, put serious pressure on Britain's ability to maintain force levels in Europe; a goal that, in turn, challenged Britain's role as a military power outside Europe. Similarly, France's unsuccessful attempt to resist a Communist nationalist uprising in Vietnam had implications for France's role in Europe, as did the subsequent unsuccessful attempt to hold onto Algeria. Moreover, Britain's military role outside Europe increased the rift with India and with colonial nationalist politicians who linked in the Non-Aligned Movement declared at the Bandung Conference in 1955. This rift made any post-imperial defence agreement implausible.

From 1948, a major and eventually successful military effort was made by Britain and the empire to resist a Communist insurrection in the economically crucial colony of Malaya, which, it was hoped, would serve as the basis for a Dominion of South-East Asia that would include Sarawak, Singapore, and North Borneo. The British also ensured a positive political context by not allowing what was termed the Emergency to deter them from moving Malaya towards independence in 1957, a process that helped ensure that most of the Malayan public supported Britain. British assertiveness also included, in late 1952, RAF overflights of Buraimi oasis, an oil-rich part of the Arabian peninsula, then in dispute between British-backed Sultan Said bin Taimur of Oman and Saudi Arabia, which looked to American support. In Antarctica, the Churchill government funded expeditions to consolidate territorial claims, and thus to rebut rival claims notably by Argentina. No more colonies were granted independence under the Churchill ministry (1951–55), and change was 'kept within bounds'. However, copious preparations were laid for self-government during these years. Moreover, in 1954, the government abandoned its military commitment over Buraimi, while, that year, against the wishes of some Conservative politicians, British troops were withdrawn from the Suez Canal Zone, after fighting two years earlier had indicated the cost of staying on. Also in 1954, Britain had to accept the end of its oil interests in Iran. Nevertheless, further east, Britain underlined its willingness to take an active role in collective defence when it became a founder member, with the USA, Australia, New Zealand, Pakistan, France, Thailand, and the Philippines, of the Southeast Asia Treaty Organization (SEATO). While the Americans sought to manage European decolonisation as a means of thwarting Communism and increasing their informal control, the British government, notably Anthony Eden as Foreign Secretary from 1951 to 1955, hoped they could safeguard their interests in the Middle East and South East Asia, and get the Americans to bear much of the cost.

Naval bases remained a key part of the articulation of imperial influence and power. Their fate was therefore of consequence. In 1955, Britain agreed to transfer the Simon's Town naval base from British to South African control. This was a measure that Churchill had strongly opposed, not least because the Cape route to the Indian Ocean was seen as the alternative to the Suez route, and thus as strategically significant. Under the agreement, Britain retained important naval advantages, including South African consent to make the base available to Britain in war, even if South Africa itself was neutral, as well as South African responsibility for the maintenance of the base, orders for warships from British yards, and acceptance of British views on the development of the South African navy. Significantly, the British had earlier hoped to win a South African commitment to the defence of the Middle East, a commitment that would help replace the loss of Indian backing. However, no such commitment played a role in the agreement.[13]

The assertive British policy in the Middle East, directed against the Soviets and the challenge from Arab nationalism, and intended to impress the Americans, led to the creation of the British-backed Baghdad Pact in 1955, which, by the end of the year, linked Britain, Iran, Iraq, Pakistan, and Turkey. This policy also led to plans for intelligence operations designed to overthrow the governments of Egypt, Syria, and Saudi Arabia, plans that culminated with the unsuccessful Suez invasion of 1956 directed against Egypt.[14] This was a particularly dramatic instance of Britain's failure to address the hopes of nationalist politicians.

In sub-Saharan Africa, the most important confrontation occurred in Kenya, where the British harshly suppressed the Mau Mau uprising in 1952–57. In this 'success', a success that involved much civilian hardship, the British benefited from a wide-ranging social-reform policy. This included land reform, in which the government distanced itself from the white colonists whose acquisition of land created much unrest both in Kenya and in other parts of Africa, for example Nyasaland (Malawi). The British also benefited from the assistance of loyal Africans, including former insurgents. The latter element was subsequently downplayed in Kenyan accounts of the uprising. Yet, it proved significant, both as an aspect of winning hearts and minds and in providing troops. Alongside British regular army units and the white settler Kenya Regiment, there were loyal Africans: the King's African Rifles, Kenya

13 R. Hyam and P. Henshaw, *The Lion and the Springbok: Britain and South Africa since the Boer War* (Cambridge, 2003), pp. 236–49.

14 D.R. Devereux, *The Formulation of British Defence Policy towards the Middle East, 1948–56* (1990); P. Darby, *British Defence Policy East of Suez 1947–1968* (Oxford, 1973).

Police, Kikuyu Home Guards, and former insurgents. From 1955, success led to the withdrawal of troops and in 1956 the police took over responsibility for operations.[15] The harshness of British attempts to separate the guerrillas from popular support, including the detention of possibly over 160,000 Kikuyu, as well as widespread brutality, notably the use of torture, has led to criticism at the crossover between public and academic history and legal action that has received much attention.[16] At the time, the abuses resulted in criticism by colonial officials and army officers, as well as parliamentary debate and public outrage. To others, the policies appeared an appropriate response to a murderous insurrection. Recent references to 'Britain's *gulag*' reflect a lack of nuance and of comparative awareness, notably of the terrible death rate and long prison sentences in the Soviet *gulags*. Moreover, the British use of torture, while disgusting, was less than that of the French in tackling insurrection in Algeria. The integral role of repression and corrupt patronage in the subsequent politics of independent Kenya are also of note.[17]

Force was also applied in Cyprus from 1955, in response to communal tensions between Greek and Turkish communities, and the development among the former of the EOKA Greek Cypriot terrorist movement, which sought union with Greece. The new governor, Field-Marshal Sir John Harding (who had replaced a civilian), saw the situation in large part in a military light. This response appears anachronistic from the perspective of the imminent decolonisation of Cyprus, but did not seem so to many in the 1950s when Cyprus offered a military base to compensate for the loss of that in Egypt. Indeed, there was a parallel between policies then and those in the inter-war period.

British security policies, however, were increasingly set without reference to empire. Canada was a founder member of the North Atlantic Treaty Organization (NATO) established in 1949, but it was a security framework for Western Europe, not one focused on the empire. Moreover, although both Britain and Canada wanted NATO to have a North Atlantic identity, this goal was undermined by successive enlargements: Greece and Turkey in 1952, and

---

15 D. Branch, *Defeating Mau Mau, Creating Kenya: Counterinsurgency, Civil War, and Decolonization* (Cambridge, 2009); H. Bennett, *Fighting the Mau Mau: The British Army and Counter-Insurgency in the Kenya Emergency* (Cambridge, 2013).

16 C. Elkins, *Imperial Reckoning: The Untold Story of Britain's Gulag in Kenya* (London, 2005); D. Anderson, *Histories of the Hanged: The Dirty War in Kenya and the End of Empire* (London, 2005); B. Grob-Fitzgibbon, *Imperial Endgame: Britain's Dirty Wars and the End of Empire* (Basingstoke, 2011), p. 4.

17 D. Branch, *Kenya: Between Hope and Despair, 1963–2011* (New Haven, Connecticut, 2011).

West Germany in 1955.[18] As a more obvious sign of Britain's lesser role and prestige for the Dominions, in 1951, Australia and New Zealand, concerned about possible challenges from China, Indonesia, and Japan, independently entered into a defence pact with the USA: ANZUS. In the event, the USA was unwilling to heed the views of Australia and New Zealand. The USA wanted the alliance to be part of a range of security agreements, not a partnership, and this attitude helped to maintain Australian and New Zealand interest in continued good relations with Britain. The fate of these allies indeed prefigured problems Britain was to encounter with the USA. Meanwhile, South Africa unsuccessfully sought to supplement its naval links with Britain by others with Western powers. The military basis of the empire during the world wars was unravelling.

The Americans were unwilling to let Britain join ANZUS because, in 1950, the British government had recognised the newly established Communist government of China, beginning a pattern of difference with the USA over policy towards China that, in part, reflected clashing conceptions of the role of ideology and the nature of pragmatism in international politics.[19] This was not the limit of differences between the two powers, for the British wish to preserve the empire, still seen by both the Labour and Conservative leaderships as the basis for Britain's international and economic position, contrasted with American interest in a new world order of capitalist democracies, an order that challenged imperial rule as much as Communism. For example, the CIA-supported 'Asia Foundation' produced anti-imperialist propaganda in Singapore on the model of the anti-Soviet 'Radio Free Europe'.

While British governments saw the empire as a way to demonstrate to the USA the value of the 'special relationship' between Britain and the USA as a global asset, the Americans both encouraged what they saw as orderly decolonisation and sought to manage the decolonisation as a means of thwarting Communism and increasing informal American control.[20] Thus, former colonies received American military assistance, as Pakistan did from 1953. Indeed, Pakistan was to become a military ally of the USA and/or China, with Britain no longer having a role. There were also different views between Britain and the USA on the liberalisation of trade and air routes, while the USA had taken an unwelcome position on Palestine, and had helped to weaken Britain's position in Iran.

---

18 M. Smith, *NATO Enlargement during the Cold War: Strategy and System in the Western Alliance* (Basingstoke, 2000).

19 V.S. Kaufman, *Confronting Communism: US and British Policies toward China* (Columbia, Missouri, 2001).

20 C. Fraser, 'The "New Frontier" of Empire in the Caribbean: The Transfer of Power in British Guiana, 1961–1964', *International History Review*, 22 (2000), pp. 583–610.

Nevertheless, the two powers were united in opposition to Communism, especially in the establishment of NATO. Moreover, in 1950, the British contributed the second-largest foreign contingent (after the Americans) to the American-led United Nations Army that resisted the Communist North Korean invasion of South Korea, a departure from pre-war imperial geopolitics for Britain and one that was expensive.[21] This was a commitment and conflict that was not to lead to any expansion of the empire. Instead, Britain as a military power became in large part a servant of wider interests. In turn, this stance weakened the practical and emotional weight of imperial commitments and the relevance of the empire.

The high cost of the military build-up of these years lessened the resources available both for economic development and for social welfare, contributing to a crisis in public finances in the early 1950s. This crisis provided another instance of the tensions between welfarism, military expenditure, and financial/taxation considerations also seen with the Liberal government of the late 1900s and early 1910s during the naval race with Germany. Furthermore, Britain lacked the resources to sustain the Colonial Office policies outlined in the successive Colonial Development and Welfare Acts of 1940, 1945, 1949, 1950, and 1959, and government action was able to provide only a portion of the investment necessary for colonial economic development. In 1956, Harold Macmillan, then Chancellor of the Exchequer, revealed anxiety about the cost of colonial aid; while other ministries opposed colonial industrialisation as a threat to British economic interests.

Suez and After, 1956–1964

Britain still saw itself as a major imperial power. In 1956, however, under Churchill's lacklustre Conservative successor, Anthony Eden, the weakness of the imperial response and the limited domestic popularity of empire were exposed in the Suez Crisis. Britain and France attacked Egypt, an intervention publicly justified at the time as a way of safeguarding the Suez Canal, which had been nationalised by the aggressive Egyptian leader Gamal Abdel Nasser in defiance of the 1954 agreement between Britain and Egypt under which Britain had withdrawn its garrison from the Suez Canal Zone. Nasser was regarded as a threat to British and French imperial interests, to the conservative Arab ruling houses allied to Britain, notably in Jordan, to the British imperial position in

21 A. Farrar-Hockley, *The British Part in the Korean War* (London, 1990).

Aden, and to the French position in Algeria. Eden was determined to protect Britain's position in the Middle East in order to provide a basis for continued imperial strength.

The invasion was poorly planned, but was a major display of British military power. It was not abandoned because of failure on the ground, although it was unclear how the invaders were going to consolidate any success. Instead, the invasion was abandoned in large part because of American opposition. Concerned about the impact of the invasion on attitudes in the Third World, the Americans, who were ambivalent about many aspects of British policy, refused to extend any credits to support sterling, blocked British access to the International Monetary Fund until she withdrew her troops from Suez, and were unwilling to provide oil to compensate for interrupted supplies from the Middle East. American opposition, which underlined the vulnerability of the British economy, was crucial in weakening British resolve and led to a humiliating withdrawal that provided a clear indication of Britain's loss of world power.[22]

Failure in the Suez Crisis can be seen as the end of Britain's ability to act wholly independently; from then on, there was an implicit reliance on American acceptance of British initiatives, even at the time of the Falklands War in 1982, and a related stress on a 'special relationship'. Decolonisation and greater Dominion autonomy also ensured that Britain could bring less to the strategic table. Indian independence in 1947 was particularly important, as Indian troops had been crucial to Britain's expeditionary capacity in Asia, Africa, and the Middle East. There were no Indian troops to help in the Suez Crisis, nor, later, to participate in the Vietnam War, had that been a goal. Thanks in part to the fact that, with the exception of the Gurkhas, Britain could no longer deploy imperial military resources, intervention in the two Gulf Wars (1991, 2003), was very much as a junior partner of the USA, and with Britain as much a symbolic partner as a crucial supplier of support, notably so in 2003. By then, the idea that Britain might have fought in part by deploying Indian troops was no more than a distant memory. It was not only a lack of allied and imperial assistance that was at issue in the Suez Crisis. In addition, there had been a major shift in the military and political contexts. That the British had been far more successful when they attacked Egypt in 1882 than in 1956 reflected a major shift both in Western attitudes towards force projection and in the ability to coerce a compliant response. Changes in the attitude to the use of force played a role, but so also did the rise of nationalist attitudes in the Third World. In his novel

---

22 K. Kyle, *The Suez Conflict* (London, 1989); W.R. Louis and R. Owen (eds), *Suez 1956: The Crisis and its Consequences* (Oxford, 1989).

Landed Gently (1957), Alan Hunter referred to jingoism as doomed alongside other aspects of the old world, notably the satanic mills and social injustice.

Suez is usually treated as the turning-point, but, as with the end of empire in South Asia in 1947–48, the British government dug in elsewhere, this time, eventually, in Aden and the Gulf. This point raises the question of when empire ended: with the loss of Singapore in 1942 or of India in 1947, with the Suez Crisis in 1956, or the 'wind of change' on which Britain left much of Africa in the early 1960s, with the abandonment of Aden and an east of Suez policy in 1967–68, or independence of Rhodesia/Zimbabwe in 1980, or with the cession of Hong Kong in 1997? Each major loss was highly significant for its region, and also, less obviously, had an impact on what was left. This staggered retreat reflected the heterogeneity of Britain's empire and what became, notably after an animating principle and strength was gone, a group of dependencies to which power was devolved at different times for various reasons.

Prior to Suez, the British government had already decided to grant independence to the Gold Coast (Ghana) and Malaya in 1957. Government attitudes to empire nevertheless changed significantly after the Suez decade in what was certainly a transformation in Britain's global position. As Conservative prime minister from 1957 to 1963, Harold Macmillan, who had backed Suez, explicitly set out to restore relations with the USA. This goal took priority over the preservation, let alone strengthening, of the empire, although the active management of imperial transformation into a pro-British Commonwealth was still seen as a major task. In 1957, Macmillan decided to reduce the size of the army. Conscription was ended, although this was as part of a change intended to enhance military effectiveness at a lower cost. One flaw was the assumption that colonial governments and those of newly independent states would be willing and able to deploy forces to serve imperial purposes elsewhere in the world.[23] In response to what Macmillan, speaking to the South African parliament on 3 February 1960, referred to as a 'wind of change', much of the empire was dismantled in a rush. This was especially so in Africa, but also in the West Indies, as well as for other colonies including Cyprus. Churchill would have been less willing to abandon the empire at this rate. Decolonisation was hastened by a strong upsurge in colonial demands for independence, which the government did not know how to confront. In particular, the simultaneous demands for change posed a challenge and, although a frequently deployed account, managed decolonisation did not describe a more difficult and often violent

23 D. French, *Army, Empire, and Cold War: The British Army and Military Policy, 1945–1971* (Oxford, 2012).

process.[24] Thus, in Nyasaland (Malawi), Hastings Banda won much support in 1959 for his campaign against British colonial policy, notably over land rights. Action by the governor led to riots. The crisis encouraged an angry Macmillan to support the transfer of more authority to those Africans who could be recruited to Britain's ends.

Although criticised by some right-wing Conservatives, particularly the Marquess of Salisbury, decolonisation was not a central issue in British politics, and notably not after the Suez crisis. There was fighting in the last stages of empire, particularly resistance to nationalists in Malaya (which gained independence in 1957), Kenya (gained in 1963), and, unsuccessfully, Aden (gained in 1967). Moreover, military deployments continued in the defence and protection of the formal and informal empire, especially in Jordan (1958), Kuwait (1961), Brunei (1962), Malaysia (1963–66),[25] Aden (1963–67), East Africa (1964),[26] Anguilla (1969), and Oman (1970–76),[27] and this pattern related to an ambitious sense of British power.

Aden, however, proved a conspicuous failure for British power, and offers one clear view of the end of empire. Nationalist agitation there, which had been increasingly strident from 1956, turned into revolt in 1963. The British deployed 19,000 troops, the bulk of the men then allocated to colonial garrisons, but their position was undermined by the failure to sustain local support. The British-officered Federal Reserve Army proved unreliable, and, in June 1967, the South Arabian Police and the Aden Armed Police rebelled in the city of Aden. Furthermore, the British were unable to support allied sheikhs in the interior against the guerrilla attacks of the National Liberation Front (NLF). The air power, scorched earth tactics, and resettlement policies seen in Malaya in the 1950s were used, but the NLF's inroads forced an abandonment of the interior in the early summer of 1967. Once the British were clearly on the way out, they found it hard to obtain accurate intelligence, and this made mounting operations difficult. Reduced to holding on to Aden, where the garrison itself had to be protected, the only initiative left was to abandon the position, which was done in November 1967, bringing to an end a rule that had begun in 1839.

---

24 M. Thomas, *Fight or Flight: Britain, France, and their Roads from Empire* (Oxford, 2014), p. 350.

25 H.D. James and D. Sheil-Small, *The Undeclared War: The Story of the Indonesian Confrontation, 1962–66* (London, 1971).

26 T.H. Parsons, *The 1964 Army Mutinies and the Making of Modern East Africa* (Westport, Connecticut, 2003).

27 J. Akehurst, *We Won a War: The Campaign in Oman, 1965–75* (Salisbury, 1982).

On the other hand, a very different impression was created by the successful use of British and Commonwealth forces to resist the Indonesian attack on Malaysia in 1963–66, although ultimate success depended on the unrelated overthrow of the nationalist regime in Indonesia. At any rate, Britain faced nothing on the scale that the French confronted in their attempt to retain Indo-China (1946–54) and Algeria (1954–62), nor that the Portuguese confronted in their African pretensions. Nor, in Africa, was there chaos comparable to what occurred in Congo (Zaire) immediately after its independence from Belgium in 1960. The examples of Algeria and Congo certainly influenced Macmillan. It is unclear how far a major nationalist rising in, or foreign invasion of, a British colony would have led to a substantial response that might have proved bitterly divisive within Britain. Certainly, decolonisation did not prove as divisive for the Conservatives as relations with Europe did from the late 1980s. In part, this was because, despite what can be regarded as the anomaly of the Falklands War in 1982, the empire was seen as being transformed into the Commonwealth, rather than lost. Thus, the logic of Britain's imperial mission, allegedly bringing civilisation to backward areas of the globe, allowed the presentation of independence as the inevitable terminus of empire. This argument was more than simply a case of presentation as the government reshaped its imperial mission to respond to the conditions, needs, and opportunities of the post-war world.[28]

This end to empire was also relatively painless in Britain because interest in much of it was increasingly relatively limited within Britain from the 1950s. Given that empire was always both a matter of attitudes as well as policies, the former require extensive discussion. A lack of interest was not the case with some traditional Conservative groups, such as the military, but was the case with much of the Party's middle-class support. Moreover, this support became more important for the Party. Leaders such as Edward Heath and Reginald Maudling (Colonial Secretary in 1961–62), neither of whom came from the traditional ruling group, felt little commitment to the empire. The wartime experience of many orientated them more towards Europe than the empire. Conservative disengagement from empire was also related to 'New' Commonwealth immigration, notably from the West Indies, and to the empire 'coming home' in ways in which certain politicians (and some of their constituents) found distinctly troubling. The balance between the generations was also important, with the young not experiencing in the end of empire the sense of discontinuity

28 B. Grob-Fitzgibbon, *Imperial Endgame: Britain's Dirty Wars and the End of Empire* (Basingstoke, 2011), p. 376.

felt by their elders. Generational shifts also related to specific points, for example attitudes to British settlers in Africa. Differences between the generations constituted an instructive contrast between the historical memory and imagination of the generations. The discontinuity, however, was far greater in the former colonies, especially, but not only, if violence was involved. In Britain, the empire served as a foil for defining the national character: commitment to empire was increasingly perceived as the antithesis of what it meant to be 'modern', as an obstacle to economic reform, an emblem of outdated social values, and a view out of kilter with 'democratic' political values. It appeared redundant. The decline of religious ideas of legitimate authority meant that the empire no longer had a divine underpinning and a Providential purpose.

Although post-imperial nostalgia was to be another matter, public opinion and domestic politics were generally indifferent to the ending of empire at the time it ended. Nevertheless, the politics focused on the settler colonies was problematic. Indeed the fate of both Kenya and the Central African Federation could have brought down Macmillan in 1959. In the summer of 1959, Sir Patrick Devlin's damning report on the Nyasaland Emergency, coinciding with revelations of the Hola Camp massacre in Kenya, threatened to split both the Cabinet and the Party. Alan Lennox-Boyd, the Colonial Secretary from 1954 to 1959, offered his resignation several times and, had he gone, the other Colonial Office ministers (Julian Amery and Lord Perth) could doubtless have followed. From the back benches, Enoch Powell attacked the government's colonial policy in the debate over Hola. With an eye to an autumnal general election, Macmillan regarded the Devlin report as 'dynamite. It may well blow this Government out of office' (Diary, 13 July 1959). There are some similarities with the Westland affair in 1986. In the event, Macmillan (unlike Margaret Thatcher in 1986) suffered no ministerial losses, but (like Thatcher in 1987) he went on to win a landslide at the election in October 1959. This may suggest that, while colonial (especially African) crises dogged Macmillan in the Party, the electorate was hardly troubled by them. The insoluble problems of Central Africa continued to distract Macmillan in his second administration. Ian MacLeod, Lennox-Boyd's more progressive successor as Colonial Secretary in 1959–61, was on the point of resignation in early 1961. Had he done so, Macmillan recorded, 'I think the Government would have fallen. All the younger men in the Party would have gone against us' (Diary, 22 February 1961). Instead, MacLeod went on to be Chairman of the Party (1961–63).

As empire receded fast, Britain appeared a diminished power, although it had an enhanced military capability as a result of becoming the third state in the world to develop the atom bomb (1952), followed by being the third with the hydrogen bomb (1957). The outnumbered nature of the British Army on the Rhine ensured that it would need to use tactical nuclear weapons in the event of Soviet attack. The nuclear dimension linked Britain closely with the USA, notably because of the failure in 1960 of 'Blue Streak', the initiative for a British nuclear missile. From 1960, American nuclear submarines equipped with Polaris intercontinental missiles began to operate from the Holy Loch in Scotland. Moreover, in 1962, Macmillan persuaded President Kennedy to provide Britain with the submarine-launched Polaris missile system, which offered Britain a global naval capability, although American agreement was dependent on the British force being primarily allocated for NATO duties. Indeed, if imperial diehards, such as the Suez Group within the Conservative Party, opposed for example to concessions over Cyprus,[29] represented one critique of government policy and the foreign policy consensus, another was provided by the Campaign for Nuclear Disarmament (CND) launched in 1958. That year, 9,000 people marched in protest from London to the Atomic Weapons Research Establishment at Aldermaston. In 1960, the philosopher Bertrand Russell organised a campaign of non-violent civil disobedience. Its impact, however, was limited.

Support for joining the European Economic Community (EEC) became more widespread in British political circles in the early 1960s as it became clear that the organisation would be a success, especially in terms of the level of economic growth enjoyed by the member states. Rapid growth in the economies of Germany, France, and Italy, and, outside the EEC, Japan, helped make Britain appear unsuccessful. The relative decline of the British economy was particularly pronounced in manufacturing, although in some sectors, such as pharmaceuticals, British technology remained a market leader. Economic discussions increasingly were held without any serious consideration of empire. The loss of British influence in Washington was also an issue, as America was keen for Britain to join the EEC, and, indeed, continues to press Britain to support European integration under the assumption that Britain might be able to exercise significant influence while the British would be an Anglo-American voice in European economic and foreign policy. Instead, in 1963, the French President, Charles de Gaulle, vetoed the British application, declaring at a press conference, 'England is insular ... the nature and structure and economic context of England differ profoundly from those of the other states of the Continent'. De Gaulle also argued that Britain was too close to America. Again, empire was no longer the key issue, or, indeed, a key issue.

29 P. Ziegler, *Edward Heath* (London, 2010), pp. 107–8.

Labour to the Fore: Into Europe 1964–1973

Even though there was a degree of opposition in the Conservative Party to entry into the EEC, the Labour Party was more ambivalent. In part, this opposition reflected the fear that Continental workers would accept lower levels of social protection and welfare, and thus price their British counterparts out of work; a process that was to be more clearly the case with East and South Asian competition on the global scale. There were also political concerns as an aspect of an anti-EEC internationalism that aspired to create and sustain Labour values elsewhere in the world, notably in the former empire.[30] Hugh Gaitskell, Labour's leader, declared in 1962, significantly in a television interview, that entry into the EEC 'means the end of Britain as an independent nation; we become no more than Texas or California in the United States of Europe. It means the end of a thousand years of history'.

There was a rethink about British policy when Labour came to power in October 1964 under a new leader, Harold Wilson, a self-proclaimed moderniser. He had initially hoped to maintain Britain's role as a major independent power, and, grandiloquently, sought to act as a leading figure on the international stage, not least by revitalising the Commonwealth and pursuing a broader international role for it. In support of India against China, which had successfully attacked the former in 1962 in a limited war, Wilson, in June 1965, declared: 'Britain's frontiers are on the Himalayas'. Although special forces were allegedly sent to Vietnam, the government used Britain's continuing post-imperial commitment in support of Malaysia against Indonesia as a reason for not getting involved in support of the USA in Vietnam, despite considerable pressure from President Lyndon B. Johnson.

However, the attempt to act as a major independent player, and to be great accordingly, failed. This goal had to be abandoned in part because Britain lacked the necessary diplomatic strength, for example to mediate over Vietnam, but also in the face of the country's severe financial problems, which included a serious sterling crisis in July 1966 and a devaluation of sterling by 15 per cent on 18 November 1967. This blow made Britain look very weak. Britain lacked imperial strength or any substitute. The inability to end the secession from the empire of Southern Rhodesia, a colony dominated by a minority white population that had unilaterally declared independence in November 1965, contributed to a sense of failure. This issue weakened Britain internationally and notably within

30 B. Frank, C. Horner, and D. Stewart (eds), *The British Labour Movement and Imperialism* (Cambridge, 2010).

the Commonwealth,[31] as well as being highly contentious politically. Wilson was not prepared to risk mutiny by sending troops into Southern Rhodesia and successive negotiations revealed that the rebel regime was unwilling to accept British plans for African representation.

As a result of a new sense of overreach, the government decided in January 1968 to abandon Britain's military position 'east of Suez'. The decision to withdraw from Singapore had been taken by the Cabinet in June 1965, but American pressure led to the abandonment of this plan and to the announcement in 1966 that British forces would remain in Malaysia and Singapore. However, the 1967 devaluation resulted in a change in policy, with withdrawal seen as a way to sell a broader programme of austerity necessary for recovery. On 16 January 1968, Wilson announced the end of East of Suez: both in the Gulf and in South-East Asia.[32] British forces were withdrawn from Aden in 1967,[33] and from the Gulf[34] and (largely) Singapore in 1971. The refusal to come to the assistance of the USA in Vietnam was an aspect of this policy, and separated Britain from Australia and New Zealand, which did send troops. Meanwhile, decolonisation continued, and, by 1971, there was little left of the empire, apart from such far-flung outposts as the Falkland Islands, Gibraltar, Hong Kong, and some small islands in the South Atlantic and West Indies, including Ascension, Tristan da Cunha, and St Helena. Britain had controlled far more territory in 1700. Moreover, the merger of the Foreign Office and the Commonwealth Office in October 1968 reflected a significant change and further led to the dominance of the views of the former.

Britain's international commitments and defence priorities were increasingly focused on Western Europe from 1966–67, with the focus on NATO tasks a military equivalent to a drive to join the EEC, which came to fruition in 1973. Britain surrendered the economic interests of empire to meet the requirements of the EEC. This was notably so in the case of lamb imports from New Zealand. At sea, a focus on the NATO area was a consequence of the drawing back from imperial consequences east of Suez and of the build-up of the Soviet navy from the 1950s, and much of the British fleet was allocated to the Naval Force Atlantic, a NATO command established in 1967. Multilateralism within NATO, which,

---

31 R. Coggins, 'Wilson and Rhodesia: UDI and British Policy Towards Africa', *Contemporary British History*, 20 (2006), pp. 363–81.

32 P.L. Pham, *Ending 'East of Suez': The British Decision to Withdraw from Malaysia and Singapore 1964–1968* (Oxford, 2010).

33 S. Harper, *Last Sunset: What Happened in Aden* (London, 1978).

34 S.C. Smith, *Britain's Revival and Fall in the Gulf: Kuwait, Qatar and the Trucial States 1950–1971* (London, 2004).

replacing empire, progressively became the consensus for Britain's defence in the 1960s, greatly diminished the independent role of British strategy. This process was taken further in 1966 with the cancellation of the planned CVA-01 fleet carrier, which would have been the first large carrier to be built in Britain since World War Two. The Minister of Defence (Navy) resigned over the decision to end an independent British intervention capability.[35] It was envisaged that, after the existing aircraft carriers, with their distant strike capability, came to an end of their service, naval air power would amount essentially to helicopters designed to act against Soviet submarines in the North Atlantic. An ability to support amphibious operations no longer seemed necessary, which amounted to a major shift in military tasking reflecting the abandonment of empire.

Indeed, the British forces were already in Western Europe, in the former occupation zone within West Germany, as the British Army of the Rhine, so that, in the event of a conflict, there would be no equivalent to the need to move troops to the Continent seen in 1914 and 1939 when troops had been moved to France. British defence priorities were focused on Western Europe and the North Atlantic, the British being obliged to maintain 55,000 troops in Germany in order to man 65 kilometres of the West German border with East Germany. If numbers were reduced, for example to help in the situation in Northern Ireland, it was necessary to seek NATO permission and to promise to restore the agreed strength. The army as a whole was equipped and trained primarily for this task, with the strategic, operational, and tactical emphasis on resisting heavily armed and more numerous Soviet forces. No longer an imperial force, the British military had moved far from its role during Victoria's reign, although from the perspective of Irish nationalists, the military acted as an imperial force in Northern Ireland where reinforcements were sent in 1969 in response to sectarian rioting. The army succeeded in 1972 in ending the 'no-go' areas in Belfast and Londonderry that the Provisional IRA had created as a standard stage in the Maoist theory of revolutionary warfare. In its effort to end British sovereignty, the Provisional IRA then turned to terrorism, which ensured a long-term commitment for the military. There was confusion as to whether this was a counter-insurgency or a law-and-order situation. Eventually, the latter view prevailed as part of a strategy to end the crisis by political means.[36]

---

35 A. Gorst, 'CVA-01', in R. Harding (ed.), *The Royal Navy, 1930–2000: Innovation and Defence* (Abingdon, 2005), pp. 170–92.

36 C. Townshend, *Britain's Civil Wars: Counterinsurgency in the Twentieth Century* (London, 1986); J. Wilsey, *The Ulster Tales: A Tribute to Those Who Served, 1969–2000* (Barnsley, 2011).

The end of imperial power projection, the devaluation of sterling, and entry into the EEC, encouraged former colonies to articulate post-imperial identities and policies. In turn, this process made imperial echoes appear increasingly redundant. Alex Douglas-Home, the Foreign Secretary (1970–74) and former prime minister (1963–64), argued that Britain's destiny was 'European', in part because of changes in the Commonwealth.[37]

Imperial Collapse, 1973–1980

'END OF AN ERA', proclaimed the British satirical journal *Private Eye* on its front cover on 2 April 1976. It marked the resignation of Harold Wilson as Labour prime minister by depicting a largely submerged battleship with only the superstructure showing. The bubble coming from the boat had Wilson saying to James Callaghan, his successor, 'Alright, Jim, you can take over now'; but the legacy he was being offered was of a wrecked state, one that made global pretensions appear unrealistic, if not ridiculous. The photograph, ironically, was of a German dreadnought scuttled in Scapa Flow in 1919, while Britain's last battleship, the *Vanguard*, had been scrapped in 1960, but shipwreck appeared an appropriate metaphor for a country that had lost direction and a state that could no longer function adequately. By 1976, both Labour (1964–70, 1974–79) and Conservative (1970–74) hopes of economic modernisation had failed, and Britain's prestige and economic position were in marked decline. The Conservative government of Edward Heath had fallen in 1974 having failed to overcome economic problems and trade union militancy. Hit hard by the oil-price shock of 1973–74 and by a failure to control inflation and trade-union militancy, the Labour government had to turn, in 1976, to the International Monetary Fund for a loan, and to accept cuts in government spending in return. Although there was then an improvement in labour relations and in political stability, this ended when in 1978–79, in the 'Winter of Discontent', the economic and trade-union crises of the decade appeared to culminate in a political and social breakdown.

Outside Europe, the Labour governments of 1974–79 took a much less assertive stance than their predecessors of 1964–70 had done. Britain participated in the CENTO naval exercise, Midlink 74, in the Arabian Sea in 1974, but, despite the hopes of the Singapore government, the last forces were withdrawn from Singapore, SEATO was dissolved in 1977, and there was no pretence that Hong Kong could be defended against China. Callaghan, prime

37 A. Douglas-Home, *Our European Destiny* (London, 1971).

minister from 1976 to 1979, nevertheless, ordered a continued naval presence in the South Atlantic in order to deter the Argentinians from action against the Falklands. Imperial fragments remained reliant upon Britain, many in practice post-imperial dependencies loath to be cast to the four winds. Some of these fragments continued to gain independence – the Bahamas in 1973, Grenada in 1974, the Solomon Islands, the Ellice Islands (as Tuvalu), and Dominica in 1978, the Gilbert Islands (as part of Kiribati), St Lucia, and St Vincent in 1979, Antigua and British Honduras in 1981, and St Kitts–Nevis in 1983. Moreover, Brunei, hitherto a protectorate, with Britain responsible, under a 1971 treaty, for defence and foreign policy, became fully independent in 1984. The abandonment of the overseas system of bases continued in 1975, with the termination of the Simon's Town agreements, and with the departure, in 1979, of the navy from Malta, where it had continued to use facilities after independence in 1964 under the Military Facilities Agreement. Both steps were linked to the withdrawal from 'East of Suez' and marked the closure of the long-established network of imperial naval bases. A concrete expression of British power, or at least the British presence, was also lost. Malta had been crucial to the British role in the Mediterranean and the change there very much marked the move towards the American naval dominance of that strategic region.

The failure to reconcile European and global interests was a more serious issue. Although the British government had hoped that it would be possible to bridge the Commonwealth and the EEC, which had been joined in 1973, not least by making the latter more 'outward-looking', British entry into the EEC was understandably seen by many former colonies as a deliberate rejection of their interests. Indeed, prior to entry, British trade with the Commonwealth was greater than that with Europe. Links with former colonies were further frayed because of serious divisions within the Commonwealth over British government policy towards South Africa and Southern Rhodesia, which provided the occasion and spark for disagreements within an already-problematic system, as well as being an issue in Conservative politics in Britain. The Right was repeatedly unhappy about what it saw as a failure to stand by 'kith and kin', and very much saw southern Africa in terms of resistance to Communist advance in the Cold War. Due to her political position, Margaret Thatcher, prime minister from 1979 to 1990, who was also a pragmatist, was better able than other Conservative politicians to push through change.[38] The empire briefly expanded when independent white rule in Southern Rhodesia was undermined by the overthrow

38 C. Moore, *Margaret Thatcher. The Authorised Biography. I: Not For Turning* (London, 2013), p. 454.

of Portuguese colonial rule in neighbouring Mozambique and Angola and by the loss of South African support. With the collapse of UDI (the Unilateral Declaration of Independence), British control was reintroduced in 1979 as part of an independence settlement based on majority rule. Democratic elections were followed by the grant of independence in 1980 to what became Zimbabwe.

Although the Commonwealth Secretariat was established in 1965, while the first Commonwealth Heads of Government meeting was held, in Singapore, in 1971, the Commonwealth amounted to little in the international system, or even in British foreign policy. The rapid expansion of the Commonwealth to include a large number of newly independent colonies also affected the status within the Commonwealth of the Dominions, especially Australia and New Zealand. Successive British governments did not appreciate pressure to take action against white minority regimes in southern Africa, and this difference reached a highpoint with Thatcher's refusal, in the 1987 and 1989 meetings of Commonwealth Heads of Government, to accept the Commonwealth policy on sanctions against South Africa and the conference communiqués' resulting clause 'with the exception of Britain'. From the outset, the Commonwealth had not included all former colonies. Burma refused to join when it became independent in 1948, while Ireland, South Africa, and Pakistan left in 1949, 1961, and 1972 respectively. South Africa rejoined in 1994 after the end of the apartheid regime. Mozambique, which was admitted in 1995, had never been a British colony, instead being ruled by Portugal. Gambia left in 2013 in response to criticisms of the autocratic nature of its government.

More generally, the Commonwealth did not meet British hopes that it would serve as a continuation of imperial cohesion, not least because of a reluctance to follow the British lead that reflected a scepticism about British intentions and moral authority.[39] Newly independent states had developed their own views on international relations and foreign policy, and the Non-Aligned Movement sapped the willingness of some to follow the British lead. India was more interested in the Non-Aligned Movement than the Commonwealth, while Mahathir bin Mohamad, prime minister of Malaysia from 1981 to 2003, did not attend the Commonwealth Heads of Government meetings in 1981 and 1983, as he claimed to prefer to 'look east' to Japan.

In addition, the British were unable or unwilling to compensate for political estrangement by large amounts of economic aid and financial support.[40]

---

39 R.J. Moore, *Making the New Commonwealth* (Oxford, 1987); W.D. McIntyre, *The Significance of the Commonwealth, 1965–90* (Basingstoke, 1991).

40 D.A. Low, *Eclipse of Empire* (Cambridge, 1991), p. 332.

The creation of an equal partnership proved a goal that was incompatible with British leadership. It was symbolic that the Commonwealth Institute in West London, visited by generations of schoolchildren as a guide to a progressive future, seemed increasingly tired and eventually closed.

In some respects, the Conservative government of Margaret Thatcher, which was elected to power in 1979, represented a self-conscious return to earlier values and interests, but there was to be no revival of imperial concerns. Instead, Thatcher sought a clear alignment with the USA in the Cold War, and this issue dominated her view of the world. East–West tensions had revived markedly with the Soviet intervention in Afghanistan at the close of 1979; although the USA, not Britain, took the major role in supporting opposition there. Nevertheless, concern about Soviet plans led the British to return in strength to the Indian Ocean in 1980, to participate in 'Beacon Compass', a joint exercise with the American navy. The settlement of the Southern Rhodesia dispute in 1980 further helped ensure the British focus on the Cold War, notably as East–West tensions increased in 1979–83, with war close in 1983. British concern in 1983 about the American invasion of Grenada, a Caribbean island, and member of the Commonwealth, that had been violently taken over by a hard-line left-wing group, did not have a major impact on Anglo-American relations, although the American failure to consult Britain was regarded as a humiliation, not least by the Queen. However, on the part of Britain, there was a more general withdrawal from intervention in former colonies: the British government did not take a major role when Fiji had two coups in 1987.

The Falklands War, 1982

That Britain was to fight a last imperial war in 1982 was totally unexpected. Although contested with Spain in the late eighteenth century, a contest that nearly led to war with France and Spain in 1770, the Falklands had been under British control from 1833. They were claimed, as the Malvinas, by the Argentinians, whose ruling military *junta* was convinced that, because the British government was uncertain of the desirability of holding onto the colony, it would accept its seizure by the Argentinians. The decision, in 1981, to withdraw the Antarctic patrol ship *Endurance* was seen as a sign of British lack of interest in the South Atlantic, and, on 2 April 1982, the virtually undefended islands were successfully invaded. The next day, Thatcher told the Commons that the islands would be returned to British administration and stated, 'The people of the Falkland Islands, like the people of the United Kingdom, are an island race'. When General Alexander Haig, the American Secretary of State, visited Thatcher on 8 April 1982 in an effort to mediate over the Falklands, Thatcher showed him what she told him were 'very appropriate', recently hung, portraits of Nelson and Wellington.[41]

A successful British reconquest began with that of South Georgia on 25 April. British troops landed in the Falklands on 21 May and fighting culminated with the surrender of the Argentinean garrison on 14 June. During the war, 255 British servicemen died. The speed with which the operation was mounted contrasted markedly with the length of time taken for the preparations for the Suez expedition in 1956; and this rapidity helped limit the possibilities for domestic and international criticism. There was a degree of support in 1982 not seen in subsequent British military deployments. The opposition Labour Party leader, Michael Foot, regarded the Argentinean *junta* as Fascists and denied that the British position was imperialist. The French ambassador took a different view.[42] Only a minority of the Labour Party, led by Tony Benn, opposed the war, and there were very few criticisms from Conservatives. The Americans proved far more problematic, leading to British complaints,[43] but, in the event, provided logistical and intelligence support of great value. The French provided information on the Exocet missiles sold to Argentina. However, the campaign matched those of the earlier defence of empire in depending on British fighting resolve and quality.

The gut patriotism released and displayed in 1982 made some commentators uncomfortable, but Thatcher knew how to respond. War helped give her leadership a dynamic reputation enjoyed by no Conservative leader since Churchill, and cemented her already-strong relations with Party activists. Thatcher's defence of national interests struck a chord across Party boundaries, and most of the Labour Party supported the recovery of the Falklands. She was able to link the 1980s to the formative experiences of her youth and those of many of her listeners, notably World War Two, its aftermath, and the last stages of Britain as a great power and an empire. The war provided her with an opportunity to deploy a strong and uncomplicated patriotism, one that was related to military activity. At the same time, her government proved far less successful in taking forward this patriotism for the next generation, which reflected not only its failure but also the complexities of British society and

---

41 Moore, *Thatcher*, p. 687.

42 Moore, *Thatcher*, p. 678.

43 L. Freedman, *The Official History of the Falklands Campaign* (2 vols, London, 2005), I, 191.

public culture. Indeed, when she died in 2013, there was a clear generational contrast in the response to the memories of the war that were reignited.

The Falklands War led, among much of the population, to an imperial glow that, alongside serious opposition divisions, helped the Conservatives win re-election in 1983 with a much greater majority, but to many it seemed anachronistic. This was even more true of the former empire. New Zealand had offered naval support, a welcome step, but Britain fought alone. For logistical and timing reasons, the provision of troops by former colonies would not have been of much value, but had Canada maintained its earlier naval strength, and been willing to help, that would have been useful. However, under Pierre Trudeau, prime minister from 1968 to 1979 and 1980 to 1984, there was a stronger neutralism in Canadian policy. As part of the change in links, the Canadian constitution was patriated in 1982.

1983 to the Present

After the war, the Falklands were developed, at considerable expense, as a military base, 'Fortress Falklands', with a new runway and a garrison of 3,000 men. Nevertheless, territorial control was no longer a key issue in Britain's foreign relations or international strength. Despite repeated Spanish (peaceful) pressure and persistent border harassment, Gibraltar was retained. Spain itself has comparable positions in Morocco: at Ceuta and Melilla. In contrast, Hong Kong, on much of which Britain had only a 99-year lease, was turned over to China in 1997 after a negotiated settlement. There was no attempt to hand the issue over for decision to local views, and China was not interested in the British idea of renewing the lease. In the face of concern about the authoritarian nature of Chinese rule, the desire to win the goodwill of the Chinese government, and an acceptance of the dominant position of China, prevailed. Relations with China had improved considerably after the death of its radical leader Mao Zedong in 1976. In an agreement reached in 1984, China agreed that Hong Kong would have administrative and financial autonomy as well as its own legal system, key elements of a 'one country, two systems' solution.[44]

China also became influential in the naval affairs of former British colonies. The Chinese developed a naval base at Gwadar on the Baluchi coast for Pakistan, from which it could overlook the approaches to the Gulf, and they also played

44 J. Brown and R. Foot (eds), *Hong Kong's Transitions 1842–1997* (Basingstoke, 1997).

a role on the coast of Myanmar, developing an offshore listening station to keep an eye on Indian naval moves, and in Sri Lanka. Chinese territorial claims in the South China Sea were seen as threatening by Malaysia and Singapore and, as they could not rely on British assistance, encouraged development of their naval power. The response to China was very different to that to rising Japanese naval strength in the 1920s and 1930s. Chinese expansionism in the East China Sea in the 2010s was a matter for local powers and the USA. Britain did not take a role.

Britain was to return to 'east of Suez' from 1990, and even more from 2003, initially taking a prominent role in 1991 in driving the Iraqis from Kuwait, a former British Protectorate; but this stance was very much as part of American-led coalition activity. The same was true of the intervention in Iraq in 2003, while that in Afghanistan was also as part of an international force. There was a major attempt to avoid echoes of imperialism in relations with the Islamic world. The 2003 Defence White Paper argued that 'priority must be given to meeting a wider range of expeditionary tasks, at greater range from the United Kingdom and with an ever-increasing strategic, operational and tactical tempo'; but the idea of an independent military role had ended other than against weak opponents, as in the brief intervention in Sierra Leone. This intervention did not lead to the imposition of direct rule as would have been the case in the nineteenth century. The situation was not changed under the Strategic Review held by the Conservative-led Coalition government in 2010. Instead, there were major military cuts, notably with the end, for a while, of aircraft carrier capacity.

That the end of an independent imperial role, as opposed to peacekeeping activity, was also true of France, while the Dutch, Belgium, Portugal, and Spain all lost their empires between 1945 and 1980, did not lessen the significance of the issue for Britain. A major strand of continuity in British history and in Britain's impact in the world was no more. Britain had a military capacity that was greater than that in 1850, but scarcely had a capacity for independent action. A different ethos, in Britain and elsewhere in the world, as well as declining relative power in the global power order that followed World War Two, were the key elements in the retreat from empire; while the practice of multilateralism was a crucial means. There was talk of European identity, internationalism, and a special or essential relationship with the USA. The reality for Britain was a loss of independence and a lack of autonomy. Empire as an expression of power, identity, and independence, was no more.

Chapter 7

Britain and America: Parallels and Contrasts

With America in rebellion from 1775, the readers of Edward Gibbon's *Decline and Fall of the Roman Empire* (1776–88) were well aware that his historic tale was an account pregnant with meaning for contemporary Britain even if he was reluctant to draw direct links.[1] The habit of looking back to the fate of former greatness is a frequent one, and for most of the history of the West it focused on Rome, Republican and/or Imperial, as present-day developments could be inscribed into its past. However, this tendency has become far less frequent over the last century, in large part because of the collapse of the imaginative grasp of the Ancient world on societies whose historical memory, instead, has been dramatically foreshortened. This loss of the ability to identify resonating themes, part of the impoverishment of modern political and cultural discourse, has ensured that the frame of historical reference is now far smaller than in the past, and is presented in a simpler fashion.

In particular, the British empire has become the essential comparator for modern America. In many respects, this may seem absurd. America, the most populous state in the New World, and the third most populous on Earth, one that stretches from the Atlantic to the Pacific and has, throughout its independent history from 1776, been a democracy, may seem to have little in common with a small monarchy off the coast of Europe that became, through conquest, the greatest empire the world had hitherto known, only to lose all bar a few fragments in a half century. However, aside from the important links of a shared history until 1776 and a resulting legacy which was shared to a considerable extent, comparisons can be assisted by pointing out British naval predominance before the American age, as well as the federal character of the 'white' British empire by the early twentieth century, the Dominion system, and the extent to which, more generally, imperial rule was intended as a stage to

1 J. Robertson, 'Gibbon's Roman Empire as a Universal Monarchy: The *Decline and Fall* and the Imperial Idea in Early Modern Europe', in R. McKitterick and R. Quinault (eds), *Edward Gibbon and Empire* (Cambridge, 1997), pp. 249–50.

self-determination. At any rate, the comparison resonates because there appears to be no other. But is it appropriate?

Discussion of America as an empire is longstanding, and developed in particular from the major military successes and territorial gains of the Spanish–American War of 1898. This was the key episode in American power projection in Latin America and across the Pacific, both of which were, and are, seen in terms of imperialism.[2] The peace treaty left Puerto Rico, Guam, and the Philippines to the United States. America readily employed force to support its interests. For example, in 1912, marines were sent into Cuba in order to protect American property in the face of a large-scale, mostly black, peasant uprising motivated by the strains of economic change, social pressure, and political discrimination. In Cuba, annexation was no longer an option, but, as in Nicaragua, the disruptive consequences of American activity remained acute.[3]

The imperial argument came to the fore, in a very different form, that of America as *the* empire, rather than America as an empire, after the collapse of the Soviet Union in the early 1990s. Indeed, the 1990s and early 2000s witnessed a degree of American power, particularly military strength, that led domestic and foreign critics to complain about the existence of a 'hyper-power', a critical variant on the term 'superpower'. Thus, in trying to position himself in Latin American history and ideology, Hugo Chávez, the populist president of Venezuela from 1999 to 2013, claimed to be leading a 'Bolivarian' revolution against the 'empire', the latter no longer the colonial power, Spain, that Simón Bolívar (1783–1830) had successfully overthrown, but now the USA. In foreign policy, Chávez drew on Bolívar for the title of his anti-American Bolívarian Alliance for the Americans. He claimed that, immediately before he gained power, Venezuela had been weakened by a neo-liberalism that he blamed on the USA. In 2000, Chávez gave Fidel Castro, the prominently anti-American ruler of Cuba, a replica of Bolívar's diamond-studded sword.

At the same time, in a variant of earlier discussion, notably about Britain, there was concern in the USA, particularly from the 1970s, that the country was in relative decline, and that American hegemony, if it existed, was precarious. In 1987, in *The Rise and Fall of the Great Powers*,[4] Paul Kennedy advanced

2 L.D. Langley, *The Banana Wars: An Inner History of American Empire, 1900–1934* (Lexington, Kentucky, 1983); M.A. Renda, *Taking Haiti: Military Occupation and the Culture of U.S. Imperialism, 1915–1940* (Chapel Hill, North Carolina, 2001).

3 M. Gobat, *Confronting the American Dream: Nicaragua under U.S. Imperial Rule* (Durham, North Carolina, 2005).

4 P. Kennedy, *The Rise and Fall of the Great Powers: Economic Change and Military Conflict from 1500 to 2000* (London, 1987).

an account of America's likely future that was criticised the following year by Samuel P. Huntington for declinism. In 1997, Kennedy observed in the *Atlantic Monthly*:

> The United States now runs the risk, so familiar to historians of the rise and fall of Great Powers, of what might be called "imperial overstretch": that is to say, decision-makers in Washington must face the awkward and enduring fact that the total of the United States' global interests and obligations is nowadays far too large for the country to be able to defend them all simultaneously.[5]

This concern rose to a height from the mid-2000s as serious problems in Iraq and Afghanistan, the rise in Chinese strength, a sustained crisis in American public finances, and the inability of the political system to solve this crisis, interacted to cause considerable anxiety. Discussion about decline led to an assessment by American commentators of the earlier British case.

Thus, there have been several narratives of America as an imperial power, and each has invited attention to Britain. Aside from important comparisons across time, there were also significant similarities in particular periods. For example, the spread of settlement and subjugation of indigenous people in the nineteenth- and early twentieth century that was such an important feature in transforming America was also seen within the British empire, notably in Canada, Australia, New Zealand, and South Africa.[6] This spread of settlement was linked to ideas of identity focused on agrarianism. The latter was apparent with American advocates, notably Thomas Jefferson, president from 1801 to 1809, and with British counterparts. The latter included Tories, for example in their encouragement from the 1810s of settlement in Canada, which was seen as the way to anchor it in the empire. As another parallel, the segregation of blacks in the USA has also been compared with the treatment of Untouchables in India.[7]

The practice of informal empire, or of control short of territorial rule, also offers a comparison. This can be seen after World War One, with American policy in Latin America and that of Britain across much of Eurasia. For example, the British General Staff, advocating a greater effort on behalf of

5 For a critique of Kennedy, J. Black, *Great Powers and the Quest for Hegemony: The World Order since 1500* (Abingdon, 2008), esp. pp. 1–26.

6 J. Belich, *Replenishing the World: The Settler Revolution and the Rise of the Angloworld, 1783–1939* (Oxford, 2011).

7 G. Pandy, *A History of Prejudice: Race, Caste, and Difference in India and the United States* (Cambridge, 2013).

the anti-Communist whites in southern Russia in 1919, linked influence, geopolitics, and a sense of international threat:

> Taking the long view, it is unquestionable that what the British Empire has most reason to fear in the future is a Russo-German combination, which, starting as a commercial and economic organisation, will ultimately develop into a military alliance. We have at the present time a great opportunity of establishing on a permanent footing British influence and British trade connections in South Russia, where British prestige is high ... may well prove a permanent counterpoise to German penetration ... Nor should it be forgotten that the rich districts of the Don and the Donetz have a peculiar significance for the British people, situated as they are on one of the principal avenues of approach to our Eastern Empire.[8]

The last remark was a somewhat implausible account of the forward protection of India, one that captured the longstanding tendency to treat Eastern European and Asian power politics in that light. This interest in influence as a means to protect both particular geographical commitments and a more general sense of balance was to be important to America.

Britain and, more particularly, its empire have provided those discussing America not so much with a frame of reference for detailed discussion, as with a source of images and examples that can be plundered by those seeking historical resonance for their arguments. In a different context, this was seen with the references to the British National Health Service during the discussion about health reform in America in the early 2010s. Caution was/is generally absent. Phrases such as the age of British or American empire, or power, do not invite qualification and therefore tend to treat checks or defeats for this power as aspects of structural and cultural 'overstretch' and inherent failure, if not the end of the age. The assumption of a distinct age, moreover, is crucial to the idea of a sequence of hegemonic powers, such as Britain, America, China; although that idea neglects the significant co-terminous nature of imperial or great-power status, as well as the degree of co-operation, even co-dependency, that can exist.

In addition, aside from realist criteria of strength, power is in part a matter of perception and will. This point helps explain the importance of declinist accounts. Ironically, for those who sought comparisons, the rise of American power had itself affected, if not helped determine, the trajectory of British power. Thus, American hegemony from the 1940s had played a major part in British

---

8 General Staff, 'The Military Situation in Russia', 22 July 1918, NA. CAB. 24/84 fol. 285.

decolonisation and the decline of Britain's informal empire, and also benefited greatly from these processes. Earlier, America had benefited greatly from British strength. By allying with Britain in 1917 and 1941, the USA automatically allied with the world's largest navy and with Canada, and both greatly increased American security. In going to war in 1917, the USA constructed national interest in terms of the freedom of international trade from the unrestricted submarine warfare declared by Germany, a construction that aligned the USA with Britain.

The term empire was employed to discuss America in part because it was an arresting one. It could also serve writers on the Right and, more commonly and with a longer pedigree, notably back to the Progressive movement, the Left.[9] They could employ the language of empire to argue that it reflected and encouraged undesirable aspects of culture and society, akin to the Orientalism and Ornamentalism castigated in the case of earlier European imperialism.[10] International rivals were also critical of American imperialism. In February 2007, President Putin of Russia, no mean bully towards his neighbours, as Georgia (2008) and Ukraine (2014–15) were to testify, publicly attacked the USA for seeking global dominance, for bellicosity, resorting to force, ignoring the sovereignty of other powers, and overstepping 'its national borders in every way'.

The original American empire, that across North America to the Pacific, became, thanks to settlement by European Americans, especially from the 1840s, America, and did not seem an empire, not least because it was contiguous. Thereafter, there was an overseas empire from the late 1860s, notably of Alaska, Pacific island possessions, and Puerto Rico. Settlement, independence for the Philippines, statehood for Alaska and Hawaii, and assimilation ensured, however, that the American empire was not one expressed through rule over occupied territory.

On this criterion, indeed, it is worth reconsidering how best to define empire. One criterion refers to the ability to project power. In that light, aside from the USA, the continued capability of one-time territorial imperial powers for power projection was notable in the 2000s and 2010s, certainly in the case of Britain

---

9 A.J. Bacevich, *American Empire: The Realities and Consequences of U.S. Diplomacy* (Cambridge, Mass., 2002); D. Harvey, *The New Imperialism* (New York, 2003); N. Smith, *American Empire: Roosevelt's Geography and the Prelude to Globalization* (Berkeley, California, 2003); N. Ferguson, *Empire: How Britain Made the Modern World* (London, 2003) and *Colossus: The Price of America's Empire* (New York, 2004); A. Johnson, *Blowback: The Costs and Consequences of American Empire* (2nd edn, New York, 2004).

10 E.W. Said, *Orientalism* (New York, 1979); D. Cannadine, *Ornamentalism: How the British Saw their Empire* (London, 2001).

and France. British forces were sent to Iraq and Afghanistan, and French to Mali and the Central African Republic. Moreover, a practice of drawing parallels between American and British policy, or at least discussing the former in terms of imperialism, encourages a fresh assessment of the British empire.

Supporters of an active American role in the world in the 2000s and 2010s were prone to adopt a highly sympathetic account of the British empire. For example, in 2003, a year of hubris about American power, Niall Ferguson's book *Empire: How Britain Made the Modern World* and his linked television series and books on the empire received considerable attention. Ferguson, an American-based conservative British historian with a family background in the empire, drew eloquent attention to what he presented as its long-term benefits: 'no organisation in history has done more to promote the free movement of goods, capital and labour ... and to impose Western norms of law, order and governance around the world'. Ferguson was apt to make comparisons between British policy and American imperialism, for example between the British conquest of Egypt in 1882 and the occupation of Iraq after the 2003 invasion, and to reflect credit, or, at least, credibility, on the latter from the former.[11] In turn, there was well-founded criticism that Ferguson had failed to give due weight to the disadvantages of British empire, both to the areas that experienced imperialism and to the metropole.[12]

The disadvantages and costs of empire, and its consequences for culture, society, economy, and politics, attracted the attention of critics. This critique of British imperialism was presented as pertinent for an understanding of American power. Indeed, critics of American power amplified their criticism and gave it historical depth by attacks on the British empire, which was also blamed for many of the aspects of modernisation and globalisation judged unwelcome.

As with the British, especially in the nineteenth century, American global policy had developed in the twentieth century, more particularly from 1941, with a pursuit of morality linked to the furtherance of international goals.[13]

11 N. Ferguson, 'Egypt 1882: A fine template for running Baghdad today', *Sunday Times*, 1 June 2003, p. 8, *Empire: How Britain Made the Modern World* (London, 2003), and 'The Unconscious Colossus: Limits of (and Alternatives to) American Empire', *Daedalus*, 134/2 (2005), pp. 18–33. On Ferguson, see J. Wilson, 'Niall Ferguson's Imperial Passion', *History Workshop Journal*, 56/1 (2003), pp. 175–83.

12 For example, F. Cooper, 'Empire Multiplied: A Review Essay', *Comparative Studies in Society and History*, 46 (2004), pp. 247–72 and A. Sartori, 'The British Empire and Its Liberal Mission', *Journal of Modern History*, 78 (2006), pp. 641–2.

13 P.K. O'Brien and A. Clesse (eds), *Two Hegemonies: Britain 1846–1914 and the United States 1941–2001* (Aldershot, 2002).

There was a quest for an open world, in the shape of free trade and the unfettered movement of money, an engagement with modernisation,[14] and a confidence that technology endorses, as much as it underlines, a privileged position in the international order. The latter led to controversy in 2013–14 over the extent to which technology, in the shape of the ability to scrutinise the Internet, gave the USA unparalleled power in surveillance. From a critical viewpoint, the power of the British and American empires can be presented in instrumental terms as protection systems for economic self-interest, including in both formal and informal empire.[15] Moreover, this approach can serve as a way, in criticising these empires, to attack globalisation.

However, for both Britain and the USA, the idea of empire included not only specific national interests but also the pursuit of a benign and mutually beneficial world order. In each case, there was a willingness to use major efforts to engage with rival empires that were also, correctly, seen as authoritarian, if not, in some cases, tyrannical: Napoleonic France, Wilhelmine and Nazi Germany, Imperial Japan, and the Soviet Union. The self-image of British power was of Britain as the defender of small states against tyranny. This proved a way to link national history to present purposes, suggesting, moreover, that Britain was the friend of liberty and its power given meaning by this role. The defence of the Dutch against Spain from 1585 to 1604 was thus linked to opposition to Louis XIV of France, Napoleon, Wilhelm II, Hitler, and Soviet expansionism. The defence of the weak against the strong could be presented as both moral and prudential. David Cameron, the prime minister, offered this account of Britain in speeches in 2013.

Yet, however plausible this account of Britain, the terms of the mutual benefit offered by the British and American empires were unwelcome to many. This point was more particularly so in the British case as its empire rested, and more clearly than its American counterpart, on control, constraint, and coercion. However much affected by the exigencies of political and economic competition, there was a democratic objective at the heart of American capitalism that was seen as in America's and the world's interests, and that helped foster American opposition to the European colonial empires. Moreover, many of the liberal

---

14 M.E. Latham, *Modernisation as Ideology: American Social Science and 'Nation Building' in the Kennedy Era* (Chapel Hill, North Carolina, 2000) and *The Right Kind of Revolution: Modernisation, Development, and U.S. Foreign Policy from the Cold War to the Present* (Ithaca, New York, 2011); N. Gilman, *Mandarins of the Future: Modernisation Theory in Cold War America* (Baltimore, Maryland, 2003).

15 G.A. Barton, *Informal Empire and the Rise of One World Culture* (Basingstoke, 2014), p. 168.

ideas that played a central role in British assumptions in the nineteenth century were taken up by American writers and policymakers from the 1940s, in part, initially, in criticism of the protectionism then shown by the British empire. The focus was on free trade, but now as part of a world of sovereign democracies, a different definition of liberty to that offered by most British commentators in the nineteenth century with the important exceptions of Europe and Latin America. The Americans hoped that newly independent peoples would support democratic capitalism, and thus look to the USA. They were to have more success with the one-time client-states of the Soviet Union, such as Georgia, than with many former colonies of the European trans-oceanic empires, such as India and Egypt. From the American perspective, the British empire appeared both alien and redundant. In 1776, Britain had been the enemy against which independence was defined with the Declaration of Independence. As a minor echo, British accents and actors seemed obvious trademarks of villainy through the democratising lens of Hollywood.

Patterns of immigration into the two countries constitute a key difference. Immigration has been central to the American experience and world-view from the outset, whereas the political, social, and cultural impact of immigration into modern Britain has not become prominent until recent decades. As a consequence, the process by which the empire formally 'came home' has proved very troubling for Britain. At the same time, the centrality of the empire in the debate over British immigration and identity declined as immigration from Eastern Europe became a more prominent theme from the 2000s. This shift indicated the role of changing contexts, in this case the European Union, but also the way in which established languages of political concern and debate could be re-used in new circumstances. This was an aspect of the way in which discussion of imperial links in part reflected other tensions.

The relationship that is perceived between the British and American empires[16] depends in part upon which state and stage of each is to be the focus of attention. There were certainly contrasts between the two, but far less than between the two and other empires, for example Nazi Germany, the Soviet Union, or modern China. Attempts to argue functional comparisons between empires[17] need to bear such points about state and stage in mind. More specifically, the vexed relationship between commitments and resources seen with all empires had, in

---

16 C.S. Maier, *Among Empires: American Ascendancy and its Predecessors* (Cambridge, Mass., 2006).

17 T. Parsons, *The Rule of Empires: Those Who Built Them, Those Who Endured Them, and Why They Always Fall* (New York, 2010).

the case of Britain and the USA, the particular problems created by the need to address the democratic politics and free public culture of the metropole. Thus, on 6 April 1933, the (British) Committee of Imperial Defence met to discuss a report of 31 March from the Chiefs of Staff on the situation in the Far East. The military pressed for greater defence preparations, noting, 'Singapore is the indispensable base for naval operations to protect the trade and territory of the British Commonwealth of Nations in the Eastern Hemisphere', only for Neville Chamberlain, the Chancellor of the Exchequer, in offering support, to note also that, 'at the Treasury, it was felt that the risks of the financial situation were perhaps more pressing than the risks from Japanese aggression'.[18] Chamberlain, who was to go on to be prime minister in 1937–40, was very concerned to keep taxation low, for economic and ideological reasons, but also to ensure domestic political support for the national government. It had to face re-election.

From the perspective of empire, or at least power, advocates of military capability and intervention in both Britain and the USA were frequently to criticise the consequences of politics, specifically public opinion, in the metropole. However, policy choices or parameters that were thus explained or criticised frequently owed much to the usual issues of prioritisation between commitment and the related pressure of resource issues. Geopolitical and strategic considerations played a major role in the discussion of these questions. The very discussion of strategic choices in the 1930s suggests a difference in goals and means between the British and American empires. As the Chiefs of Staff noted on 12 October 1933, 'the maintenance of sea communications is the first principle of the system of Imperial Defence',[19] although by the late 1930s, and with Chamberlain taking a major role, there was a major effort to build up British air power. America was to succeed Britain in the 1940s as the world's leading naval power, a position it continues to hold, but air and space (rocket) power was to be more important for the USA.

'Lessons' from the past are always problematic, not least due to the need to understand the past in its own terms and circumstances, and because the process of drawing lessons is generally overly didactic and is prone to overlook the multi-dimensional character, not to say ambivalence, of past episodes. One key lesson that can be drawn is that of the need, in both past and present, to make choices and to accept the difficulties and discipline entailed. This process is particularly difficult in societies with well-developed public politics, such as Britain and the USA now and, in different forms, since the eighteenth century, because in these

18 NA. CAB. 24/239 fols 283, 287.
19 NA. CAB. 24/244 fol. 136.

societies most choices have ardent protagonists. The nature of public debate, with its emphasis on clarity, rights, entitlements, and morality, does not lend itself to the complexities and exigencies bound up in fiscal and military issues, notably questions of prioritisation and related compromises.

Looking back to the problems of the British empire provides insights for America,[20] and indeed Britain, today. It makes it clear that the choices were, and are, generally not between good and evil, as was rather crudely suggested by the liberal interventionists of the 1990s and the neo-conservatives in the 2000s, notably, but not only, in the discussion of 1930s' Appeasement. It is instructive, for example, to consider the 'Military Appreciation of the Present World Situation' produced by the Chief of the Imperial General Staff in October 1932. Concerned about the threat posed by German rearmament and revisionism directed against the Versailles peace settlement of 1919, he argued the need for Britain to consider the implications of developments in the Far East. The argument was of a prudent need to choose between difficult options:

> The extension of Japanese control in Manchuria must inevitably result in a diminution of Russian influence in that country and in the Far East generally. As the contrary is equally true there can be no doubt which is preferable to the British Empire. Though we do not wish and in fact are morally unable to condone Japan's disregard of her obligations under the Covenant [of the League of Nations], the Nine Power Treaty [for China] and the Kellogg Pact, and cannot even justify the methods she has thought fit to employ, it must remain beyond dispute that the extension of Japanese control in Manchuria would be less inimical to the British Empire than the inevitable alternative – an increase of Soviet influence.
>
> To maintain our position in the world and our possessions in the Far East a friendly Japan is an essential requisite, and it seems to me that our interests lie in the direction of attempting to regain the confidence of that country as a prelude to a return of British influence in Japanese policy.[21]

The details of this argument, which looked back to the view that Britain should not have broken with its 1902 alliance with Japan at the time of the 1922 Washington Naval Treaty, can be challenged. Japanese militarism can be seen as inherently aggressive and overly unpredictable, while the long-term willingness

20 A.J. Bacevich, *The Limits of Power: The End of American Exceptionalism* (New York, 2008).

21 NA. CAB. 24/234 fol. 162.

of the USA to intervene against Japan in the Far East, as it did with diplomatic pressure prior to the Japanese attack in 1941, can be regarded as more important than short-term American isolationism and appeasement. What, however, the episode indicates is the repeated need to choose between unwelcome options, something that commentators were prone to ignore in the 1990s, 2000s, and 2010s. There is a longstanding tendency to 'have your cake' and leave someone else to pay for it. An incautious use of imperial comparisons does not contribute to a quality debate, but is an aspect of the wider porosity of the past and the presentness of history, the way in which the latter is deployed from current perspectives and in order to support the political issues of the day. Discussion about decline proves particularly seductive, as decline and failure can be blamed on opponents and/or bad choices, and lend particular urgency to the demand for political support.[22]

In the case of the USA today, there is a relative decline from the situation in the 1990s, just as, earlier, there had been a relative decline in the 1960s from the position in the late 1940s and 1950s. It is unclear that there is a value in comparing these specific developments (which owed much to particular political and economic conjunctures in America and other states), with the very different circumstances of British imperial decline. Living beyond means entails different things in the public politics, international system, and demographics of the 2010s to the situation in the 1890s or, even, 1950s. There is, however, a common need to ensure that people understand that actions and policies have consequences that cannot be wished away by rhetoric. The quality of leadership therefore is a key factor. Thinking about ends, and not sufficiently about means, was true, for example, of several generations of British and American policymakers. Ultimately, however, the value of the past emerges not in terms of a lesson through comparison but, rather, of the need to understand and try to mould the uncertainty and unpredictability of the future in a mature fashion.

---

22 For scepticism, J. Joffe, *The Myth of America's Decline: Politics, Economics, and a Half Century of False Prophecies* (New York, 2013).

Chapter 8

Competing Histories and the British Empire

An overly critical and somewhat ahistorical account of British imperial history prevails in political discussion, education, colonial and post-colonial literature, and the media. This account reflects changes in Britain, as well as the extent to which the overthrowing, or at least end, of British rule is important to the foundation accounts of so many states, ranging from the USA to India, Ireland to Israel. In particular, there is a widespread failure to appreciate the extent to which Britain was not the conqueror of native peoples ruling themselves in a democratic fashion. There is also a misleading tendency to blame British imperial rule for many of today's pressures and problems, which, in reality, stem, more usually, from population increase, modernisation, and globalisation. Moreover, as an empire, Britain engaged with rival powers, the contours and purposes of whose imperial rule was sometimes harsher than those of Britain. This situation pertained in particular to Britain's leading role in opposition to the genocidal tyranny of Nazi Germany, but Wilhelmine Germany's policies in East and South-West Africa in the 1900s were far harsher than those of Britain. Moreover, the brutality used by the Italians in the 1920s and 1930s to suppress resistance in Libya and to conquer Ethiopia, and that of the Japanese in China, were each far worse than that seen with the British empire in the early twentieth century.

However, across the political spectrum, the tendency to read the past to satisfy the present has often led to a harsh portrayal of empire and, specifically, of the British empire. Furthermore, there is an assumption that the empire, indeed all empires, was/were uniformly brutal. Thus, India is seen through the lens of the Mutiny and the Amritsar massacre, without regard for the relatively peaceful and benign years in between. Empire and imperialism thereby become defined by brutality rather than the rule of law or other criteria. Empire is no longer regarded as a community. It has passed into history; and, as such, the controversies about goals and identities that were there from the outset, and often very significant to policy, have been replaced by others about character and consequences. This process is an aspect of a wider criticism, if not rejection, of the imperial legacy. In 2011, when visiting Pakistan, David Cameron was questioned about the Kashmir question, the most sensitive issue in Pakistani–Indian relations. Underplaying the extent to which the dispute is really about sectarian and geopolitical disputes between the two powers and also arises from politics within them, Cameron replied: 'I don't want to try to insert Britain in some leading role where, as with so many of the world's problems, we are responsible for the issue in the first place'.[1] Empire in 2014 was linked in *The Guardian* to a bellicosity that was also, allegedly, bad for British society.[2]

Renaming

The rejection of the imperial memory is symbolic as well as practical. Names have been widely discarded as part of a process of denying imperial memorialisation. Whereas the settlement colonies, Australia, Canada, and New Zealand, retained imperial names, such as Sydney and Perth, Vancouver and Waterloo, and Wellington and Nelson, these names were frequently rejected in some newly independent states where such settlement had been limited. The renaming of states was an important break in continuity, as also with the French empire, where, for example, Upper Volta became Burkina Faso. In the British empire, Nyasaland was renamed Malawi on independence in 1964, and Northern Rhodesia became Zambia, Southern Rhodesia eventually becoming Zimbabwe in 1980.[3] Nine years later, Burma became Myanmar, the name of the country in Burmese. Cities were renamed. The capital of Southern Rhodesia, Salisbury, became Harare; while, in 2002, the life-sized bronze statue of the British explorer David Livingstone located near the Victoria Falls was defaced. In India, Bombay became Mumbai in 1995, and Madras Chennai in 1996, provinces were renamed, and imperial statues junked. On the other hand, there were also many names that did not change, for example Blantyre in Malawi and Kingston in Jamaica.

New Identities

The process of renaming, however, was not simply directed against Britain, other imperial powers, and colonialism. Instead, opposition to British rule was an

1 *Daily Telegraph*, 5 Apr. 2011.
2 *The Guardian*, 13 Feb. 2014.
3 D. Maylam, *The Cult of Rhodes: Remembering an Imperialist in Africa* (Claremont, South Africa, 2005).

aspect of defining a new identity. While this was presented as a throwing off of the imperial yoke, this definition was also an aspect of the struggle for influence and control among indigenous groups and political movements that could be seen generally in post-colonial societies. Thus, renaming in India owed something to the Hindu nationalism of the Bharatiya Janata Party (BJP), a nationalism seen in opposition to earlier rule by Muslim empires, notably the Lodis and the Mughals, and also reflected local separatism in parts of southern India. Just as the onset and continuance of imperial rule were closely related to the use of the outside power by existing forces (and vice versa), so the same process occurred as imperial rule ended and also thereafter. In independent states, such as India, the idea of statehood and political legitimacy was (misleadingly) presented as resting on an historical continuity that had allegedly been ruptured by British conquest and rule. Thus, a negative account of British imperialism was necessary, not only to give additional meaning to the process of national liberation, but also in order to provide a stronger logic for both state and country.

In contrast, the extent to which the territorial scope, and thus ethnic composition, of many states were the work of British conquerors and negotiators, and, therefore, relatively recent, created problems for the presentation of both history and the present. Ironically, British territorialisation and concepts of identity and political authority were used to particular ends by colonial and post-colonial societies,[4] and by the post-colonial states, notably with the retention of imperial frontiers. At the same time, this issue became a way to blame British rule, both in the newly independent states and when British commentators were discussing difficulties in former colonies. In addition, the post-independence rethinking of the colonial period led to a greater emphasis on resistance to colonial rule, for example the Maroons of Jamaica and the Indian 'Rebellion' or 'First War of Independence'; although this emphasis tended to involve a misleading treatment of much resistance in terms of later, nationalistic, anti-colonialism. Moreover, the standard account in former colonies frequently underplays the emergence of local colonial élites. Consideration of the colonial period, anyway, was politically problematic as it posed a major question mark against the success of post-colonial governments in improving living standards, maintaining stability and the rule of law, notably the integrity of contracts, and in limiting corruption.

There is a tendency to blame imperialism for all the problems of post-colonial states. Such a tendency can be well grounded, not least because of the extent to which the imperial borders used by post-colonial states have, at least, helped

4 A.S. Rush, *Bonds of Empire: West Indians and Britishness from Victoria to Decolonization* (Oxford, 2011).

accentuate many problems. At the same time, there are contentious issues of longer-term genesis, or that have risen to the fore since independence. Independence frequently occurred many years ago, such as in India and Pakistan in 1947, and there have been significant changes since independence. For example, corruption appears to have become worse since imperial rule ended in many countries, including India where corruption has become especially prominent over the last decade. Corruption is linked to the use of the post-independence state to advance particular interests, notably religious, ethnic, and regional. There is, indeed, an inherent sectarianism in countries such as Nigeria.

Yet, in part, ethnic tensions, as in Fiji, and sectarianism are linked to population movements during the colonial period, which helps account for the blame heaped on Britain. In Sri Lanka, where the emphasis on a Sinhalese Buddhist national cultural identity has led to a downplaying of the integral role of the Tamil population, many of whom are Hindu, the (accurate) presentation of the Tamils as more likely to serve the British colonial rulers from 1795 to 1948 also serves to imply that they were, and therefore are, somehow less patriotic and nationalist, and, instead, are un-Sri Lankan, like the British themselves. The two themes are linked in British colonial support for education, which proved of particular benefit to Tamils seeking employment in public service, while the Sinhalese then preferred to focus on agriculture. A harsher tone is offered by seeing this as an instance of alleged British policies of 'divide and rule', an approach that criticises Britain but also serves to present Tamil assertiveness, let alone separatism, as a legacy of imperial misgovernment and one that is out of place in modern Sri Lanka.

Repeatedly, it is far easier to criticise the past, and to present current grievances in its (alleged) light, than it is to consider how to confront problems in the present. It is instructive to contrast the extensive (and appropriate) memorialisation of the iniquities of the slave trade in Britain and the far more hesitant engagement with modern slavery or quasi-slavery and the reasons why Africans seek to flee Africa today.[5] Similarly, with India, there is a highly selective account of independence and massacres in public memorialisation.

There are powerful reasons for attacking imperial rule. In particular, it appears necessary in many countries to advance their national account by arguing that the British empire overthrew an earlier more benign situation. This situation is variously presented, in terms of peaceful, environmentally sound natives, notably in North America, Australasia, and the Pacific islands, or of a developed state

---

5 K. Bales, *Disposable People: New Slavery in the Global Economy* (Berkeley, California, 1999).

system. This latter argument, however, underplays the extent of porosity in the states of the past, including the British empire. Modern concepts of nationality have been employed misleadingly to interpret the polities and politics of the past. In practice, there was considerable migration across what have since been constructed as national borders. Moreover, there was a willingness, in what were in fact 'composite states', to seek support where it could be found. This situation eased imperial penetration by Britain and other empires or, looked at differently, underlined the processes of compromise that, in part, constituted imperialism. In turn, precisely because, during and after decolonisation, it was not clear how 'peoples' were to be defined, there was an emphasis, instead, on the allegedly national character of states and proto-states.

Ireland

The process of criticising empire is not simply something to be seen in Africa or India, but can also be noted in the British Isles. There, critics of Britishness present it as an aspect of empire. In Ireland, the positive aspects of English control and then participation in Britain, from the twelfth century to 1921, are underrated. Museum displays on Irish history concentrate on the glories of Celtic civilisation in the 'Dark Ages' of the second half of the first millennium CE, emphasising Ireland's contribution to English culture at a time when Europe was assailed by 'barbarians'. In contrast, there is then relatively little on the period of English rule and participation in Britain, until the story resumes with the struggle for independence and subsequent history.

As a consequence, the positive aspects of the English rule, and of Irish participation in Britain, are neglected in favour of an image of lost centuries, their gloom punctuated by cruel episodes, notably the fate of the besieged towns of Wexford and Waterford at the hands of Oliver Cromwell and his invading English Protestant troops in 1649, and the deadly Irish Famine of 1846–48.[6] This approach fails to present either of the latter episodes in context, and also neglects the major part taken by the Irish in the development of the English, and then the British, empire. The survival of the Irish union in the nineteenth century has been described as 'the great elephant in the room of modern Irish historiography'.[7] Alongside the hardships and suffering associated with empire

6 J. Montano, *The Roots of English Colonialism in Ireland* (Cambridge, 2011).

7 A. Jackson, 'Ireland's Long Nineteenth Century of Union', *Journal of Modern History*, 86 (2014), p. 125.

in Ireland, there were also opportunities at all levels of society.[8] This was true both for Protestant Irish and for their Catholic counterparts. Opportunities for both varied and were generally far from equal, but they existed, not least in military service, which provided state-supported lives, trade, and migration. As a result, the demobilisation of much of the army when the Napoleonic Wars ended in 1815 caused acute problems in Ireland.

While some Irish colonial civil servants were affected by Irish nationalism, and sufficiently so to criticise aspects of British rule, notably in India, the commitment of most to the British empire, albeit an improved empire, was clear.[9] Thus, in the Punjab in the late nineteenth century, Irish civil servants played a central role in carrying through an economic development that included the provision of security of tenure, while Irish doctors also took a crucial role in the Indian Medical Service.[10] The underplaying of the imperial connection ensures that the riches of Anglo-Irish culture, famously represented by the writers Jonathan Swift and Oscar Wilde, are undervalued, or are treated essentially as Irish, which misrepresents them. The networks created by the Irish within the empire bridged with those created outside the empire, notably in the USA, and served the individual and family strategies of large numbers, leading to an experience that was at once individual and varied.

The emphasis on Irish nationalism in the twentieth century also led to a marked neglect of the large numbers of Irish Catholic volunteers who had fought for George V in World War One. This neglect extended to a failure to put much effort into constructing or maintaining war memorials. In contrast, the far smaller number involved in the Easter Rising of 1916 against British rule were actively commemorated. Their defiance was seen as a central episode in winning Irish independence, and thus was a crucial element in the Irish foundation myth. That a survivor of the rising, Eamonn de Valera, leader of

8 S. Howe, *Ireland and Empire: Colonial Legacies in Irish History and Culture* (Oxford, 2000).

9 P.A. Townend, 'Between Two Worlds: Irish Nationalists and Imperial Crisis 1878–1880', *Past and Present*, 194 (2007), pp. 139–74; S.B. Cook, 'The Irish Raj: Social Origins and Careers of Irishmen in the Indian Civil Service, 1855–1914', *Journal of Social History*, 20 (1987), pp. 507–29.

10 K. Jeffery, *An Irish Empire? Aspects of Ireland and the British Empire* (Manchester, 1996); K. Kenny, *Ireland in the British Empire* (Oxford, 2006); T. Foley and M. O'Connor (eds), *Ireland and India: Colonies, Culture and Empire* (Dublin, 2006); M. Silvestri, *Ireland and India: Nationalism, Empire and Memory* (Basingstoke, 2009); B. Crosbie, *Irish Imperial Networks: Migration, Social Communication and Exchange in Nineteenth-Century India* (Cambridge, 2012); P. O'Leary, *Servants of the Empire: The Irish in Punjab 1881–1921* (Manchester, 2011).

Sinn Féin from 1917 to 1926, was in power for much of the period from 1932 to 1973, contributed greatly to this situation. It also contributed to the related continuing ambivalence about the commemoration of the Irish Civil War of 1922–23 as he had been a member of the defeated rebels in the latter, rebels who had rejected the compromise, partition, peace with Britain. The many Irish who volunteered to fight in the British military in World War Two were also ignored until recently. An academic revisionism critical of the IRA and the eulogisation of armed struggle became pronounced in some scholarly circles from the 1970s. This revisionism was both eventually challenged in some academic circles and had a less potent impact on the public use of history.[11] Nevertheless, signs of a more positive account of the relationship with Britain, one that was definitely post-imperial, were seen with Queen Elizabeth II's successful state visit to Ireland in 2011. In this, the first by a British sovereign since Irish independence, the Queen publicly honoured the Republican dead in Parnell Square West. There was a return visit, the first by an Irish President, in 2014.

Scotland

In Scotland, there was also a rejection of the imperial legacy as part of an anti-British and anti-English nationalism. In the Victorian period and the early twentieth century, an emphasis on William Wallace, Robert the Bruce, and the 'war of independence', was not a form of victim history, but, rather, an account of why Scotland was a fit partner in Union, and not a colony. In contrast, the increased expression from the 1960s of a distinctive historical tradition separate to that of Britain was widely linked to pressure for increased autonomy, if not independence. Much opprobrium focused on the Anglo-Scottish Union of 1707. This was presented as an episode of English imperialism, indeed as a reprise, in a different form, of the successive English attempts to subjugate Scotland from the 1290s to the 1540s. The Union was widely discussed as a measure detrimental to Scotland and maybe obtained partly through bribery. The theme of disunity, indeed treason, as a cause of national weakness was one that was employed in presenting the Union and, from then, could also be applied to current issues. The positive and nationalist reception of the American film *Braveheart* (1995), a wildly inaccurate account of Wallace's life, was indicative of a more general pattern of opposition to 'betrayal' from within.

11 J. Regan, *Myth and the Irish State* (Sallins, 2013).

In practice, this approach represented a serious failure to appreciate the situation in 1706–07. The Union was an English move to extend the Act of Settlement to Scotland and to end the threat posed by the Scottish parliament's capacity for separate legislation, notably the 1705 Act allowing Scotland to choose a successor to the Scottish Crown. Although the passage of the Act of Union through the Scottish Parliament in 1706 in part depended on successful political management as well as corruption, there were also important issues of self-interest. The Scottish economy was in a very poor state, there was a determination not to be shut out from English and colonial markets, the bitter civil war of 1689–91 had underlined the difficulty of independence from England, and the powerful leadership of the Presbyterian Church, whose privileged position in a seriously divided Scotland was written into the treaty, accepted the Union as a political necessity because there was no good Protestant alternative. The refusal of the exiled Stuarts to convert to Protestantism gravely lessened Scottish options.

These points, however, were not well ventilated in public discussion, where, indeed, academic caveats about the invention of Scottish history,[12] were unwelcome. A victim model of Scottish history proved far more attractive. With the creation, after the referendum following the Labour victory in the general election of 1997, of a Scottish parliament and Executive in 1999, the drift became very much away from a British identity, not least as self-government became an incremental process. The Executive became a de facto government from 2007, and in 2012, under the Scotland Act, became a de jure government. Although there was valuable historical work on Scotland's major role in the British empire, this was less the case with public history. The new National Museum of Scotland, opened in its current building in Edinburgh in 2011, greatly downplays the role of the Scots in the British empire. Pressure for Scottish independence has accentuated this presentation, while nationalists attacked what they presented as an Anglicisation, or Englishisation, of Great Britain, and, with it, Scotland, by what they saw as an English-dominated Lesser Britain.

Without the drive for independence, Wales, which also played a major role in the British empire,[13] has witnessed a similar process as far as its British identity and role are concerned. The fad of Celticism – Celtic Christianity, Celtic pottery, and so on – is an attempt to invent a pre-British past for Wales.

---

12 H.R. Trevor-Roper, *The Invention of Scotland* (London, 2008).

13 H.V. Bowen (ed.), *Wales and the British Overseas Empire: Interactions and Influences, 1650–1830* (Manchester, 2011).

The Attack on the Past

Thus, the multi-faceted nature of the British imperial past and its impact has been largely lost. This was a multi-faceted nature that contributed to the pluralistic character of the empire. Instead, a politics of rejection ensures that the imperial past serves for themes and images as part of an empowerment through real, remembered, or, sometimes, constructed, grievance. This approach provides not only the recovery of terrible episodes, but also ready reflexes of anger and newsworthy copy, as with the harsh treatment of rebels, rebel sympathisers, and innocent bystanders in the Mau Mau rebellion in Kenya, an issue that took on new energy as demands for compensation were fuelled by revelations of harsh British policy from 2011.

The criticism of the past was multi-centred. Australia, notably, continues to be a sphere for vexed debates about imperialism. These focused on the treatment of the earlier population. In 2011, new tensions arose when the Left-dominated Sydney City Council insisted that the words 'European arrival' be replaced in official documents with the term 'invasion or illegal colonisation'. This decision was reached after pressure from the council's Aboriginal and Torres Strait Islander Advisory Panel, and the council voted 7:2 in favour of the change. Academic opinion was also divided, the historian Alan Frost pointing out that the intentions of William Pitt the Younger, the British prime minister, could not be accurately described as an invasion:

> My notion of invasion is armed forces arriving to dispossess someone else. What happened to the Aborigines subsequently was dispossession but that was not the intention of the Pitt Administration. For the first 15 to 20 years, Sydney was just a tiny thing on the edge of a vast continent. It seems to me that to use the word "invasion" to describe it is an abuse of language.[14]

Such an abuse is very common.

Britain

Similarly, there has been a significant change in tone and content in the discussion of the imperial past in Britain. A sense of irrelevance was captured in the Al Stewart song 'On the Border' (1976):

---

14 *The Times*, 29 June 2011, p. 27.

> On my wall the colours of the map are running
> From Africa the winds they talk of changes coming
> ...
> In the islands where I grew up
> Nothing seems the same
> It's just the patterns that remain
> An empty shell.

For most of the public, the Commonwealth has followed the empire into irrelevance. The patriotic glow that accompanied and followed the Falklands War in 1982, a war fought to regain a part of the empire inhabited by settlers of British descent, was essentially nationalistic, not imperial. This glow was not matched for the more recent, and very different, conflicts in Iraq and Afghanistan. These have led to a marked disinclination for further expeditionary warfare. The weight of interest in this warfare felt by those associated with the military is scarcely matched elsewhere. This shift is also seen with the past. The list of 100 Great Britons produced by popular choice for the BBC in 2002 was singularly low on imperial heroes. If the winner, Churchill, was the greatest, as well as the last, of the imperial heroes, he was presented, as were Elizabeth I and Nelson, as defenders of Britain and an endangered people, rather than as exponents of the British empire. This was ironic as all three had been involved in imperial activity, Churchill conspicuously so.

A distancing was sometimes seen at the local level. Thus, in Liverpool, a key port of empire that was defined accordingly for most of its history, the celebrations of identity seen when the city was European Capital of Culture in 2008 downplayed this legacy. This was despite the fact that the city chose the slogan 'The World in One City' to mark the occasion. The cosmopolitanism that was celebrated centred on multi-culturalism, youth culture, and music, but not on the imperial legacy.[15] The situation, however, was different in the case of the 2007 commemorations in Bristol and Liverpool of the abolition of the slave trade, while the International Slavery Museum in Liverpool is very candid about the city's involvement in the empire and slavery.

The local configuration of the ebbing of empire varied greatly. The decline of the imperial identity for Liverpool matched that seen on the Clyde, and also had political consequences in terms of an end of a traditional Britishness focused on empire. Changing attitudes on the Clyde were important as far as Scottish views

15 S. Haggerty, A. Webster, and N. White (eds), *The Empire in One City? Liverpool's Inconvenient Imperial Past* (Manchester, 2008).

on the Union were concerned. In part, the working-class constituency for empire ended in Scotland and England, a change that greatly altered the overall political placing of empire and, by extension, of British history as a whole. This change was a significant aspect of the Conservative loss of traditional working-class support. From another perspective, it was a different type and stage of empire that was at issue. Linked to issues of religion and ethnicity, Scottish Unionism focused far more on the Irish issue than English Conservatism did, and the Orange vote was more important to this Unionism than the imperial one.

There was not simply a party political location for the decline of support for empire. In addition, although generally treated as separate, not least by those concerned to define a new sense of patriotism, the marked decline of support for empire, or at least sympathetic interest, was also linked to a fall in patriotic sentiment, difficult as that is to measure. Such sentiment was less frequently expressed from the 1960s. As a different, but related issue, attitudes towards abroad became less adversarial. As an interesting indication of the popular mood, it is instructive to note the extent to which it appeared normal for major football teams to have foreign players, managers, and even owners. Notions of identity and habits of expressing it have never been constant, but the last half-century has been a period of particular fluidity, one that has disorientating consequences for many. Indeed, the loss of empire, the alliance with the USA, and membership of the European Economic Community (now European Union) from 1973 were, and are, all far more than simply political issues. It became apparent that British history in many (but not all) respects had meant British empire history, and much of it passed with the loss of empire.

Until 1947, Britishness was, for many, quintessentially imperial and, as a result, empire meant an international Britishness, and not an island one. Conversely, the loss of empire in South Asia in 1947–48 saw, despite hopes, plans, and policies to the contrary, the beginning of a different state, a 'Great Britain' that came into being to run a global colonial and trading system that has since disintegrated, or, at least, to direct a Commonwealth of Nations that has also largely failed. In turn, this 'Great Britain' morphed into a fretful 'Little Britishness' that was associated, in particular by her critics, with Mrs Thatcher, prime minister from 1979 to 1990, and that her successors found it difficult to maintain. It had ceased to be possible to be Canadian and British or New Zealander and British; now it became difficult to be Scottish and British. Rephrased, both the United Kingdom and Great Britain appear to many in Britain as anachronisms, and notably so because their cohesion has been challenged by Scottish nationalism, and their purpose by the political developments of the 1990s, 2000s, and 2010s. Commentators treated Britain as a prime instance of the argument that countries were synthetic constructs. The added argument was that, as the factors that led to their construction ebbed, so they might dissolve. Britain was presented as a product of contingent relations between its constituent parts and of conflict with Europe, and its national myths as less relevant in an age of weaker nationalism.[16]

There is still point in England and Scotland, but it is unclear how far there still is in Britain. From the Scottish perspective, or, at least, that of Scottish nationalists, Scotland was regionalised from the 1940s as Great Britain was no longer seen in England as a multi-national polity, not least because of a smaller cultural engagement by and with Scots than in the eighteenth and nineteenth centuries. In short, in this view, England distorted both empire and Britishness, and certainly underplayed both Scottish culture and Scotland's contribution to Britishness. The question of who rejected and made redundant Britishness thus came into play: the English or the Scots. Britishness is certainly a separate dimension.[17] Within England, the growth of a sense of English nationalism was for long compromised by Britishness, by the national strategies of the political parties, and by the association of English nationalism with the far Right in politics. However, the Scottish issue helped lead in the mid-2010s to a much greater focus on English issues and identities. The long-term consequences of this are unclear.

Separately, the empire was, and is, not always central to processes that have affected attitudes to its role and history. For example, the impact of American culture lessened a sense of British distinctiveness, exceptionalism, and pride, and this impact had serious implications. Americanism and globalisation compromised native styles, and thus imperial models, whether in food or in diction, with all that meant for national continuity. The decline in the position, popularity, and relevance of the Established Churches, as well as of the strands of anti-Catholicism and Protestant exceptionalism that had been significant to national identity and imperial purpose, also affected links and identities that had been important to empire. With the end of patterns of imperial trade and careers, 'abroad' now is more focused on the USA and Europe than was the case in the 1950s, although there is an important exception in the case of migrants and their descendants. There is a particular lack of interest in Africa and Oceania, other than as holiday destinations such as Gambia, Kenya, or the

16 L. Colley, *Acts of Union and Disunion* (London, 2014).

17 D. Armitage, 'Greater Britain: A Useful Category of Historical Analysis?', *American Historical Review*, 104 (1999), pp. 427–45; G.A. Barton, 'The British World Model of World History', *Britain and the World*, 5 (2012), pp. 9–10.

Seychelles, or as the sources of immigration. A recent study of the empire and migration concludes:

> It seems fittingly to mark the end of empire that one of the largest locations of imported Asian contract workers is now not in Mauritius [once part of the empire from conquest from France in 1810 to independence in 1968] but in Kuwait. A growing community of expatriate British settlers is also developing, not on Canadian prairies but on the coast of southern Spain, and many of them are not workers or entrepreneurs but retired folk, seeking a place in the sun.[18]

Ignorance is also part of the response to empire, although that was also the case at the time, as the post-war Mass Observation Surveys revealed. It would surprise most readers to know that the British had had a colony in Somaliland, although British Somaliland, where Britain had declared a protectorate in 1884, only became independent, as part of the Somali Republic, in 1960. And yet, the disorder of Somalia is now linked to a humanitarian disaster, as well as the world fulcrum of piracy and large-scale migration to Britain. That former British Somaliland is less chaotic than former Italian Somaliland (the larger part of modern Somalia) is sometimes attributed to the impact of British rule.

Attitudes to the imperial past within Britain have also changed as the British have altered. By 2014, there were two million Muslims in Britain and increasingly multi-cultural Britain sees myriad tensions and alliances in which place, ethnicity, religion, class, and other factors both clash and co-exist. This is not an easy background for a positive depiction of the imperial past, although, ironically, most of the Muslims ended up in Britain because of the imperial link, notably with Pakistan. The percentage of recruits to the army from ethnic minority communities is below that of their share of the total percentage. Empire and war were downplayed as themes in British culture and history under 'New Labour', which took power in 1997, and multi-culturalism was pushed to the fore when engaging with and interpreting both. Thus, the Parekh Report of the Commission on the Future of Multi-Ethnic Britain pressed for a sense of heritage adapted to the views of recent immigrants, and this aspect of the report very much attracted comment. At times, the consequences were somewhat fanciful, and there was disproportionate emphasis both on a multi-ethnic legacy and on a positive account of it.[19] Moreover, the Britishness of immigrant communities

18 M. Harper and S. Constantine, *Migration and Empire* (Oxford, 2010), p. 349.

19 D. Dabydeen, J. Gilmore, and C. Jones (eds), *The Oxford Companion to Black British History* (Oxford, 2010).

such as West Indians was important to their identity, which was not eased by a process of attack on the imperial legacy that was a source of this Britishness.

Multi-culturalism as a political agenda often employed British imperialism as a means to criticise the history, role, and identity of Britain itself. Slavery and the slave trade played a major part in this process. Key totemic moments attracted attention, notably the murder of 132 slaves thrown overboard from the *Zong* in 1781 because they were infected with typhus and the captain wished to stop the spread of the disease aboard the ship, and because he thought he could claim them on his insurance policy. This episode was brought to court, not for these murders, but as a suit against the insurers who rejected the owners' claim that their cargo had been necessarily jettisoned. The case prompted widespread debate at the time[20] and is significant. It exemplified the very problem with Britain's history with slavery, namely whether the emphasis should be on Britain's leading role in the Atlantic slave trade or in ending the slave trade and slavery. The *Zong* incident was not just an atrocity of the slave trade carried out by Britons, but also an atrocity that galvanised the British anti-slavery movement. The combination of the two created a tension that remains problematic today. At the same time, the *Zong* can assume disproportionate attention as if it was typical of the slave trade, which was not the case. The same is true of the Morant Bay repression in Jamaica in 1865 and of the Amritsar massacre in 1919: they were not typical of imperial control in the West Indies and India, nor of imperial policing. Nevertheless, the threat of violence was an important aspect of colonial rule. Moreover, whereas religious toleration, freedom of speech, parliamentary government, and a free press had, for long, all been regarded as important to British liberty, and as ways in which Britain set a progressive example, this account was challenged from the perspective of those who experienced empire.

However, the process by which this experience was recreated was highly selective, downplaying co-operation and emphasising coercion and racism.[21] Furthermore, Britain did offer its colonies many of the advantages of British liberty. Possibly linked to this, British multi-culturalism can be seen as overly apologetic and defensive. In addition, the extent of decolonisation is such that Britain does not face problems comparable to those posed by the riots in the French West Indies in 2009: the equivalent of Guadeloupe and Martinique are neither part of Britain (as they are of France), nor ruled as imperial territories.

---

20 J. Walvin, *The Zong: A Massacre, the Law and the End of Slavery* (New Haven, Connecticut, 2011).

21 For example, E. Kolsky, *Colonial Justice in British India: White Violence and the Rule of Law* (Cambridge, 2010).

Conclusions

For a historian, it is instructive to juxtapose critical views of empire with the stadial perspective of the justifiers of British imperialism, their notion that social existence was a matter of different states of human activity, and progress a question of stages that were not reached at the same time. This latter account provided a location for the British empire, one that positioned Britain in an exemplary fashion. The selfish, self-satisfied, and self-justifying nature of this account understandably arouses hostility, contempt, and ire. Nevertheless, within that context, it is still worth considering the rationale of Britain as a spreader of allegedly civilising values and virtues, because this rationale helps explain the conditional nature of the selfishness. Imperial purpose and self-interest were believed to lie in a propagation of benign views and policies through which societies would emerge to independent statehood.[22] This was a contrast to the lack of such a prospectus in the case of the Soviet Union or modern China. Such a stadial account of British aspirations now seems objectionable as well as redundant, which is a fair account of the present, but less so for the past.

---

22 For a failure to appreciate this view, see, for example, P.K. Monod, *Imperial Island: A History of Britain and Its Empire, 1660–1837* (Malden, Mass., 2009), p. 381.

Chapter 9
Conclusions

As the nation-state ceases to have the primacy it once had as the highest form of political organisation, so empire as, in one light, a particular form of transnational organisation, deserves to be re-evaluated. Repeatedly, as indicated in this book, the legacy of empire is a fraught one. However, the tendency to underplay, if not totally ignore, the positive aspects and consequences of the British empire, alongside its drawbacks, is both misguided and unfortunate. Too often, condemning (rather than criticising) the empire is a cause of the failure to understand the past. This ahistorical condemnation also challenges attempts to create a cohesive historical sense of national identity.

Beneficial aspects of British imperial rule and participation included rising literacy rates, access to economic opportunity, an increase in standards of living and the provision of public health, the decline in disorder and rates of violent death in many colonies,[1] and the emphasis on freedoms and the rule of law in British constitutionalism. These aspects, furthermore, range from the extent to which the English language has opened the world to many, to a commitment to tolerance. One obvious legacy is the ability to debate the value of empire with people around the world, with many of them being free to express their views, often very contrary views.

However, those benefits can be questioned by suggesting that some of these developments would have occurred anyway. Indeed, concurrence is not the same as causation. The relationship between the decline in disorder and imperial rule is an example of this point, not least because such rule also led to violent opposition. Moreover, the lasting consequences of these benefits can be queried. For example, in the case of tolerance, it is noteworthy in the 2010s that religious strife is widespread in India, while Uganda passed harsh legislation against homosexuals in 2014. In addition, many of the states that were created by, and from, empire, for example Kenya, Iraq, and South Africa, have proved to be ill-conceived legacies of colonial rule that pitted and privileged certain ethnic groups against others, and with seriously divisive consequences.

---

1 I. Morris, *War. What is it Good For? The Role of Conflict in Civilisation from Primates to Robotics* (London, 2014), pp. 225–33.

Empire and the imperial experience are as much about the impact on other peoples as that on Britain, and, in many cases, more so. Manifestations range from the trivial to the more profound; the former including hobbies and foodstuffs, whether playing cricket in the Ionian Islands, now part of Greece but a British Protectorate from 1815 to 1863, or drinking gin on Minorca (British-ruled for most of the eighteenth century), or the bread and butter pudding I was given on Hawaii in 2003, which was attributed to British influence during the nineteenth century (this has also left the Union Jack on the state flag). As with much of this influence, the flavour had been 'cut' or fractured to reflect local influences and demands, in this case to produce bread and butter pudding with a tropical taste that I can recommend. Sport has been a major legacy of empire, one that bridged from white settlers to the non-white population, as with the very pronounced Indian, Sri Lankan, and West Indian interest in cricket, as well as that in Australia. Similarly, rugby is very popular in Fiji as well as in Australia, and with New Zealand Maori as well as whites.

The more profound effects of the British empire vary. They include the spread of English; major demographic movements, some involuntary and cruel; and the creation and identity of states and nations, the last generally after an earlier destruction of states or the subordination of peoples. The growth of English as the global language of business, and of international political and cultural links, has been of major importance in global integration, and has also helped disseminate not only English-language culture, but also political, economic, and social suppositions. This spread owed much to British imperial rule, especially in Africa, the Middle East, and South Asia, but, over the last half-century, has more clearly been an aspect of American influence, political, economic, and cultural. This serves to underline the difficulties in assessing the respective influence of the two in the modern world. There are important national variations. The contrasting take-up of English in China during the late nineteenth century and since 1980 is instructive in this respect: American influence is the key element in Chinese Westernisation. The influence of the USA and of the English language were taken further by technology. The Intel 4004, the first microprocessor chip, was created in the USA in 1971. The spread of the Internet as a worldwide interactive medium, and the dominance of computing by American operating systems, ensured that English became more prominent as a language than ever before.

Although, by 2014, English is still only known by a minority of the world's population (and this is particularly apparent in East Asia and Latin America), it is, nevertheless, a larger minority than ever before. Furthermore, the impact of the language spread in countries where Britain, whatever its commercial role, had never been the colonial power, such as Brazil and China. This development was significant because the English language proved a point of access not only to American culture but also to a perception, however limited or flawed, of Britain. There was also a class and age dimension. The affluent and younger have more knowledge of English than the poorer and older, and that characteristic increased its influence as a cultural medium. The pattern and language of international telephone calls reflects these linguistic links, and also bears the imprint of empire, echoing the maps of British trade a century ago. Thus, in 1991, Britain was, after Australia, the destination of the second biggest number of telephone calls made from New Zealand, with the USA coming third. This pattern is a reminder of one particular shift in the former empire, the extent to which Australia, Canada, New Zealand, the UK, and the USA now collectively represent an important sphere of interaction, being the key elements of the Anglosphere. However, in the developing network society,[2] this sphere does not define the interests of these states nor exhaust their axes of interaction.

The impact of language is one of the many ways in which it is appropriate to think of a symbiotic, as well as both real and symbolic, transfer of imperial hegemony from Britain to the USA. Symbiosis and transfer do not, however, mean sameness. With the exception of (mostly) left-wing critics, Americans have proved very resistant to the idea that they were citizens of an imperial republic from the outset or, at least, had imperial tendencies. Speaking at the United States Military Academy at West Point in November 2009, President Barack Obama differentiated American power from that of other states by saying that Americans did not come to conquer, which was part of his attempt to reclaim American military interventionism from the Bush legacy. The term 'empire of liberty' has been used to describe the USA.[3] Of course, the Native American population was subject to a brutal imperial conquest. Nevertheless, whereas much of the global spread of the English language prior to the mid-twentieth century significantly arose as a result of territorial control, and its impact on government and education, for example in India, in contrast, since then, under American hegemony, the spread has largely been due to economic advantage outside the context of any such control.

In the case of the British empire, it is repeatedly difficult to differentiate between the impact of empire, in the shape of territorial control, and that of

2 M. Castells (ed.), *The Network Society: A Cross-Cultural Perspective* (Cheltenham, 2004).

3 In 2009 alone as the title for David Reynolds's history of the United States and Gordon Wood's history of America from 1789 to 1815.

external British influence during the period of imperial dominance. Given Britain's economic and financial might, in the nineteenth century in particular, this influence would certainly have been profound without formal control, as the role of the USA today indicates. To use informal empire as a term to describe this influence is not without value. Yet, aside from its somewhat elastic, if not, at times, nebulous meaning and application, there is a problem that informal empire focuses on the role of one power, rather than the range of external influences that might well exist. For example, while Britain was the most important external force commercially in China in the 1920s and early 1930s, and was dominant in Chinese external and coastal shipping, it was not the sole non-Chinese power wielding influence there and able to apply pressure. Indeed, Britain's role in China then was considerably more benign than that of the Soviet Union, let alone Japan.

The extent of imperial influence and the commercial and liberal character of the British empire was such that transnationalism was inherent to its operations. Indeed, this characteristic helped give the empire particular range, resilience, and adaptability, while also making it difficult to define, more so, for example, than that of Ancient Rome. The British empire understood as an adaptable system of networks captures much of the activity that gave it continuity and strength. That, however, is not a theme that attracts political or popular attention when the emphasis, instead, is on anger and blame. Then, the thesis is one of conquest, control, oppression, and subordination.

Formal or informal, Britain was the dominant imperial power across much of the globe in the nineteenth- and early twentieth century, the period of the onset of modernity, as defined by such criteria as large-scale industrialisation, urbanisation, the spread of literacy, and rising living standards. The many and serious pressures and problems stemming from this process of modernisation could be accentuated by foreign rule, and frequently were, often greatly so. In addition, it is not surprising that these pressures and problems were frequently seen in these terms. However, whatever the specific manifestations in particular countries, this rule was not the root cause of the process of change. As with imperial control and colonisation, it is also difficult to separate the changes in the former colonies resulting from, or related to, decolonisation, from broader patterns of development, such as the consequences of increasing urbanisation and literacy. Moreover, much that was associated with imperialism, such as environmental change, remains important and more insistent under independent governments.[4] This assessment is not a welcoming reflection for

4 W. Beinart and L. Hughes, *Environment and Empire* (Oxford, 2007).

many, not only because it challenges the sometimes facile habit of blaming outsiders for unwelcome developments, but also because it questions the ability of post-imperial regimes to cope with the continued effects of globalisation.

More generally, criticism, if not caricature, of the British empire are freely offered, and few defenders are to be seen. There is almost a zeal to suggest that Britain was as bad as the most murderous regimes in history, as with references to 'Britain's *gulags*' when discussing the brutal response to the Mau Mau, or with discussion of the slave trade and of imperial expansion, or with comparison of the treatment of detainees in the Boer War (1899–1902), and the response to the Bengal Famine of 1943, with the actions of the Nazis. Individually, these criticisms frequently (although not always) rest to a considerable extent on emotion and hyperbole, rather than an informed knowledge of the British empire, the other regimes, or the particular circumstances of the time; but that does not prevent assertion from being believed.

As a result, politics takes precedence. Seeking and/or offering an apology for the wrongs of empire on the part of Britain is presented as a key aspect of coming to terms with the past,[5] which is in practice a very unclear process. Coming to terms or 'making peace with history', is regarded as a way to facilitate a post-colonial future and, in particular, to confront the strains of multi-culturalism and to address issues of human rights.[6] However, there is the danger that such a process, instead, leads to a reiteration of grievances and to an entrenchment of anger. Intellectually, coming to terms can be bogus, and is often ahistorical, as in the idea of the ready transference of responsibilities across the generations,[7] a theme that is to the fore in demands for compensation for the slave trade and slavery, demands very much pressed in 2014. Arguably more serious, the process can also be harmful to attempts to confront current and future issues of identity, cohesion, and social purpose.

Looked at differently, rather than focusing on trying to create an agreed narrative with concomitant politicising, including anger and apologies, attempts to engage with the diverse understandings of imperial history that will always exist provide an opportunity, instead, to return us to the complexities of the past. These complexities include those of metropole, officials, settlers, and public, as well as those who experienced imperialism, whether, for them, the

5 R. Aldrich, 'Coming to Terms with the Colonial Past: The French and Others', *Arts*, 28 (2006), pp. 91–116.

6 E. Barkan, *The Guilt of Nations: Restitution and Negotiating Historical Injustices* (New York, 2000).

7 J. Thompson, *Taking Responsibility for the Past: Reparation and Historical Justice* (Cambridge, 2002).

accent is on exploitation or co-operation, or, as more commonly, both. Public displays and academic accounts that can offer a multiplicity of views may appear confused, but can capture the extent to which the assessment of empire was, and is, inherently varied, multi-faceted, and multi-focused.[8]

This is the case not only of the contrasting views from the former colonies and the areas of informal empire, such as China, but, also, those of Britain. The varied perspectives of Scottish nationalism on British imperial history can be particularly interesting, not least as they show how difficult it is to 'fix' this nationalism. Welsh perspectives add further complexity. Another cause of a variety in perspectives is that of the ethnic composition of Britain. Polls in the early 2010s indicated that members of ethnic minority groups were unlikely to vote Conservative and were far more likely to identify as British than English, whereas members of the indigenous white minority were more likely to identify as English. This contrast had important resonances for the understanding of history, including imperial history. In addition, the nature of national history is changing at least in part because members of the ethnic minority groups comprised a growing percentage of the population, one predicted to reach nearly a third by 2050. As a consequence, there was an increased understanding of British history in terms of the trans-oceanic empire, rather than that within the British Isles. The language, meaning, and political ramifications of empire were (and are) always far from fixed.[9]

Criticism would be more impressive if it could be shown that the British were worse than other imperialists. The same point can be made about European imperialism as a whole. Although they were not alone in being trans-oceanic, the trans-oceanic character of the Western empires over the last half-millennium, as well as their global range, and association with particular commercial, and, eventually, industrial developments, gave them a particular character. However, these empires scarcely invented long-distance commerce, slavery, war, external rule, and racism. In addition, imperial pretensions and power, not self-determination, were the norm, and, whatever the ideology, remain so in parts of the world such as Tibet and Xinjiang, both still under Chinese control. Furthermore, and not only in the case of China, opposition to Western imperial rule or influence was often linked to a determination to wield such power. Thus, 'the underlying centrality of slavery in the historical

8 For an Australian perspective, B. Attwood, *Telling the Truth About Aboriginal History* (Crows Nest, 2005).

9 A. Thompson, 'The Language of Imperialism and the Meaning of Empire: Imperial Discourse in British Politics, 1895–1914', *Journal of British Studies*, 36 (1997), pp. 147–77.

relationship between Egypt and the Sudan' was such that anti-colonial nationalism in Egypt was compatible with a determination to regain power over Sudan, a power that had been exercised by Egypt with much harshness.[10] The Egyptian claim to Sudan was only disclaimed as part of the price of Britain ending its role in Egypt.

The legacy of British imperial rule varied greatly, as in the contrasting character and consequences of a key legacy, the extent of migration within, and by means of, the imperial world.[11] Control of many territories, of the nineteenth-century empire, let alone of the mandates gained after World War One, was more short-lived than was true of the Spanish empire. In many of these territories, British settlement was limited. The combined impact of empire, for example in Myanmar, was of a less profound and lasting impact than in former settlement colonies, such as Australia. These also were mostly occupied during the nineteenth century, but the bulk of the present population in these colonies is not of indigenous descent. The situation was different in colonies where the population lacked the rights or claims of Britons. In these, authority remained as a tool of imperial administrators, while institutions of representative and responsible government were granted more reluctantly. The theme of empire therefore is one of variety alongside power. This has to be remembered when there is pressure for a snap judgement of imperial control and influence, whether political or not. Should we emphasise Britain's leading role in the Atlantic slave trade or in ending slavery? At Amritsar in 2013, David Cameron expressed contrition for a 'deeply shameful event', but also said, 'I think there is an enormous amount to be proud of in what the British Empire is. But, of course, there were bad events as well as good ones'. This double judgement more generally indicates the extent to which the national past can resonate with very different themes and for different communities.[12]

Imperial conquest does not conform to current mores,[13] and there is profound ambivalence, not to say amnesia and hostility, towards Britain's imperial past. At the time, however, victories and conquests were generally deplored by few,

---

10 E.M.T. Powell, *Egypt, Great Britain, and the Mastery of the Sudan* (Berkeley, California, 2003), p. 219.

11 R. Bickers, *Settlers and Expatriates: Britons over the Seas* (Oxford, 2010); M. Harper and S. Constantine (eds), *Migration and Empire* (Oxford, 2010).

12 A. Thompson, 'The Imprint of the Empire', in Thompson (ed.), *Britain's Experience of Empire in the Twentieth Century* (Oxford, 2012), pp. 342–3.

13 For some perceptive remarks on the nature and significance of local intermediaries in the nineteenth-century Gulf, J. Onley, 'Imperial History and Political Correctness', *British Scholar*, 2 (2010), pp. 339–47.

although there was much opposition to the Boer War (1899–1902). Britain was ruled not by Quakers, who are pacifists, but by a political élite prepared to pursue national interests and destiny across the oceans, and this quest largely resonated with the aspirations of the wider political nation and their sense of the future. It is truly a world that is lost, but one that cannot be disentangled from the history of the country and people, nor separated from that of the rest of the world.

Select Bibliography

The literature on British imperialism is very extensive. The emphasis in this list is on valuable recent works. Earlier literature can be approached through their bibliographies and notes.

Alford, B.W.E., *Britain in the World Economy since 1880* (London, 1996).
Bailkin, J., *The Aftermath of Empire* (Berkeley, 2012).
Barman, J., *The West beyond the West: A History of British Columbia* (Toronto, 1996).
Bashford, A., *Imperial Hygiene: A Critical History of Colonialism, Nationalism and Public Health* (Basingstoke, 2004).
Bayly, C.A., *The Birth of the Modern World, 1780–1914: Global Connections and Comparisons* (Oxford, 2004).
Black, J., *The British Seaborne Empire* (New Haven, 2004).
Boyce, D.G., *The Irish Question and British Politics* (London, 1996).
Bridge, C. and Fedorowich, K. (eds), *The British World: Culture, Diaspora and Identity* (London, 2003).
Bruckner, P. and Francis, D. (eds), *Rediscovering the British World: Culture and Diaspora* (London, 2003).
Cain, P.J. and Hopkins, A.G., *British Imperialism, 1688–2000* (Harlow, 2001).
Darian-Smith, K., Grimshaw, P., Lindsey, K., and Mcintyre, S. (eds), *Exploring the British World: Identity, Cultural Production, Institutions* (Melbourne, 2004).
Darwin, J., *The Empire Project: The Rise and Fall of the British World-System, 1830–1970* (Cambridge, 2009).
——— *Unfinished Empire: The Global Expansion of Britain* (London, 2012).
Daunton, M.J. and Halpern, R. (eds), *Empire and Others: British Encounters with Indigenous Peoples, 1600–1850* (Philadelphia, 1998).
Ferguson, N., *Empire: How Britain Made the Modern World* (London, 2003).
Holland, R. and Stockwell, S. (eds), *Ambiguities of Empire: Essays in Honour of Andrew Porter* (London, 2009).
Howe, S., *Ireland and Empire: Colonial Legacies in Irish History and Culture* (Oxford, 2000).

Hyam, R., *Understanding the British Empire* (Cambridge, 2010).
Jackson, A., *Buildings of Empire* (Oxford, 2013).
Kelly, D. (ed.), *Lineages of Empire: The Historical Roots of British Imperial Thought* (Oxford, 2009).
Kenny, K., *Ireland in the British Empire* (Oxford, 2006).
McIntyre, W.D., *British Decolonisation 1946–1997* (London, 1998).
Magee, G.B. and Thompson, A.S., *Empire and Globalisation: Networks of People, Goods and Capital in the British World,* c.*1850–1914* (Cambridge, 2010).
Oxford History of Empire, The (Oxford, 1998–).
Porter, B., *The Absent-Minded Imperialists: Empire, Society, and Culture in Britain* (Oxford, 2004).
—— *The Lion's Share: A Short History of British Imperialism 1850–2011* (5th edn, London, 2012).
Stockwell, S. (ed.), *The British Empire: Themes and Perspectives* (Oxford, 2008).
Thompson, A. (ed.), *Britain's Experience of Empire in the Twentieth Century* (Oxford, 2012).
Thompson, A.S., *Imperial Britain: The Empire in British Politics,* c.*1880–1932* (Harlow, 2000).
—— *The Empire Strikes Back? The Impact of Imperialism on Britain from the Mid-Nineteenth Century* (Harlow, 2005).

Index